EVERY HOUR OF THE LIGHT

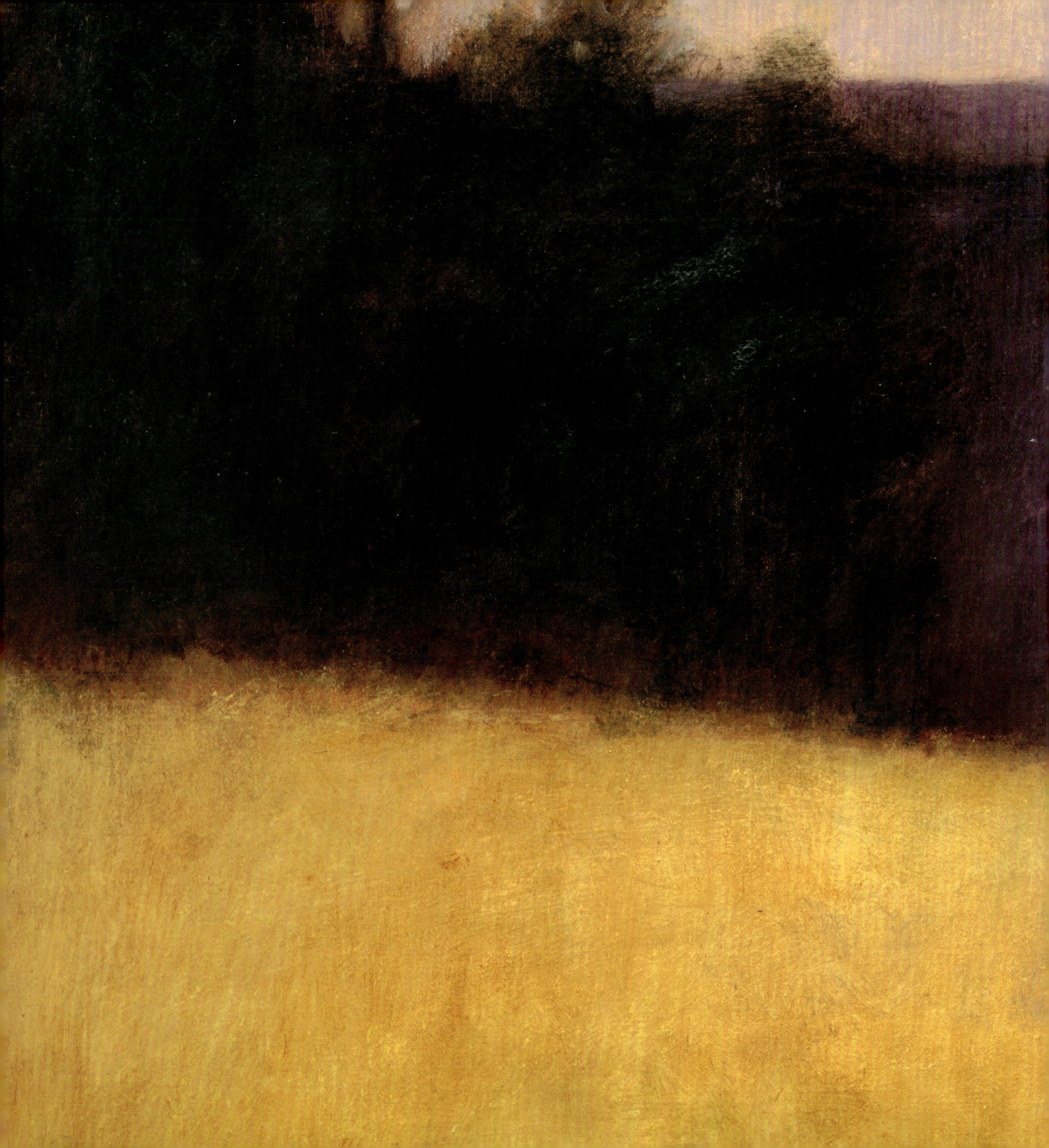

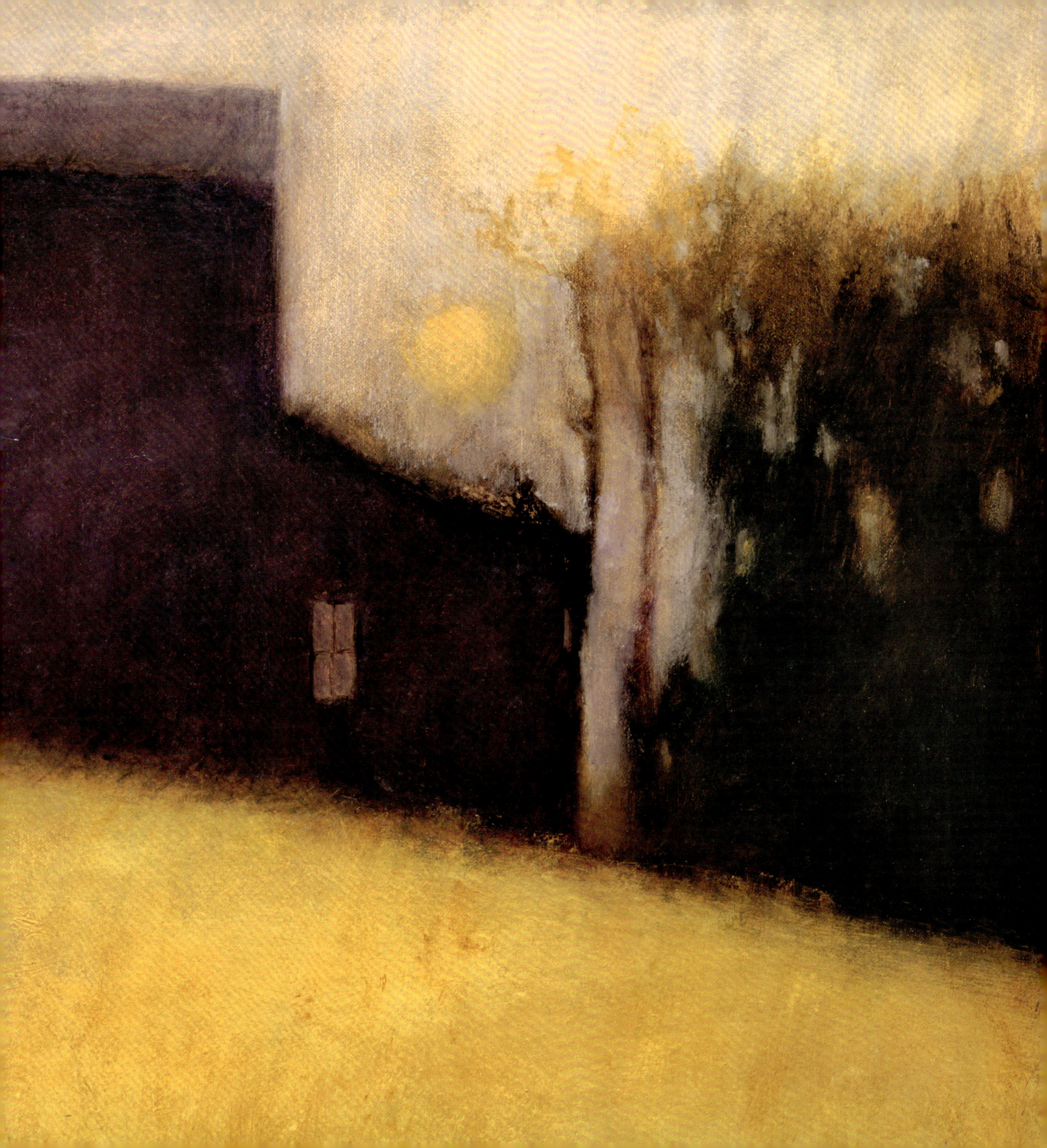

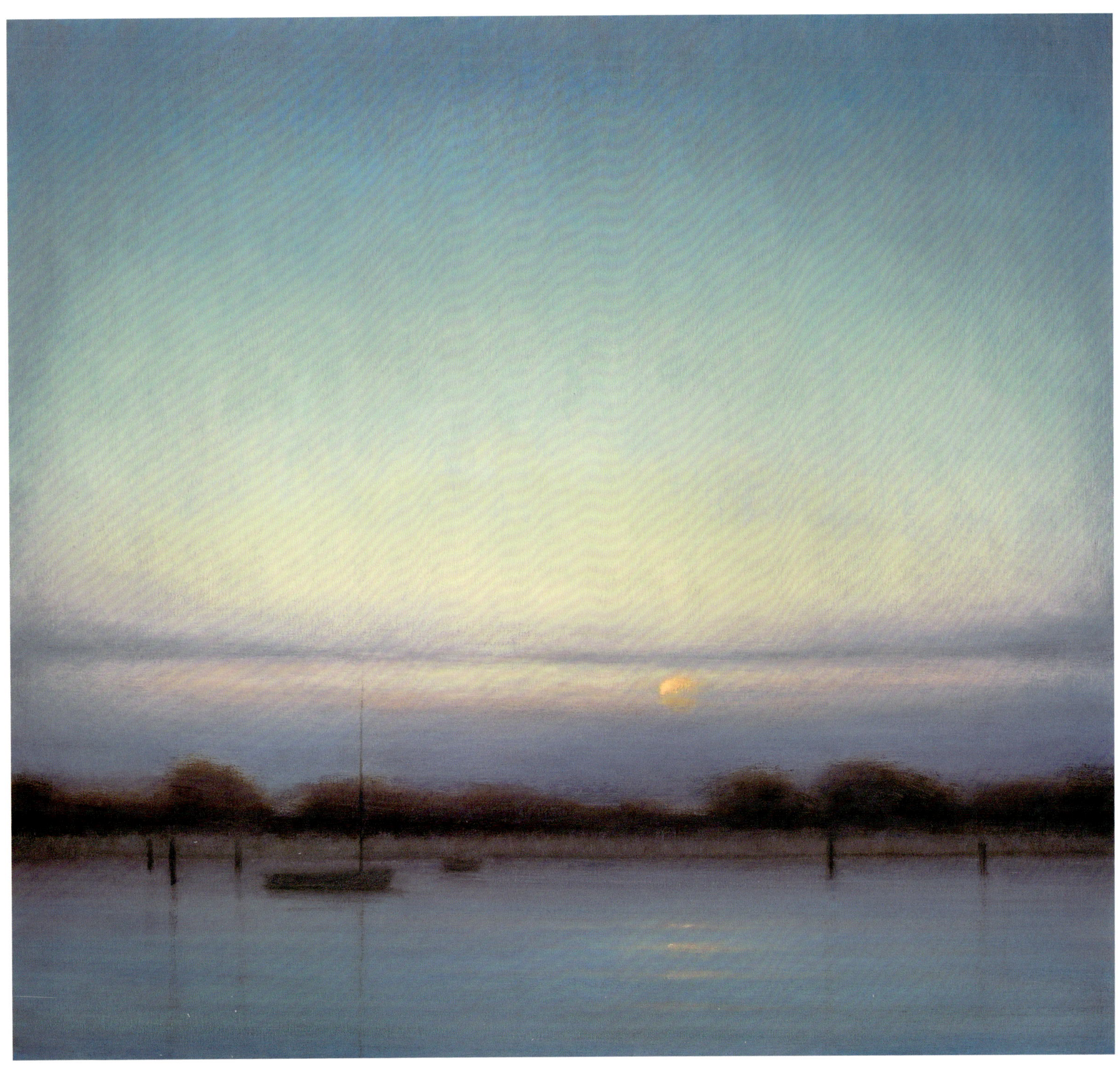

EVERY HOUR OF THE LIGHT

The Paintings of Mary Sipp Green

Foreword by Louis Zona, PhD

Essay by Beth Venn

THE ARTIST BOOK FOUNDATION

NEW YORK   LONDON   HONG KONG

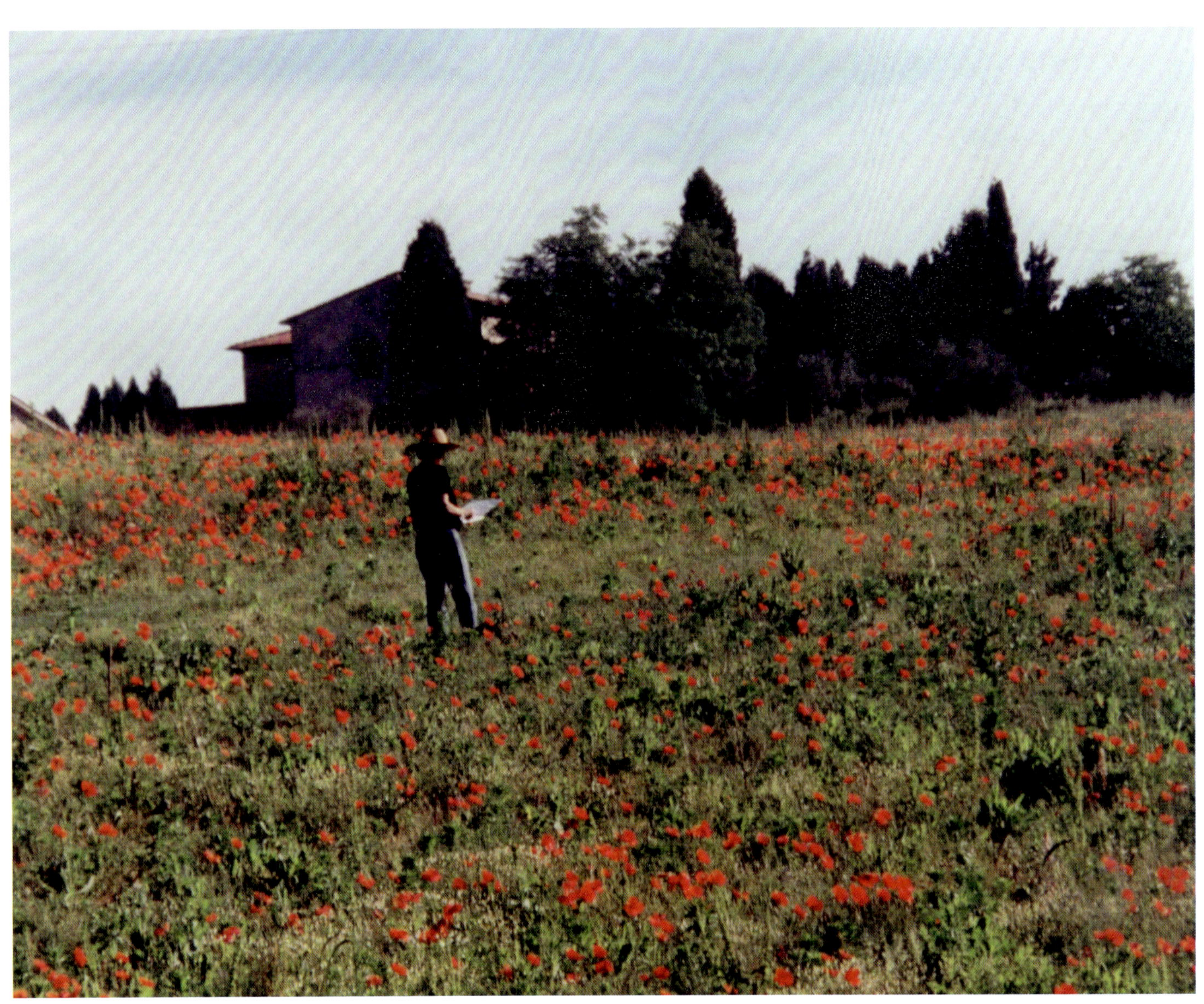

TABLE OF CONTENTS

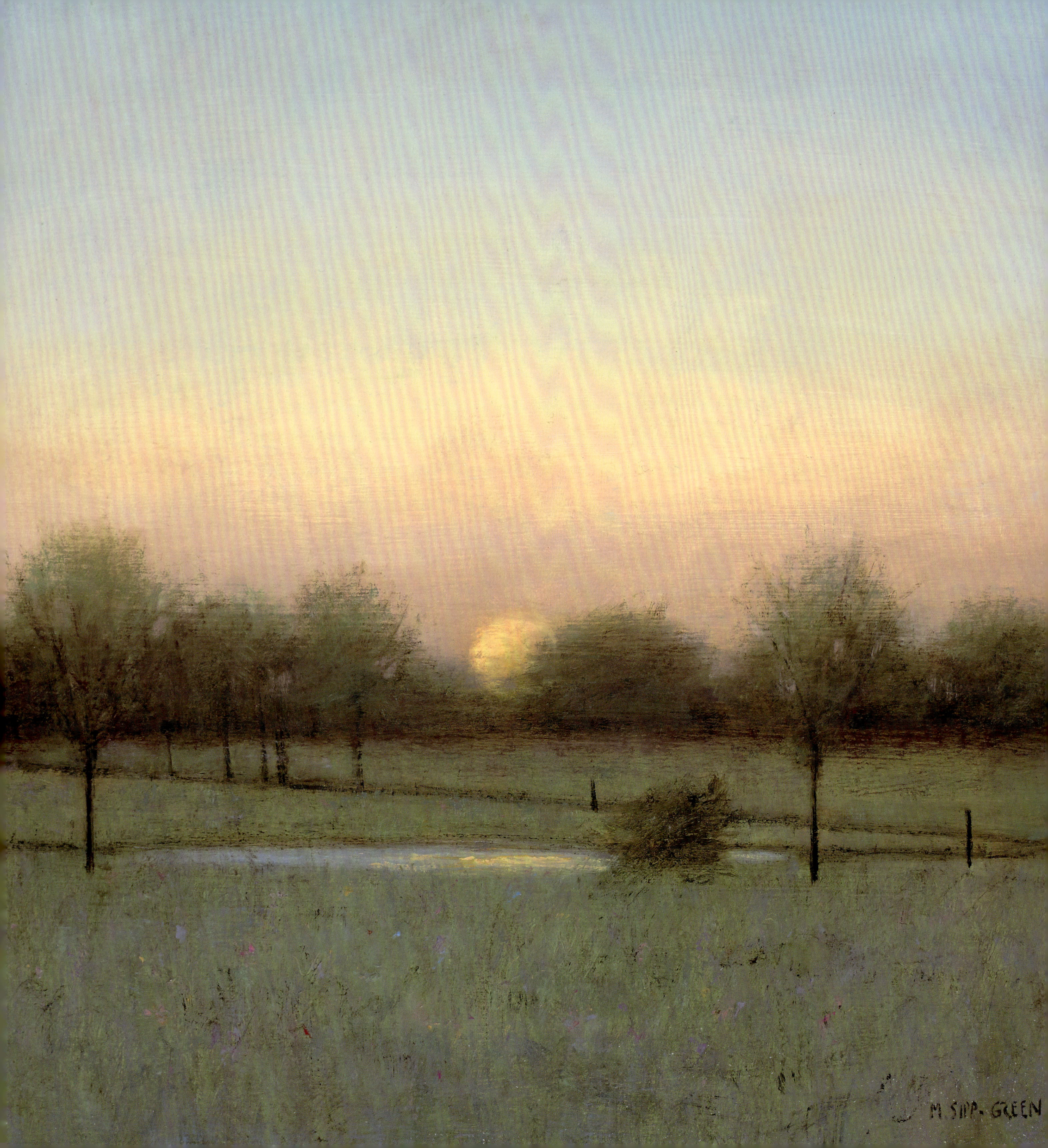
M. SIPP. GREEN

To me every hour of the light and dark is a miracle,

Every cubic inch of space is a miracle,

Every square yard of the surface of the earth is spread with
the same,

Every foot of the interior swarms with the same.

(Walt Whitman, "Miracles," stanza 2)

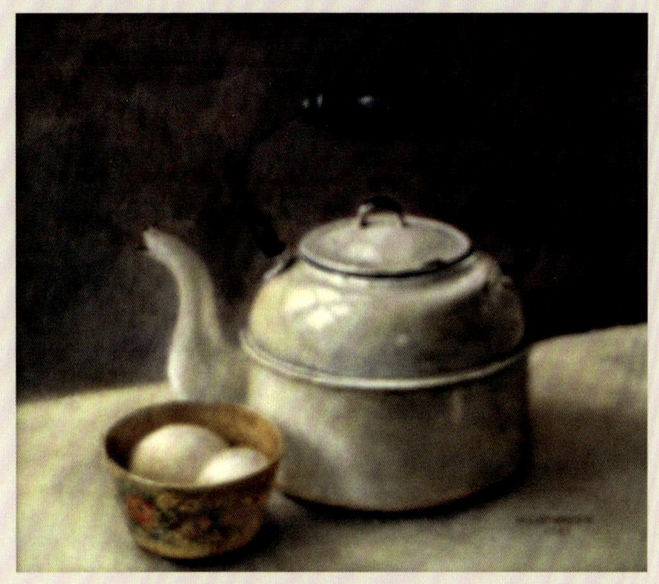

This book is dedicated to my mother Anna,

my first friend,

whose love, kindness, and encouragement never wavered.

ACKNOWLEDGMENTS

I would like to thank and acknowledge the friends and collectors who made this book possible: Dr. Eric and Wendy Vinokur; Celeste and Kent Damon; Frank Hood; Chris and Sheila Morse; Denise Grenier and Peter Kreisky; Dr. Michael Zito; Bruce and Judy Grinnell; Alan Douglas; Karen Bromley; Alix Keating; Margaret Whitton and Warren Spector; and Ken and Jill Iscol.

Many thanks to everyone who lent their invaluable time and interest to this project, in particular: my family, Jared, Laurence, Zoé, and Juliette; Eileen McDermott and Harvey Rottenberg; Martha Donovan; Rhonda Judy; Cody and Pat Troutman; William and Mary Hangley; Dr. Herbert A. Sipp; Kimberly Ragone; Gloria Henry; Anna Sipp-Bray; Margie Charles Bullock; Nick Mongiardo and his staff at Decorative Arts Studio; Lynn Sonberg and Roger Cooper; Sidney Mackenzie and John Fulop; Ross and Gail Firestone; Paulinda Schimmel; Adele and Arthur Puhn; Laura and Alvin Sinderbrand; Rosario Acquista; Michelle and Chuck Gillette; and Monica Guerra.

A very special thank-you to the galleries that represent my work and to their staff members for their generous help with this project. In particular, I would like to acknowledge James Borynack, owner of the esteemed Wally Findlay Galleries International, for his tireless efforts on my behalf and his extraordinary enthusiasm for developing my career.

I will always greatly appreciate the loyalty and support of Chris and Sheila Morse, owners of the Granary Gallery—where I have exhibited every summer since 1997—on the beautiful island of Martha's Vineyard, which continues to be the location and inspiration for much of my work.

I am indebted to Jo Ellen Harrison, owner of The Harrison Gallery in Williamstown, Massachusetts—the finest gallery in the Berkshires—for her many years of exhibiting my paintings and for her dedication to my work.

I would also like to express particular gratitude to the publisher, Leslie Pell van Breen, who guided my book throughout with her expertise, insight, encouragement, and great care; the staff at The Artist Book Foundation, for all their excellent work on my monograph; Dr. Louis Zona, for his kind words and generosity in writing the foreword; and Beth Venn, for authoring such a brilliant, thoughtful essay and for all the help she provided to this volume.

Finally, I am deeply grateful to:

My father, Herbert H. Sipp, who gave me the gifts of talent and drive as well as his love of art.

Martin I. Green, who believed in me and gave me—above all else—the gift of time.

Bessie Boris and Leo Garel, beloved mentors and friends, who informed my life and my work.

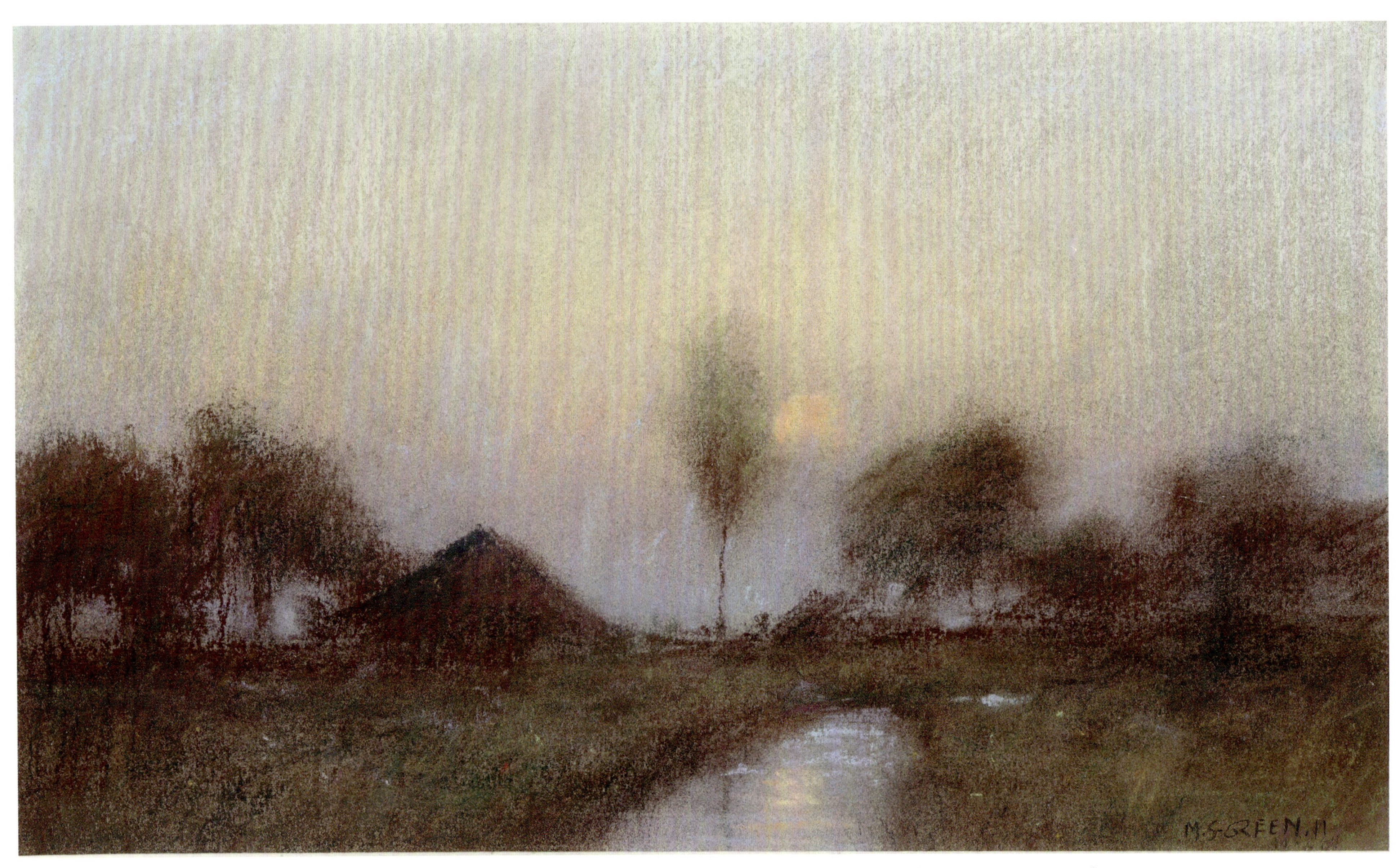

TWILIGHT FALLS, 2011 (shown actual size). Pastel on paper, 6 x 10¼ in. (15.24 x 26.03 cm). The Butler Institute of American Art, permanent collection.

FOREWORD

by Louis Zona, PhD

The landscapes of Mary Sipp Green reflect the rich legacy of American landscape painting dating back to the Hudson River School. What distinguished these early works by Thomas Cole, Asher B. Durand, Frederic Edwin Church, and others—beyond the remarkable skill they consistently displayed—was a sense of the spiritual in the land these artists loved. Indeed, American landscape painting of the 1850s simultaneously reveals the visual wonders of an unspoiled wilderness and asserts the magic felt by Ralph Waldo Emerson and his contemporaries in those magnificent vistas. Emerson and the painters of his day understood that particular kind of spirituality—those unseen forces within nature that inspire both great literature and great art.

Mary Sipp Green reminds us of the sanctity of this land. Had she lived in the nineteenth century, the masters of the Hudson River School would have welcomed her into the fold with open arms. And just as these painters strove to capture the wonder-filled imagery of the Catskill Mountains, they emphasized the importance of the sky as both a visual and a mystical element of that environment. Sipp Green, in her work, clearly places tremendous significance on the interaction of sky and earth. In one sense, her art can be seen as skyscapes, because the sky is such a dominant feature. In another sense, the sky serves as a dramatic and dynamic backdrop and the source of a magic that is felt in all of her images. No one paints the sky with such conviction, and few artists have interpreted its power within the landscape as intuitively as she has done throughout her oeuvre.

The Butler Institute of American Art, our nation's first museum of American art, has devoted much of its gallery space to views of the American landscape. The museum serves as a lasting tribute to those artists whose unique talents have preserved the appearance and the mystical qualities of our great land. Mary Sipp Green's art truly continues the tradition of landscape painting in America. The quality of her work is a beautiful reminder that landscape painting is alive and well. In fact, in the hands of Sipp Green, one of our country's most gifted painters, landscape is not only relevant again but it also reclaims its rightful place at the forefront of contemporary American painting.

Youngstown, Ohio
October 2013

SUNFLOWERS FROM TORRITA, 2007. Oil on linen, 46 x 48 in. (116.8 x 121.9 cm). Private collection.

The Pursuits of Mary Sipp Green

by Beth Venn

The Berkshires have long been fertile territory—not just for artists but for anyone seeking the uncontested beauty and spiritual allure of this part of the country. Here nature does not merely sit back and exist; it actively asserts itself in the dramatic hillsides, the roaring rivers, and even in the calmer beauty of forests and country lanes. It is against this backdrop that artist Mary Sipp Green has made her life. At first, it might seem an obvious location for someone whose paintings reveal so much about the natural world and what it has to communicate to us; however, that connection implies a far too simplistic relationship between her environment and her art, one that too easily glosses over the complicated correlation between the artist and the way she sees the world. "When you live in one place for such a long time, you come to know it well—how the light travels, when and which fields are flooded or carpeted with an interesting color, that the sky has an unusual blue in the winter at twilight or a particular violet just before a spring rainstorm. My paintings are a summation of these kinds of experiences."[1] She has not merely studied this terrain; she has internalized it, as well as that of other locales as diverse as Martha's Vineyard, Cumberland Island (Georgia), and the fields and hills of Tuscany.

It is difficult to comfortably position Green along the continuum of American landscape painting. While her work shares certain tenets of Hudson River School paintings—wide landscapes featuring vast skies and the particular plays of light at dawn and dusk—it also emphasizes the land's inherent spirituality, a quality so often seen in the work of the Luminists. At times, her brushstrokes mimic the dotting and patterning of the Impressionists and her broad strokes some of the non-objectivity of the Abstract Expressionists.

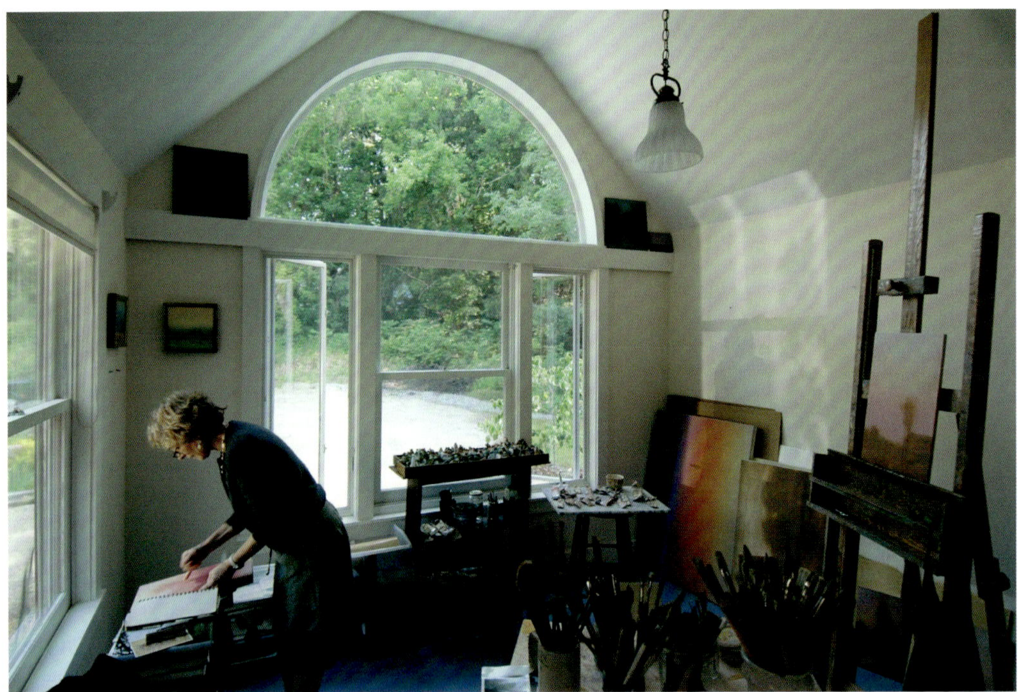

When noting her influences, Green refers to figures as divergent as the mid-nineteenth-century land-scapist George Inness, the twentieth-century color-field master Mark Rothko, and the late paintings of the enigmatic modernist Albert Pinkham Ryder.

Mary Sipp Green's home sits on a quiet lane on the banks of the Housatonic River in Stockbridge, Massachusetts. It is her world, in the broadest sense—her nearby fellow artists and the creative milieu of artist colonies, music festivals, and dance performances in this unique part of the country, in addition to the landscape itself—that provides the backdrop from which her inspiration springs. A few steps from her home, in a structure built specifically for painting, is Green's studio. This large and airy space encompasses every aspect of her practice: from the smallest scribble of a sketch on a scrap of paper to a basket of bound sketchbooks, to her raw materials of paint and primed canvas and an array of oil paints in every hue, to paintings in all stages of development on easels. It is here that the artist finds her refuge and continually refines her vision for each work (fig. 1). Green responds to how her paintings progress: she gleans valu-able insights when she deals with their development rather than how closely they conform to her original ideas. And, in turn, her landscapes engage viewers by inviting them to drift into the space, to experience the light and atmosphere, to become entranced by the cloaks of color, and to reflect upon comparable places that have punctuated their own lives.[2]

Mary Sipp Green's paintings are beautiful, serene, and often awe-inspiring. Their stillness can be meditative; their raw surge of color, breathtaking. It can be difficult to openly discuss the concept of pure beauty; much postmodern discourse finds the concept passé, and if it were truly the only thing that drew us to these works, it still might be enough. But her works are more than these formal qualities: Their intensity, their precise compositions, and their sheer virtuosity are the result of a complex web of influences, experiences, life lessons, and keen perceptions that come into play each time Green puts brush to canvas.

> *This is indeed a process in every sense of the word, and even when I am not painting, I still experience life as an artist: thinking about the work, observing my natural surroundings, learning from other artists, and searching for new expressive possibilities. At times, I am reminded of a remark John Cage once made regarding musical composition: 'Everything you do is music and everywhere is the best seat.' For me, this also says something about the fundamental appeal of a life in painting: to be always and everywhere involved in the mysterious dimensions of the everyday, in the extraordinary way in which the visible world can articulate something meaningful through the medium of paint.[3]*

As a child, Green never doubted the direction her adult life would take: "I was fortunate to grow up in a family of creative people, and I learned the skills of drawing and painting at an early age."[4] Although her formal art training would not begin until much later, she spent many a day in the family's home in Valley Stream, New York, poring over images of the world's most renown artworks via a series of stamps issued by The Metropolitan Museum of Art in the 1950s. She would also travel into the city to visit the museum itself, "walking in the rooms, seeing those dark paintings, the Impressionist works, the Modiglianis."[5] From an early age, wonder, experimentation, and curiosity—as well as trial and error—were not only accepted but encouraged: "We never had a regular Christmas tree. It was always something different. My dad would bring home all assortments of odds and ends, materials of all types, and we would make our own ornaments. Also, we were allowed to draw on the walls."

Herbert Sipp, the artist's father, graduated first in his class from New York City's Pratt Institute in the mid-1940s and went on to become a successful graphic designer. His design studio created the logos and packaging for many consumer products and pharmaceutical companies. Her mother, Anna, was equally artistic and—although not formally trained—naturally multitalented. She designed and made many of

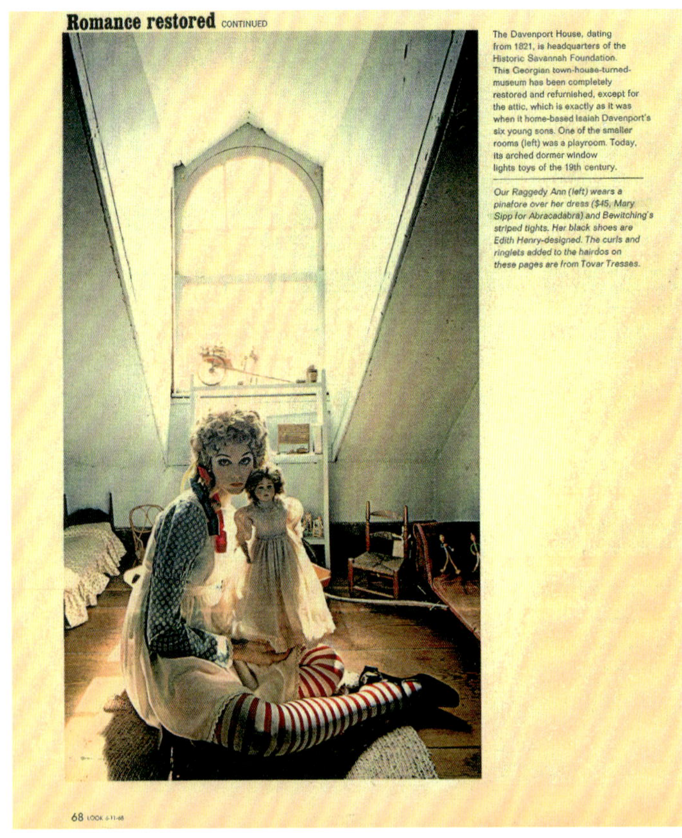

FIG. 2 *Look* magazine, June 11, 1968 article featuring designer Mary Sipp.

FIG. 3 Advertisement for Xanadu Boutique (owner-designer Mary Sipp Green), New York City, in *Village Voice*, 1969.

her children's clothes, basing them on fashions she would see in store window displays. She was a gifted singer, gardener, and baker; she even took up painting when she was well into her eighties. Green's parents bestowed if not an innate talent upon all four of their children, then at least the notion that art in all its forms was a valid and worthwhile pursuit. She also recalls both of her parents as having a generosity of spirit, a desire to help others—to bring in those who had fallen on hard times or to set up a friend with a new business. This goes a long way toward explaining Green's own earnestness; she is warm and welcoming, and very comfortable talking about her life and artistic pursuits. This same attitude carries over to her work and to her working method. She is open and nonjudgmental about her process while she works through the questions that need to be answered and the problems that need to be resolved in the early stages of her paintings. Rather than imposing her own will, she lets a painting "find itself"—to suggest what form it will ultimately take.

Green's interest in forging a creative life led her to Greenwich Village in its heyday. She fondly recalls the 1960s as a time so full of artistic expression that it was palpable on the downtown streets of New York City. In 1967, she graduated from New York's Fashion Institute of Technology with a degree in design and illustration. For the next several years she designed her own patterns and sold her one-of-a-kind fashions to such legendary New York boutiques as Abracadabra and Henri Bendel (fig. 2). While still a student, she attended an audition where models were being sought for an advertising campaign. Marty Green, an advertising executive whose company specialized in fashion and promotion, had come to FIT in search of new modeling talent. It was here that the two met, and they married in 1968. Soon they moved to a grand apartment in Chelsea and opened their own boutique in the West Village; they named their store "Xanadu" and ran ads in the *Village Voice*, characterizing it as "a paradise lost" (fig. 3). But Green's life in the late-1960s fashion world of New York was short-lived; in early 1971, she and Marty left the city and, in anticipation of the birth of their child, made a dramatic move to rural upstate New York. Throughout the 1970s, Green continued to design women's clothes, but she ultimately found the fashion world's insistence on seasonally changing styles to be calculated and too prescriptive, and she began to rethink the route her creative pursuits might take; the rigors of the design process and the compositional problem solving inherent in fashion would be instrumental to this next phase.

Green's creative childhood, artistic studies, early years as a fashion designer, and supportive parents could have shaped her life in any number of directions. For a time, she had even explored ceramics, and she once owned a darkroom where she printed her own photographs. But she always found herself drawn to the complexities and challenges of painting because, as she puts it, "it was the most difficult. The truth about it is that [one] never master[s] it. It's a search that really lasts [one's] entire life." In time, she came to understand that she really could do nothing else—that no other pursuit would intrigue her, challenge her, and force her to work through creative dilemmas and find her own path, her own solutions, quite the way painting would.

In the early 1980s, Green was part of a small group of artists who worked under the direction of a realist painter from the Berkshire area. They focused primarily on still lifes and portraits. Their working process was methodical and systematic. Initial drawings and detailed charcoal studies eventually led to finished paintings. The instruction, based largely on observation and imitation, was intended to train the

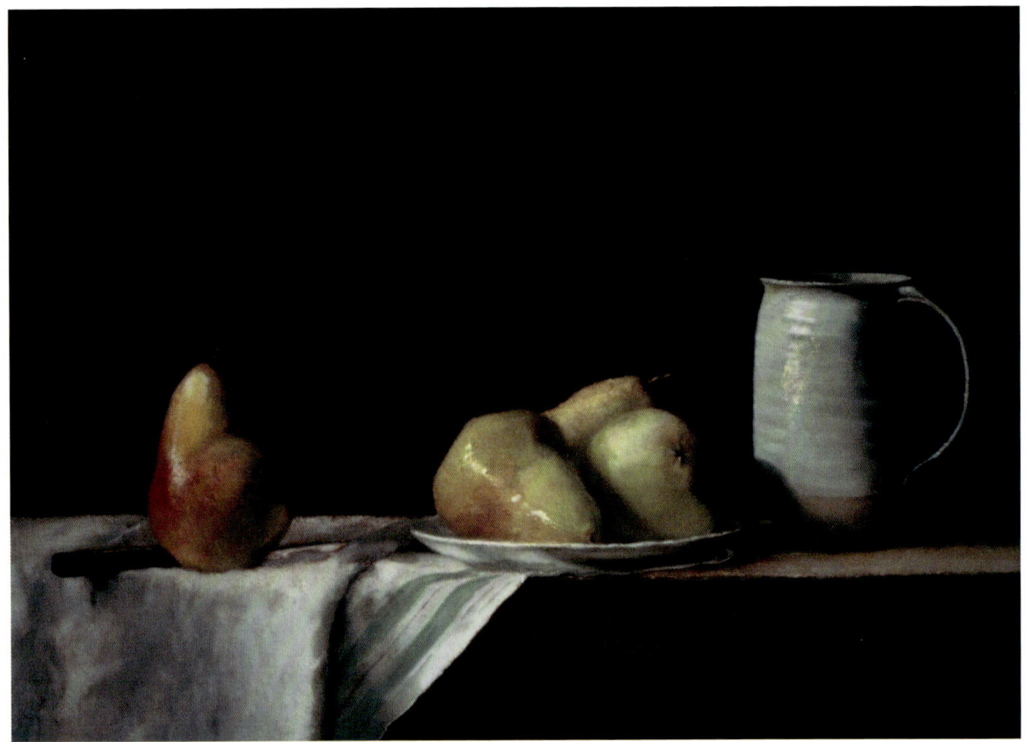

FIG. 4 *Autumn Pears,* 1983. Oil on linen, 18 x 24 in. (45.7 x 61 cm). Private collection.

painters to transfer to paper and canvas what they were seeing before them. Some of Green's work from this time has the quality of Dutch, Old Master paintings. *Autumn Pears* (1983) (fig. 4) is one of her earliest still lifes. The dramatically lit elements on the table contrast starkly with the solid dark background. The fruit, the bowl, and the cloth are all carefully articulated, their forms deftly expressed through the play of light and shadow. It was through these early studies of still objects that Green mastered the skill and gained the confidence to almost effortlessly transfer a three-dimensional view to a two-dimensional surface.

It is interesting to note that the human figure is almost never present in the artist's later paintings. Her early sketchbooks, however, are filled with the human form, and these figure studies contributed an important early role in the way Green learned to translate mass, darks, and lights onto a two-dimensional surface. Her charcoal figure studies (fig. 5) are perfectly proportioned, and she nimbly makes use of shading and contrasts to build up a sense of solid form. Although much of her early work in still lifes and figures would disappear from her oeuvre, this body of formal studies in composition, perspective, and mass

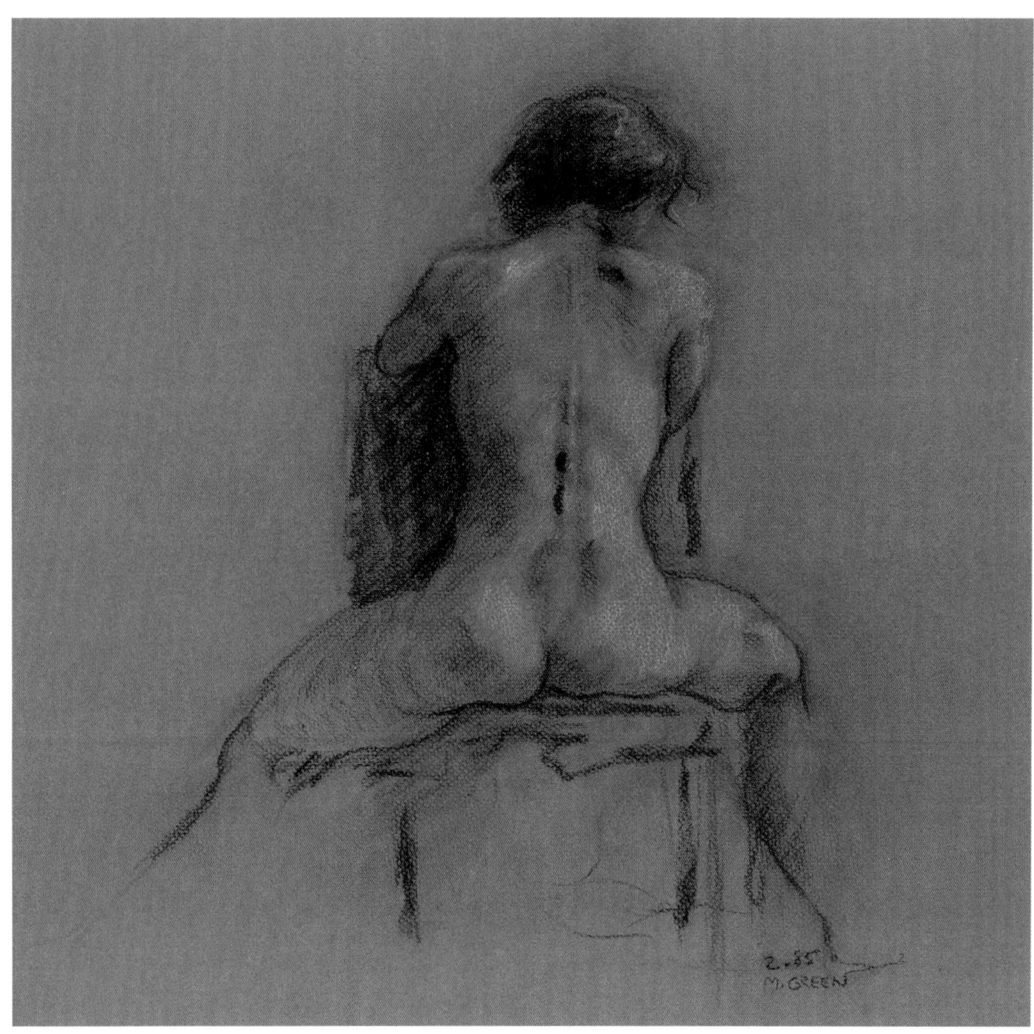

FIG. 5 *Seated Figure*, 1985. Charcoal on paper, 16¾ x 17¾ in. (42.5 x 45.1 cm). Artist's collection.

served as the foundation for Green's foray into the challenges and complexities of landscape painting. She would ultimately veer away from verisimilitude and lean toward the atmospheric and the abstract.

During these early days of painting, her artist group decided to work outdoors. She recalls that there was an initial wariness among the members because capturing a likeness proved more difficult in nature than in the more controlled still lifes: "everything—the clouds, the light, the branches, the grass—everything moved!" Green, however, loved it. She had finally found what she had been searching for; the drama as well as the unexpected, uncertain, and ever-changing nature of the outdoors was where she felt most

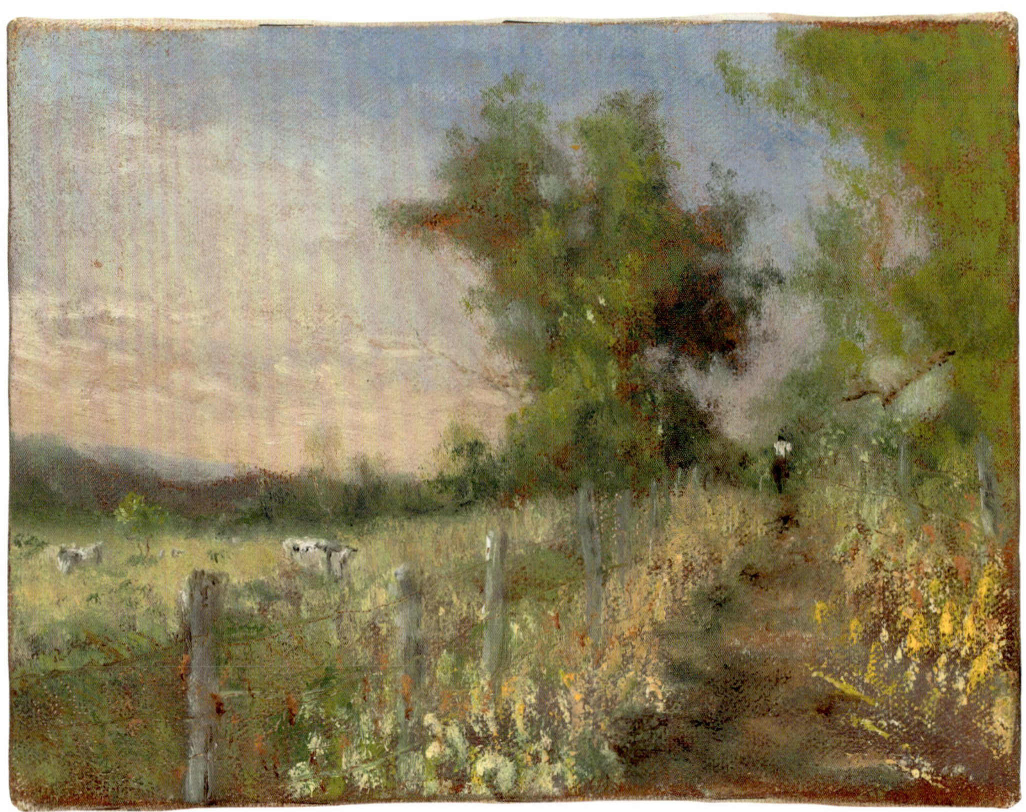

FIG. 6 *Undermountain Farm*, 1982. Oil on linen, 6 x 8 in. (15.2 x 20.3 cm). Artist's collection.

alive and most fulfilled as an artist. She reveled in how natural forms could be compositional elements and how the changing nature of light and shadows could transform a scene. But these landscapes, painted en plein air, like her 1982 painting, *Undermountain Farm* (fig. 6), affirm an early reliance on precise detail and a formal, even composition where the eye is not drawn to any one focal point but, rather, takes in the scene as a whole. The artist dotes on the field of flowers and grasses and the uneven path in the foreground, while the large trees seem to crowd out and obscure the sky—an element that would become such an important part of the artist's landscapes later. Eventually, while still painting en plein air, she would begin to take liberties with the scenes in front of her, subtly moving objects around in compositions and altering color schemes as the light changed and she learned that objects could be shifted to create more dynamic compositions. In *Early Spring at Tyringham* (1986) (fig. 7), she depicted a scene of large black cows in a field while she sat in her car along the side of the road. She painted this scene several times as the cows moved and the light of the late day changed. The cows themselves became sculptural elements, and she took the

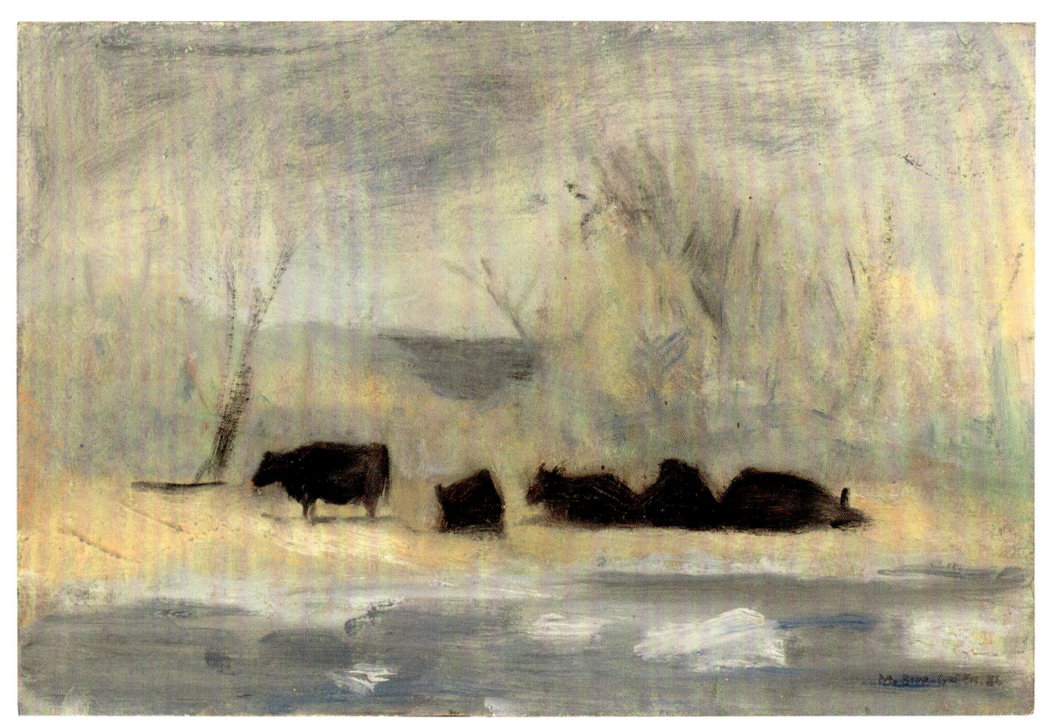

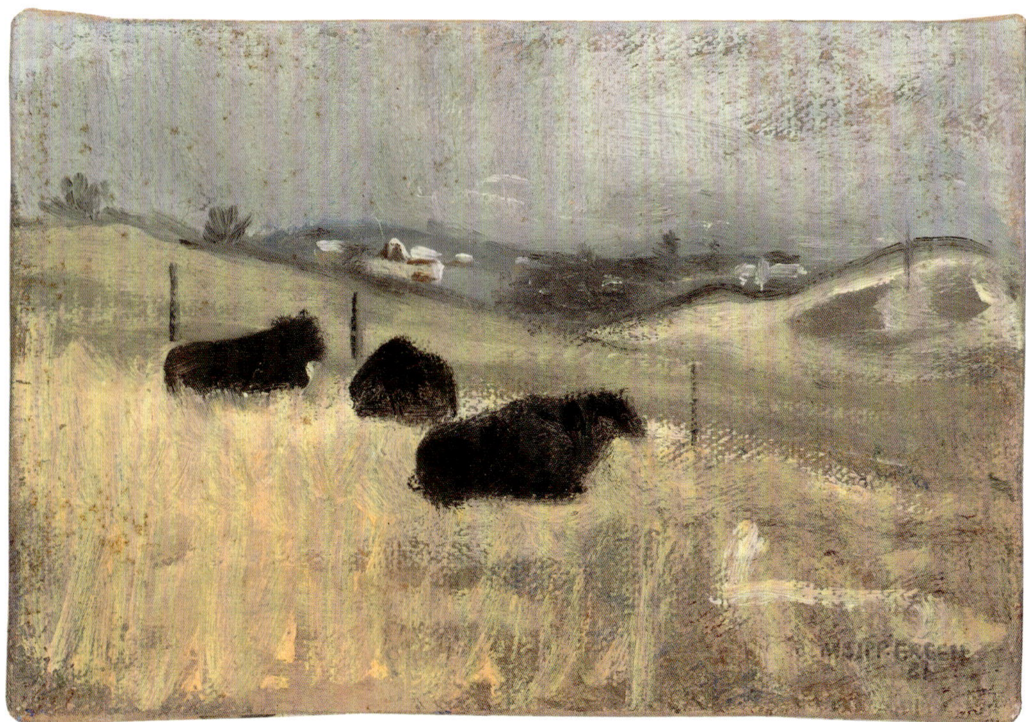

FIG. 7 *Early Spring at Tyringham*, 1986. Oil on linen, 6 x 9 in. (15.2 x 22.9 cm). Artist's collection. [bottom: 4 x 6 in. (10.2 x 15.2 cm).]

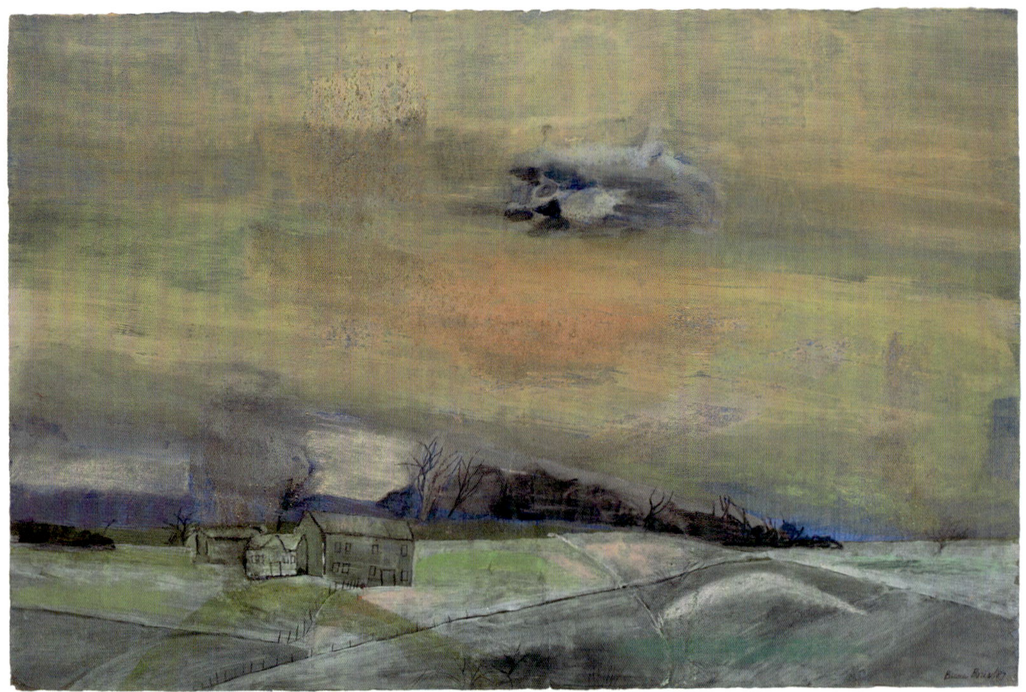

FIG. 8 Bessie Boris, *Taft Farm Fields,* 1987. Mixed media (acrylic, oil pastel, pastel charcoal, and sand) on paper, 26 x 39½ in. (66 x 100.3 cm). Artist's collection.

liberty of moving them about to experiment with different arrangements. In this work, as in others at this time, Green was just beginning to get a feel for a scene and for her own ability to render it in a way that best captured its essence.

In the late 1980s, at the Smith College Museum of Art, Green encountered for the first time the paintings of Bessie Boris, an artist Green would soon learn was also from the Berkshires and who, as it would turn out, would have much to offer a younger painter still trying to find her place and her confidence. Boris's early life as an artist was spent largely in New York City, where she had received a scholarship to study at Pratt. She later took classes at The Art Students League under the tutelage of such luminaries as George Grosz and Vaclav Vytlacil. Through her studies and later through her teaching of art classes as part of the Works Progress Administration, Boris knew many important postwar artists, including Willem de Kooning and the great mid-century portraitist Alice Neel, who painted her portrait in 1942. In the late 1970s, Boris moved to the Berkshires, where she continued to paint still lifes and portraits while delving more and more into landscape. Her confidence as an artist manifested itself in her bold use of color and

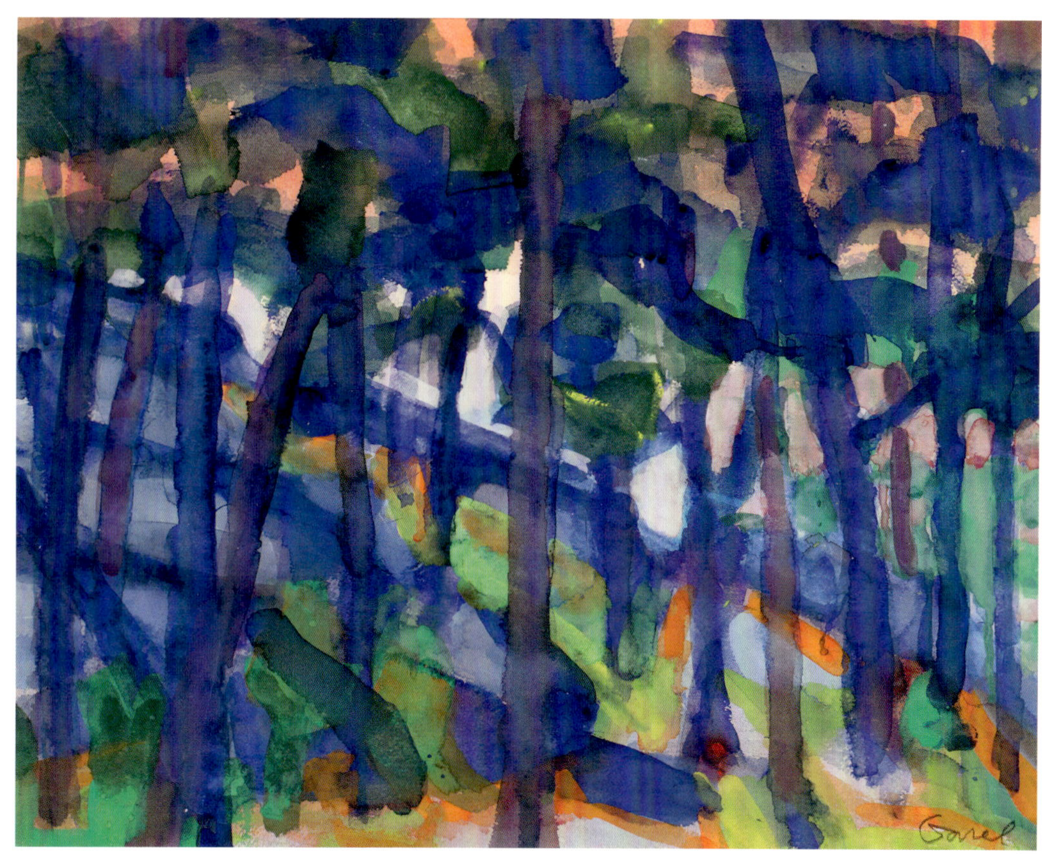

FIG. 9 Leo Garel, *Stockbridge Woods*, 1992. Gouache on paper, 18½ x 23½ in. (47 x 59.7 cm). Artist's collection.

expressive rendering of forms that, nonetheless, often gave her late paintings a melancholy character. In *Taft Farm Fields* (1987; fig. 8), the structures that form the farm appear ghostlike, caught between a sky dominated by thin washes of blues and yellows and a land of rolling, snowcapped hills. As she did with many of her works on paper, she included here sand scumbled with paint, which adds texture to this stark scene. As scholar Debra Bricker Balken wrote of Boris, "She has always had an interest in change, in meta-morphosis, in the passage of life to death … she has particularized features that pertain to adversity, deso-lation, and despair. A disquieting and often somber character pervades her work."[6]

Although Boris and Green would remain close and their artistic styles linked until Boris's death in 1993, the older artist admitted that there was not much she could do to help Green's work progress and grow more nuanced. The two enjoyed a deep friendship, painting together often at various spots in the Berkshires and visiting art galleries and museums throughout the Northeast. Boris wished to avoid the typical mentor relationship in which a student imitates the teacher's process and style; instead, she encouraged Green to be true to her own vision.

It was Boris who introduced Green to the painter who would become her most important mentor: another Stockbridge-area luminary, the artist, cartoonist, and teacher Leo Garel. Born in Brooklyn, Garel studied at Parsons School of Design and The Art Students League (like Boris, he was a student of Grosz and Vytlacil). In 1976, he moved to Stockbridge to be the director of the art department at Austen Riggs, the legendary psychiatric treatment hospital. Garel was strongly influenced by Hans Hofmann; the Abstract Expressionist's keen understanding of pictorial composition, special illusion, and color play are readily evident in Garel's paintings. In Garel's *Stockbridge Woods* (1992; fig. 9), long horizontal washes of color are interrupted by carefully placed verticals that ground the scene and draw the eye back and forth between sky and land. In some instances, tree trunks vertically dissect the composition, producing a type of rhythm across the surface. "Using simple means—broad, sometimes blocky strokes of a thick brush—he endows his pictures with deep mystery and, above all, with a magical sensuous presence."[7] This same pictorial device can be seen in many of Green's early gouaches, such as *Autumn Woods* (1992; fig. 10), where strong verticals intersect the bold colors of the land. Green is often drawn to verticals—trees, electrical poles, fence posts. They contribute to a formal arrangement that the artist views as "more than a satisfying arrangement of shapes … a palpable tension."

It was while working with Garel in the late 1980s and early 1990s that Green went through a transitional phase she sometimes refers to as her "break period"—a time when she felt she was truly coming to trust herself as an artist. At that time, she was able to take what she learned from her past experiments and from her mentors in order to find her own way with a renewed confidence. She gradually stopped trying to perfect the "facts" of the picture and instead allowed herself more freedom in the interpretation of her subjects. She recalls, "I'd been working for so many years at a high level of skill, but I came to realize that's not enough. Painting did not necessarily have to do with what I was looking at but, rather, what I was feeling. I began allowing myself to create art versus verisimilitude." She was making great strides in her art, working more intuitively in the hopes of capturing the underlying spirit of her subjects. In this transitional work, she began to understand that "art is more than just a pleasing arrangement of colors and shapes; [it is] a resolution of conflict."[8] She began to leave out the details that would only complicate her true experience of a place or a subject. She wanted to reveal a subject's essence, to keep the viewer's focus on strong, dramatic compositional elements.

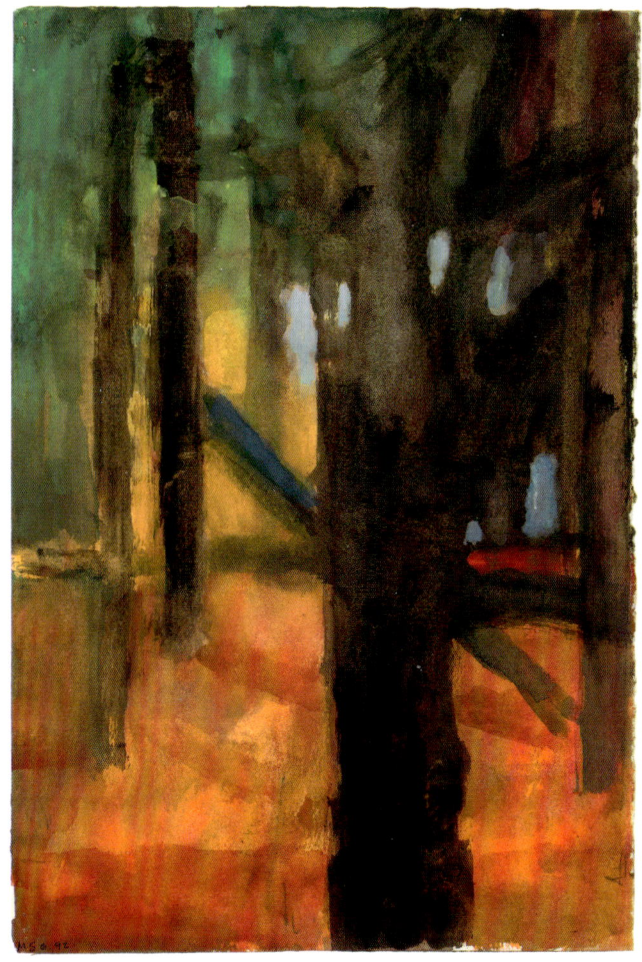

FIG. 10 *Autumn Woods*, 1992. Gouache on paper, 12 x 8 in. (30.5 x 20.3 cm).
Artist's collection.

Peonies (1986; fig. 11) is a seminal work from this period. After years of painting still-life subjects, Green looked at these simple flowers in a vase and sought to capture their very essence, their unique color and texture. Peonies is the end result of a process in which the artist first painted a well-observed scene of flowers in a vase on a table beside a window; then, with Garel's encouragement, she painted over it entirely, wiping out the original image and starting anew. It was only when she did this that she could begin to have an inner dialogue about what the painting was really about. The resulting composition directs the eye to the flowers themselves, as all secondary detail fades away. The edges of the table and the window blur into an atmospheric haze, and even the vase lacks the usual shading and highlights that

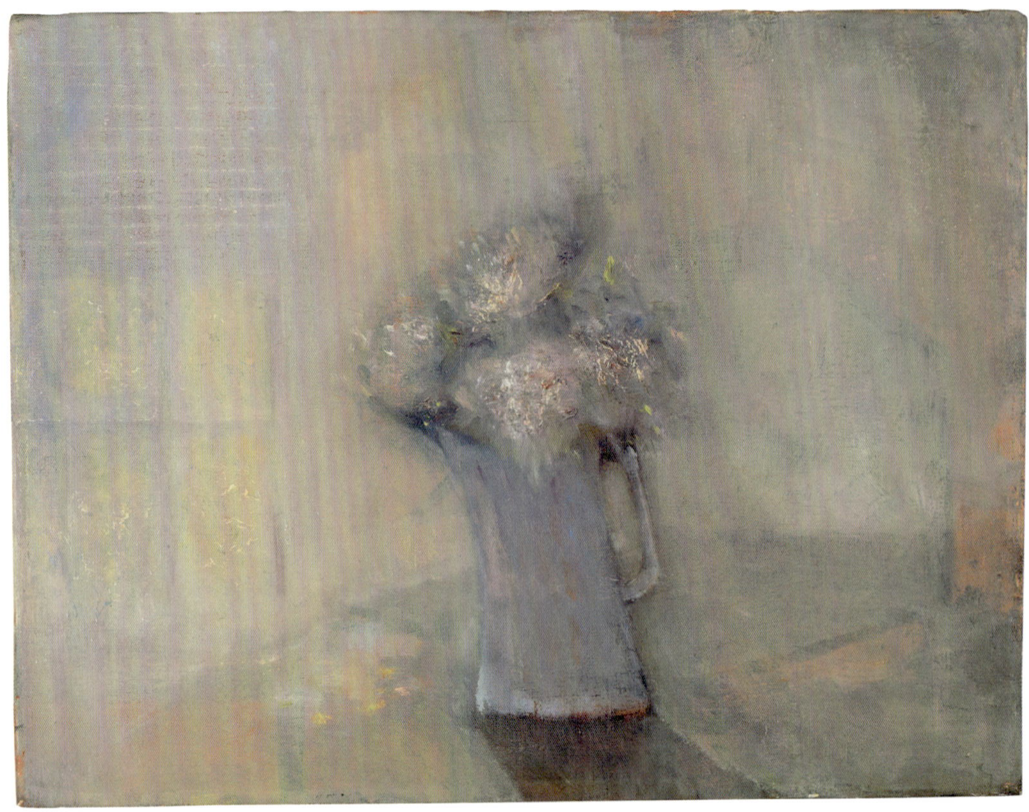

FIG. 11 *Peonies*, 1986. Oil on linen, 12 x 16 in. (30.5 x 40.6 cm). Artist's collection.

would suggest its three-dimensional form. But the peonies themselves virtually pop off the canvas, their tiny petals individualized by bright scumbles of white paint.

At this same time, Green was gradually changing the way she constructed her landscapes. She found herself marveling at the way nature could transform a familiar place through subtle changes in light in different seasons and at different times of day. She began to study landscapes on site, making detailed notations that she would then take back to her studio in order to begin her painting there. The field in *Dusk on Goldenrod* (1991; fig. 12), with its green grasses and gray barn, is one the artist crossed many times. But once she became attuned to the subtle transformations constantly taking place in the natural world, she felt compelled to capture these incidences on canvas. While walking in this field one day, she noted, "the field turned golden with the flowering goldenrod, and in the light the barn became purple."[9] She was immediately aware of the way the scene was portraying opposing colors on the color wheel. The vivid

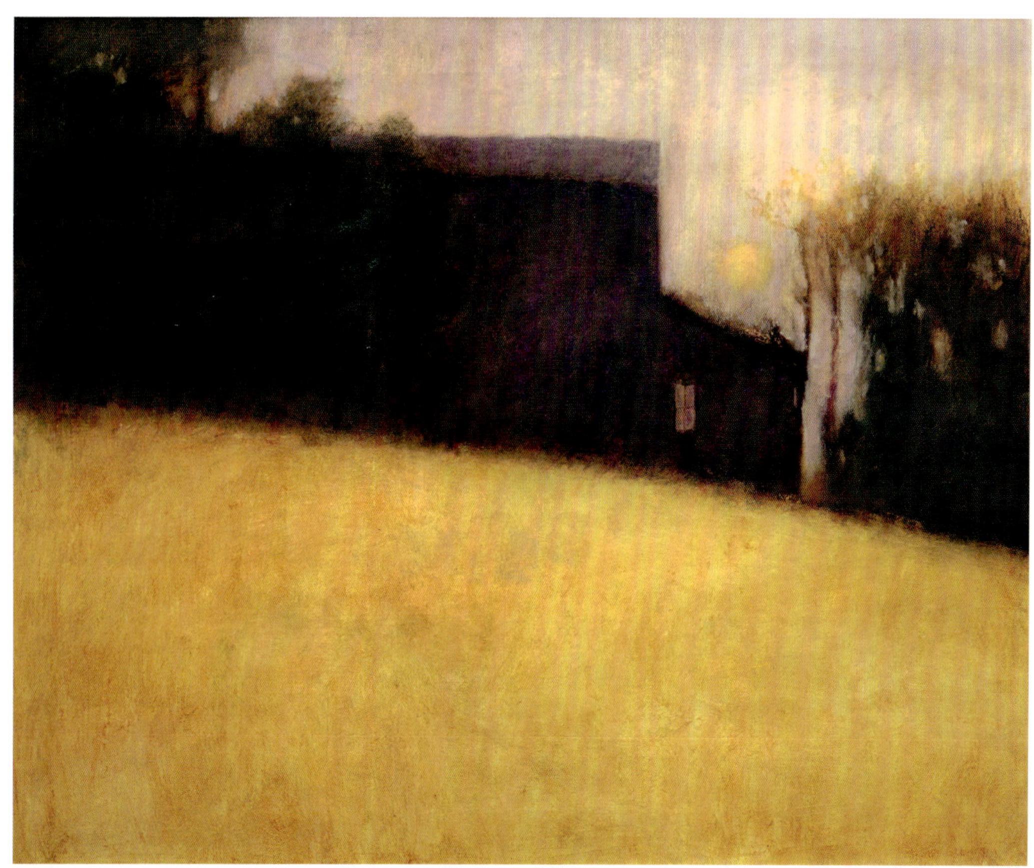

FIG. 12 *Dusk on Goldenrod*, 1991. Oil on linen, 26 x 32 in. (66 x 81.3 cm). Private collection.

violet against the blazing yellow created a tension in the work that she found pleasing and that somehow made the scene complete. "This was about all these colors of autumn—the horizontals broken by strong verticals that ground the scene."[10] It is the first painting in which she was consciously thinking about opposition and tension.

The very manner in which Green applies, scrapes back, and washes layer over layer of veiled hues speaks to her many years with artists like Garel, for whom color combinations and tensions were paramount, and to her own studied process of trial and error and her attempts to replicate colors remembered from nature—whether the light of late day, the particular violet of an iris, or the warm pinks and salmons of a seashell's interior. Although she works with standard tubes of oil paint, she custom blends each of her colors as she paints, often making notations on the backs of works in order to remind herself of her color

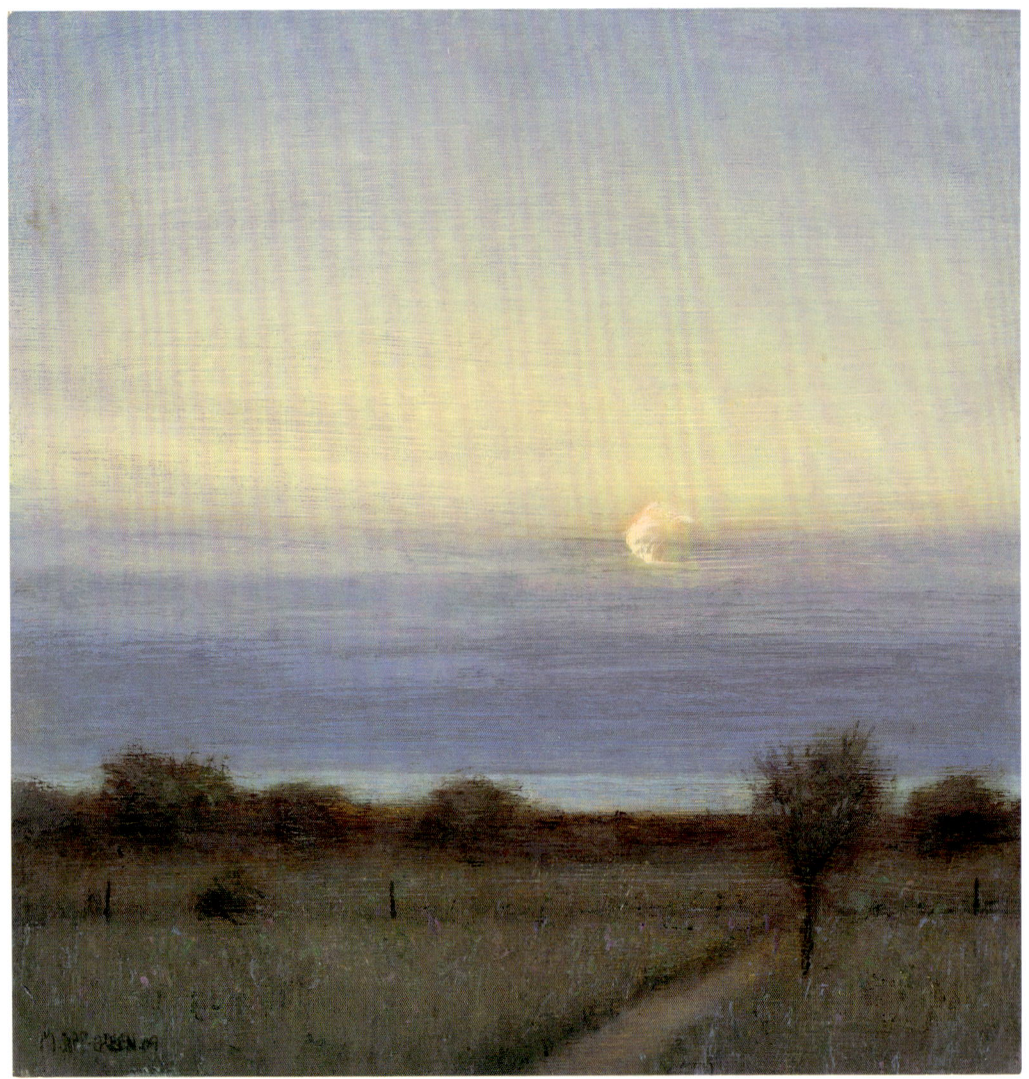

FIG. 13A *Makonikey*, 2009. Oil on board, 9 x 8¾ in. (22.9 x 22.2 cm). Private collection.

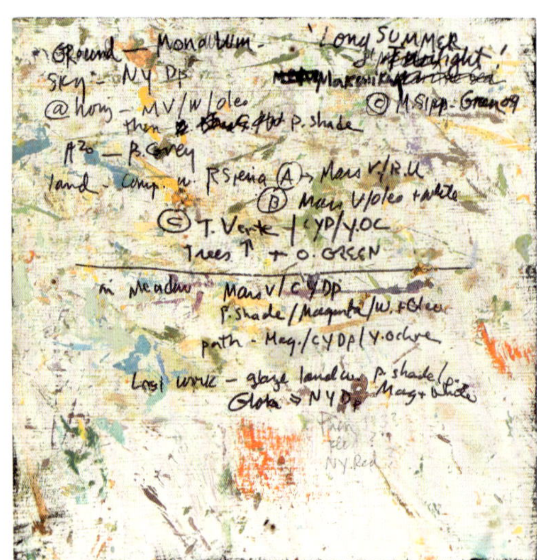

FIG. 13 *Makonikey* (back), 2009.

mixtures. These notes and small patches of color serve as a veritable recipe for the artist, should she ever want to repaint part of the work or use these specific colors to re-create the scene on a larger canvas. The back of *Makonikey* (2009; fig. 13; fig. 13a) is covered in a shorthand that begins by mentioning the painting's ground color, at the far upper-left corner, and moves to references to violet, sienna, ochers, and vert (green), before listing the tones of the glaze toward the end.

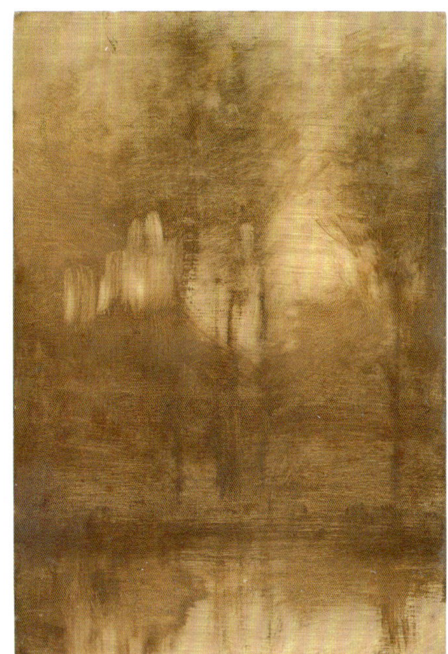

FIG. 13B *Work in Progress*, 2010. Oil on board,
16 x 11 in. (40.6 x 27.9 cm). Artist's collection.

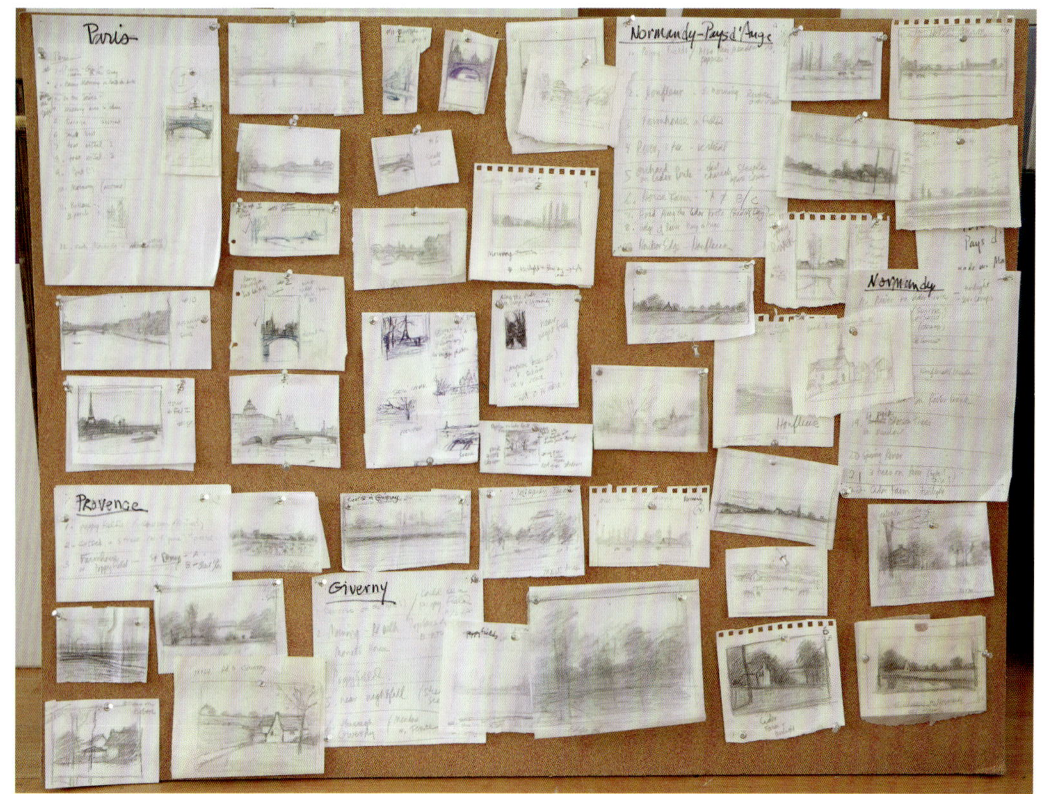

FIG. 14 Sketches pinned to cork board, 2014.

To achieve a diffuse quality of color in these paintings, I use many layers of paint, allowing each to dry before the next is applied. In this way, the colors come to resonate with one another and produce an overall depth of hue even as each remains visible as its own separate plane. This very deliberate technique is only one part of the creative process; however, it is a sort of skeleton key to the final product in which the operations of chance and accident frequently come to govern the direction of the painting. Along the way, the surface of the paint is often refigured in unpredictable ways. There is much that has to be scraped, sanded, destroyed and reapplied before the essence of a place, its mood and atmosphere finally emerges onto the canvas.[11]

Green's studio is filled with paintings in various stages of development (fig. 13b). Her paintings appear so true to their sense of place that one would assume they are painted on site. Instead—although she makes color notes and sketches in the landscape—the paintings originate in the studio "after a meditative interval that allows memory and emotion to guide"[12] her. The artist will often begin work on one

FIG. 15 *River Lights*, 2006. Oil on board, 14 x 16½ in. (35.6 x 41.9 cm). Private collection.

painting and then turn her attention to others, as she is always tending several paintings in various stages of development at any given time. Early works, unfinished studies, notebooks, and drawings—all documents of her almost thirty-five years of painting—are stacked against walls or organized neatly into large albums. A multitude of small sketches pinned to a bulletin board capture, with detailed notations, her thoughts about places, compositions, and qualities of light that she can refer back to when needed (fig. 14).

In some of Green's paintings, especially those from the early to mid-2000s, her brushwork is readily evident, and one can almost see through the various veils of paint to the dominant ground color underneath. In a group of paintings she made of evening scenes on Martha's Vineyard that includes *Quiet Dawn* (2001), *Two Boats* (2003), and *River Lights* (2006; fig. 15), dark, dramatic tones prevail, often punctuated by a single glow of light that emanates from somewhere deep in the background. Edges of buildings and trees are void of crisp lines; in their place, forms appear to blend together, to bleed into one another. But

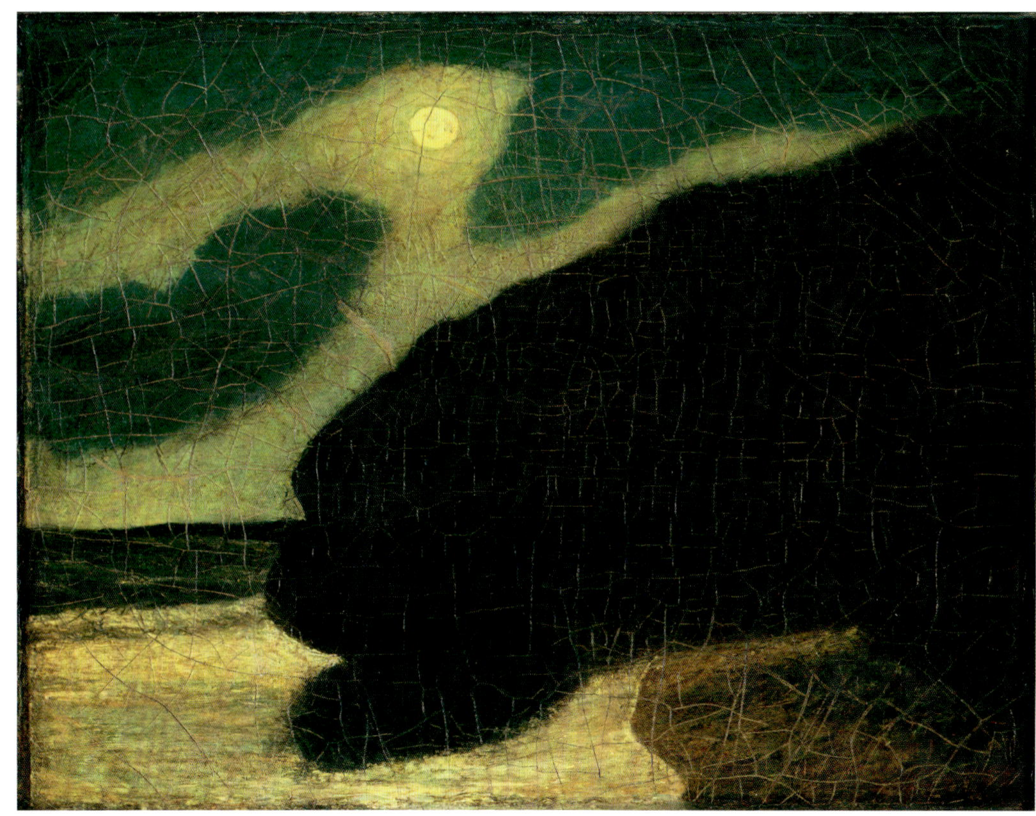

FIG.16 Albert Pinkham Ryder, *Moonlit Cove*, 1880s. Oil on canvas, 14¹/₈ x 17¹/₈ in. (35.8775 x 43.4975 cm). Acquired 1924, The Phillips Collection, Washington, DC.

despite such darkness, there is an inherent glow to these works. Green has long considered the enigmatic painter of mysterious dark scenes, Albert Pinkham Ryder, to be one of the greatest artists of all time. In particular, she extols his late work, such as *Moonlit Cove* (1880s; fig. 16), in which thick layers of paint and glaze combine with the emphasis on nighttime light to instill a powerful mood. The heavy, dark forms in Green's night scenes seem to owe a debt to Ryder and to others like Arthur Dove, who merged an element of nineteenth-century Romanticism with a thoroughly modern approach to forms in space.

Green moves easily between paintings of such nocturnal poetic intensity to scenes in which the sense of light is strong and pervasive. In *Long Twilight at Tuscany* (2009; fig. 17), although the light is just on the cusp of fading, it hangs low in the sky and spreads at a raking angle across the field. Vertical forms—buildings and trees just forward of the horizon—punctuate the scene while subtle diagonals spread out across the foreground as the light hits the planted rows. The painting is tightly composed, with elements that

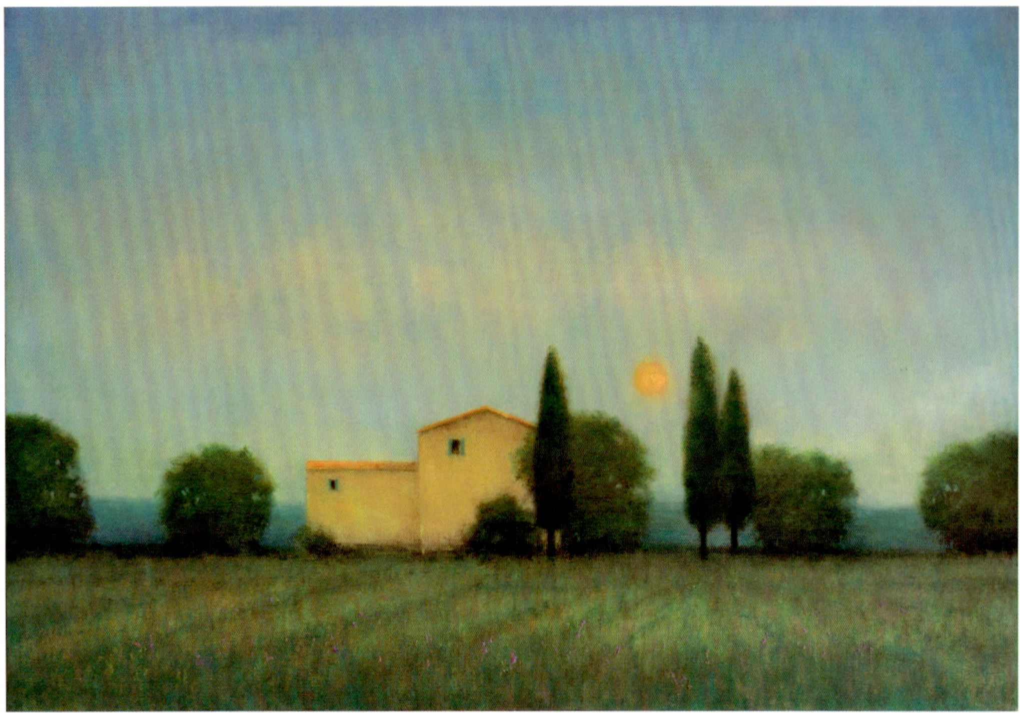

FIG. 17 *Long Twilight at Tuscany*, 2009. Oil on linen, 38 x 56 in. (96.5 x 142.2 cm). Courtesy Wally Findlay Galleries International, Inc.

tend to draw the viewer's gaze to the center of the picture. Green has admitted, "as an artist, [she'd] like to be the director of your eye, to make your eye move and be excited, to pass along [her] experience so it will also resonate in your soul."[13] This painting, too, is the result of careful notes taken by the artist—in this case, while traveling through Tuscany capturing the elements of a particular place that has been an enduring source of inspiration.

At times, Green has sought out very specific topographies for their remarkable colors and legendary beauty. In the spring in 2010, she traveled to Texas after hearing of the impressive fields of bluebonnet flowers that cover vast rolling fields in the central part of the state. There, she wandered through wildflower fields under open Western skies. She sketched furiously, capturing both the details of the individual flowers and the way endless fields of a distinctive hue of blue and ribbons of violet in the sky at dusk created a kind of abstraction. Back in her studio, she composed a series of landscapes based in equal parts on her notations, her color studies, and her memory of that color and light. *Bluebonnets in Twilight* (2010; fig. 18) is one such atmospheric construct. The deep, saturated tones in the field are separated from the sky

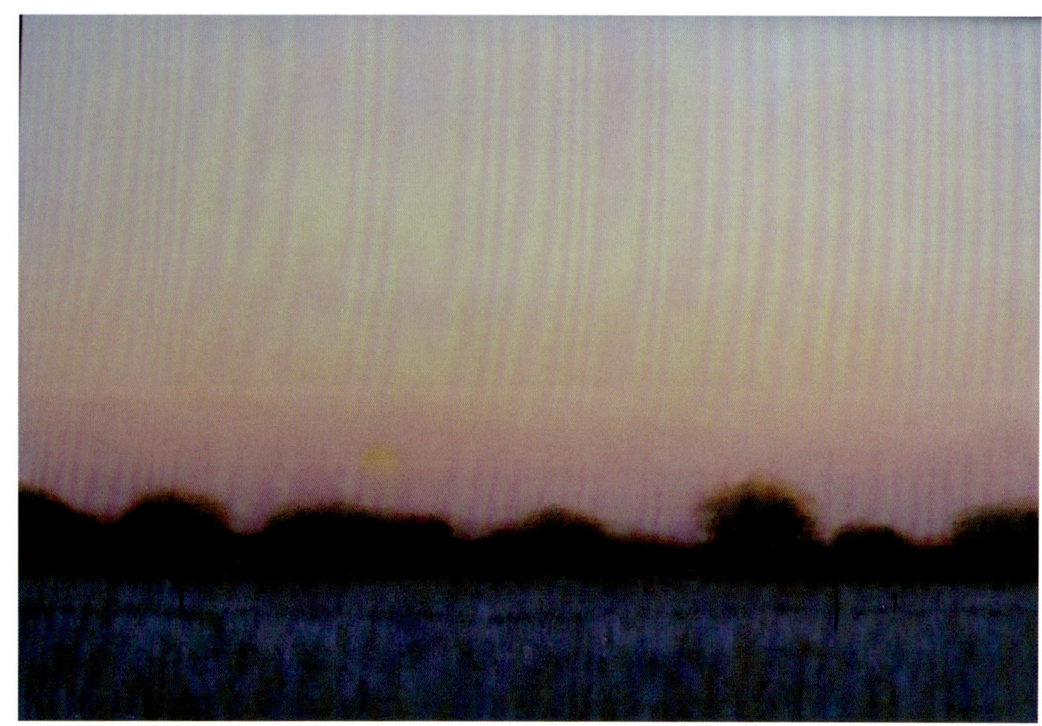

FIG. 18 *Bluebonnets in Twilight*, 2010. Oil on linen, 34 x 50 in. (86.4 x 127 cm). Private collection.

by dark abstracted forms along the horizon, from which a violet hue seems to emanate. The entire composition evokes the nocturnes of James McNeill Whistler, who accentuated tonal harmonies and deemphasized narrative content. What gives so much of Green's work its enigmatic beauty is her ability to develop paintings such as this one, which celebrates the nuances of color so prevalent in nature and encourages us to see these colors in their raw splendor, void of unnecessary detail.

When pressed to name those artists who have had the greatest impact on her work, Green makes frequent reference to the quintessential nineteenth-century American landscape painter, George Inness. Inness, who came of age during the formation of the Hudson River School, viewed nature as a manifestation of the divine and strove to represent it as faithfully as possible, but he distinguished himself from his peers in the profound degree to which philosophical and spiritual ideas inspired his work. In Green's *Berkshire Twilight* (2006; fig. 19), the most prominent feature is the bright yellow glow of the late afternoon's fading light against the simple forms of trees and a solitary farm building. Inness, in such works as *The Lonely Farm, Nantucket* (1892; fig. 20), often devoted large expanses of his canvas to the sky and, like

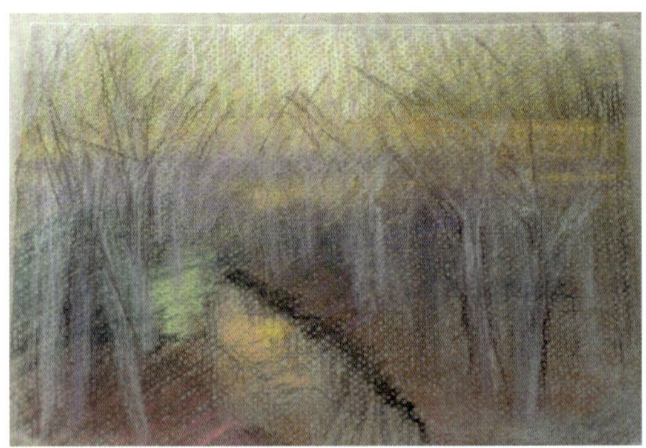

FIG. 21 *Sunset in River*, 1986. Pastel on paper, 6 x 8½ in. (15.2 x 21.6 cm). Artist's collection.

FIG. 19 *Berkshire Twilight*, 2006. Oil on linen, 42 x 56 in. (106.7 x 142.2 cm). Private collection.

Green, allowed it to nearly crowd out the land itself. In *Berkshire Twilight*, man-made structures and trees along the horizon merge with the foreground and are cast in the same deep shadow, making the glow and the spiritual suggestion of the light even more pronounced.

What is interesting to note about many of Green's recent paintings is how much, in terms of color relationships, they owe to some of her earliest pastel sketches. Although a small and rough work, *Sunset in River* (fig. 21) hints to the colors, shading, and toning Green would employ many years later in such paintings as *Berkshire Twilight*. For more than two decades, she has grappled with color relationships, testing them in pastel sketches and small gouaches. Even the notations she so thoughtfully inscribes on the backs of her works are a measure of her careful experiments and her ongoing desire to understand the minutest of changes to tone and hue.

It is the keen understanding of these subtleties and the shedding of unnecessary detail that, at times, cause so many of Green's more recent works to verge on the abstract. In some cases, horizontal bands of

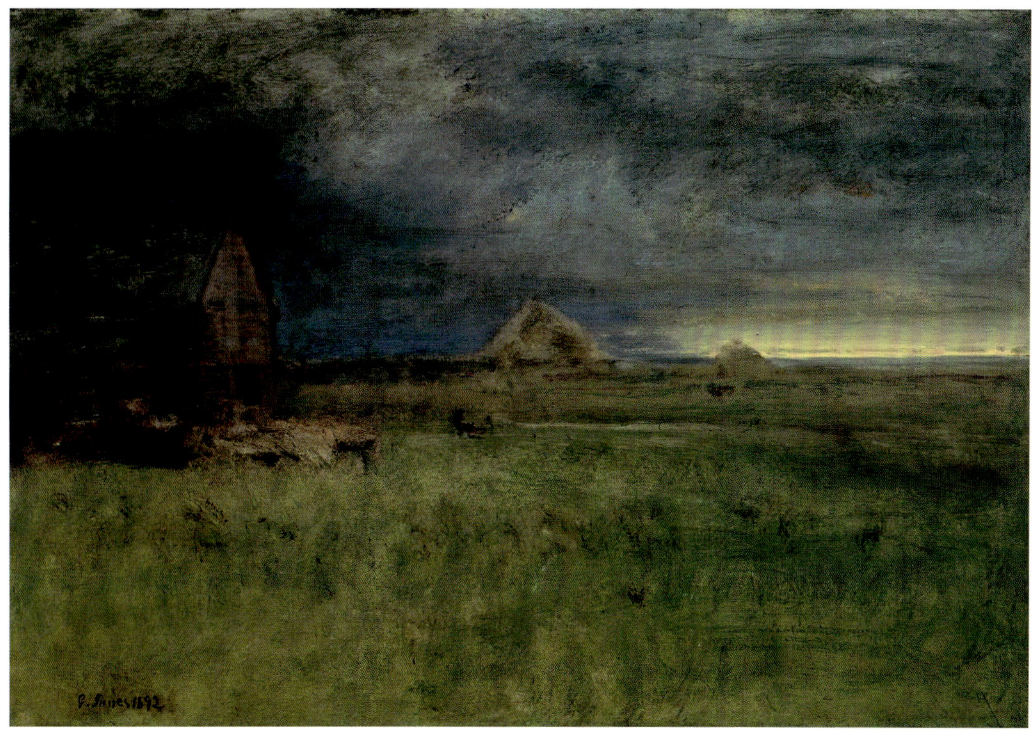

FIG. 20 George Inness, *The Lonely Farm, Nantucket*, 1892. Oil on canvas, 30¾ x 45¾ in. (78.1 x 116.2 cm). Edward B. Butler Collection, 1914.189, The Art Institute of Chicago.

color stand in for sky, horizon, and land. The visual tension created at the intersection of these forms gives the works a particular vibrancy and reminds us how little detail is really needed to convey the most salient elements of nature. As one scholar puts it, "Green enjoins us to recognize not what she has seen but rather the way of seeing that she has developed; a practice of witnessing the world rather than simply looking upon it. As we learn to see along with the artist, we are rewarded not simply with visions of the beauty of being, but also with the unfolding experience of becoming: becoming vast, becoming eternal, becoming oneself, no self, and multiple selves all at once."[14]

Although she speaks of painting not what she sees but what she feels, she also acknowledges those rare occasions when she finds herself strangely transfixed by her surroundings. In 2006, she traveled to Tuscany and visited poppy fields. The paintings she created there are among the most abstract of her career and call to mind the ethereal, floating abstractions of Mark Rothko's color fields. In Green's "atmospheric abstractions," details of individualized trees, paths, or the built environment give way in favor of an overall

FIG. 22 *Mallow in the Maremma*, 2009. Oil on linen, 48 x 46 in. (121.9 x 116.8 cm). Artist's collection.

contemplative mood. Some of the paintings from this trip were not completed for years. She felt a certain spiritual presence while driving through the Maremma in southern Tuscany. Only later did she learn that at the turn of the century, there had been a widespread epidemic in the area that had killed a large number of people. She now sees that the dark band evident in *Mallow in the Maremma* (2009; fig. 22) somehow speaks to that history:"To be in that time and that experience was awesome. And sometimes you can't do that work for years, after a meditative interval of temporal and spatial distance that allows memory and emotion to guide the work."

Green's path to her mature style has been a rich and instructive one. Whether conscious of it or not, she has been setting the stage for her current work throughout her life. As a child, she was made aware of art and the creative possibilities of self-expression. Early studies in fashion and graphics focused her attention on form, line, color, and balance. Her first attempts at painting, though focused on imitation and strict adherence to verisimilitude, gave her confidence in her eye and in her technique. But most important, Green came to an understanding, encouraged by her mentors Boris and Garel, that she could and would forge her own path in painting. She learned not only to accept but also to embrace a certain element of chance in her process. Over the years, she has built up a kind of fortitude that allows her to weather the difficult and questionable moments, to make mistakes, to suspend disbelief, and to be comfortable in the knowledge that any given painting will ultimately express the form it will take and the message it will convey. Green's works are vibrant, engaging, and imbued with a spiritual presence that is not distinct from the artist's very being: Her paintings hold a resonant earnestness and intensity precisely because she has learned to follow her vision unflinchingly and to fully embrace the discipline of a creative life.

1. Mary Sipp Green, quoted in *Mary Sipp-Green: Recent Landscapes* (Pittsfield, Massachusetts: 2005), pp. 8–9.
2. M. Stephen Doherty, "Responding to What Paintings Need," *American Artist*, May 2009, vol. 73, no. 798, pp. 36–41.
3. Mary Sipp Green, artist statement, 2009.
4. Sipp Green quoted in M. Stephen Doherty, "Responding to What Paintings Need," *American Artist*, May 2009, vol. 73, no. 798, pp. 36–41.
5. Beth Venn, conversations with the artist, December 4 and 5, 2013. All quotations by the artist are from these dates, unless otherwise noted.
6. Debra Bricker Balken, "The Sound and the Fury," in *Bessie Boris*, exh. cat., The Berkshire Museum, Pittsfield, Massachusetts, April 25–June 28, 1987.
7. Hellmut Wohl, from the art historian's introduction for a 1967 Cober Gallery exhibition catalogue.
8. Beth Venn, conversation with the artist, February 22, 2014.
9. From the text of a Wally Findlay Galleries brochure, 2014.
10. Beth Venn, conversation with the artist, January 8, 2014.
11. Mary Sipp Green, artist statement, 2010.
12. Mary Sipp Green, artist statement, 2006.
13. Beth Venn, conversation with the artist, February 22, 2014.
14. Jared Green, in *Mary Sipp-Green Selected Works: 1990–2004*, exh. cat., Springfield Museum of Fine Arts, January 26–April 2, 2005.

PAINTINGS

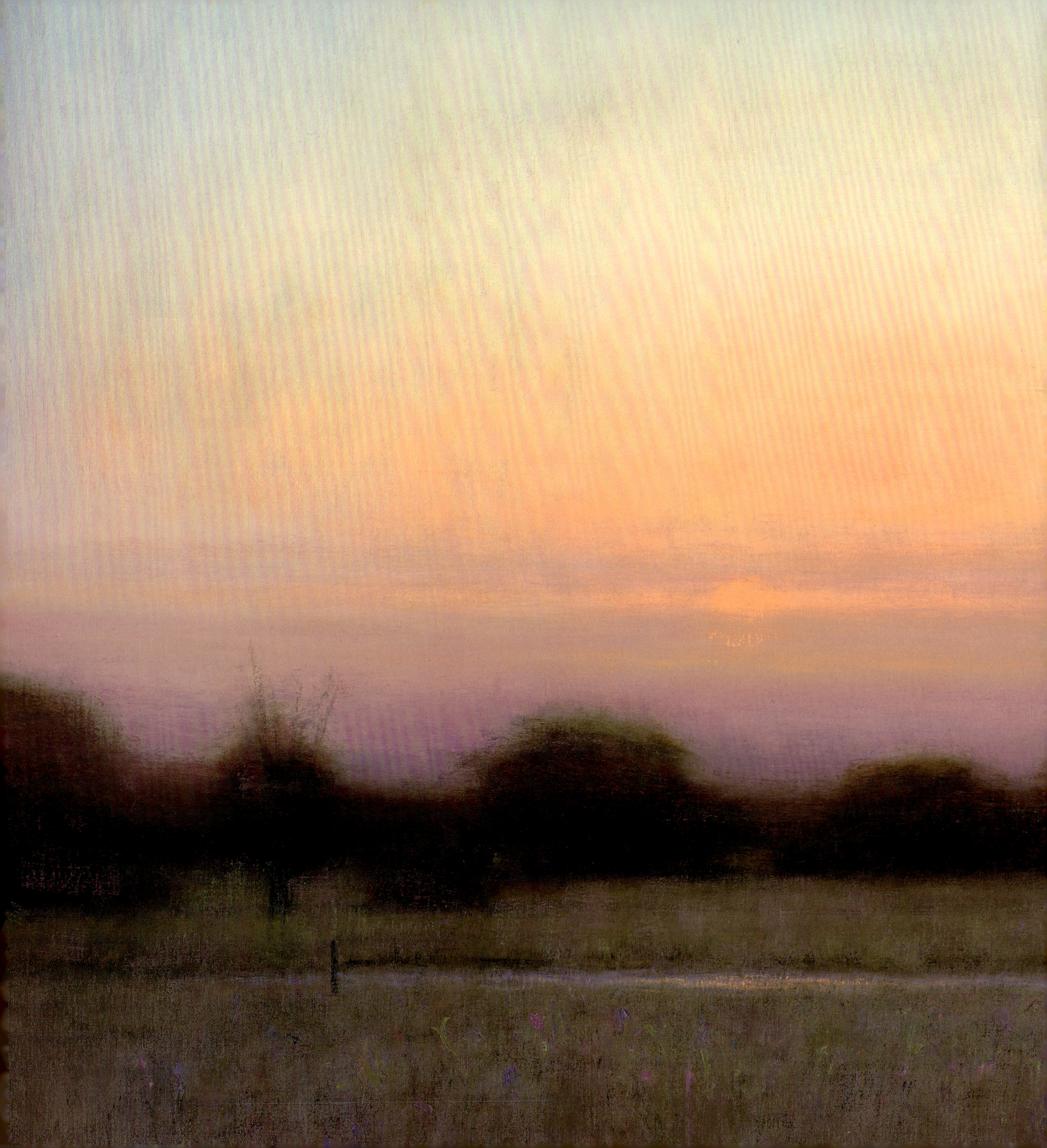

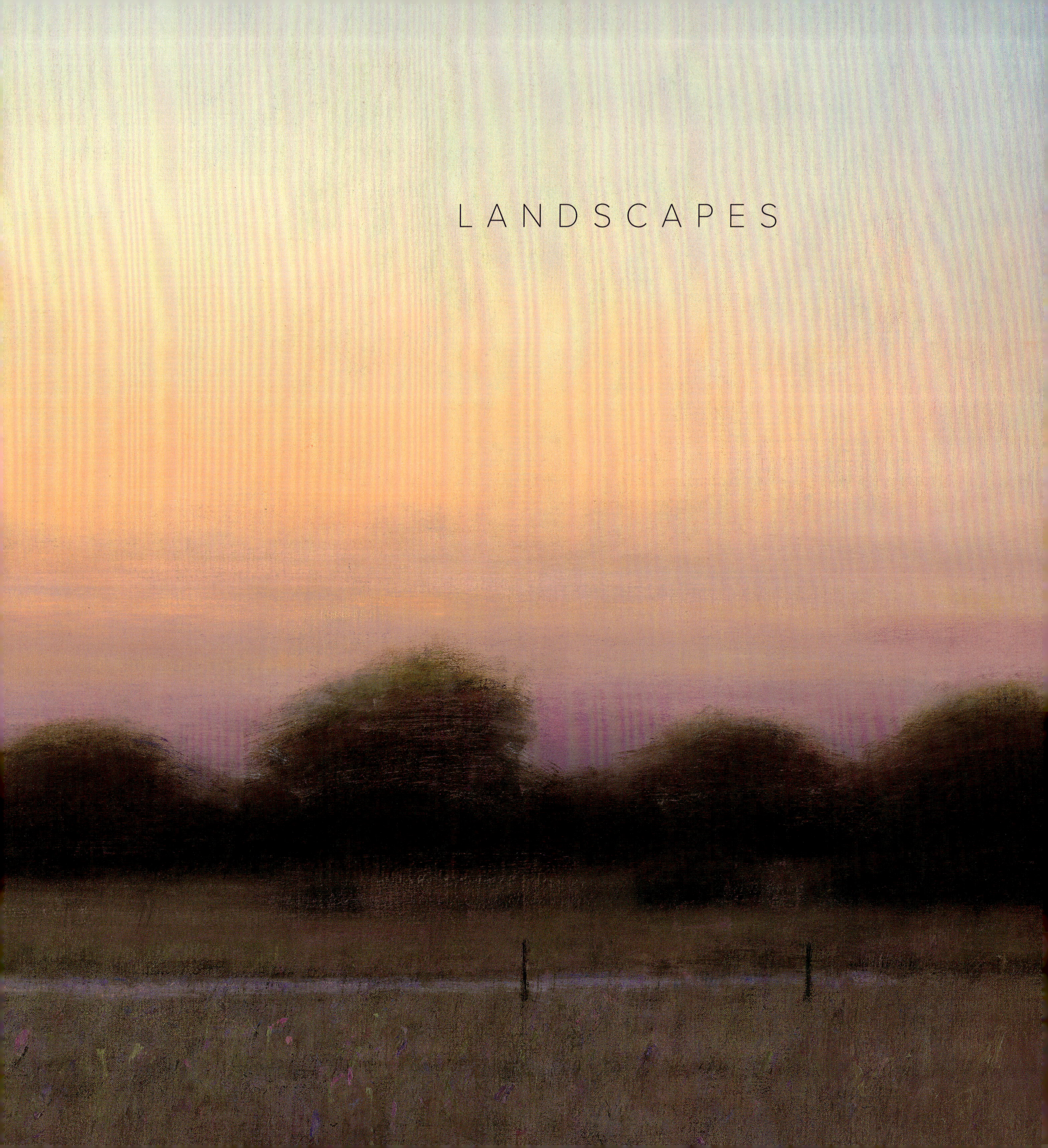
LANDSCAPES

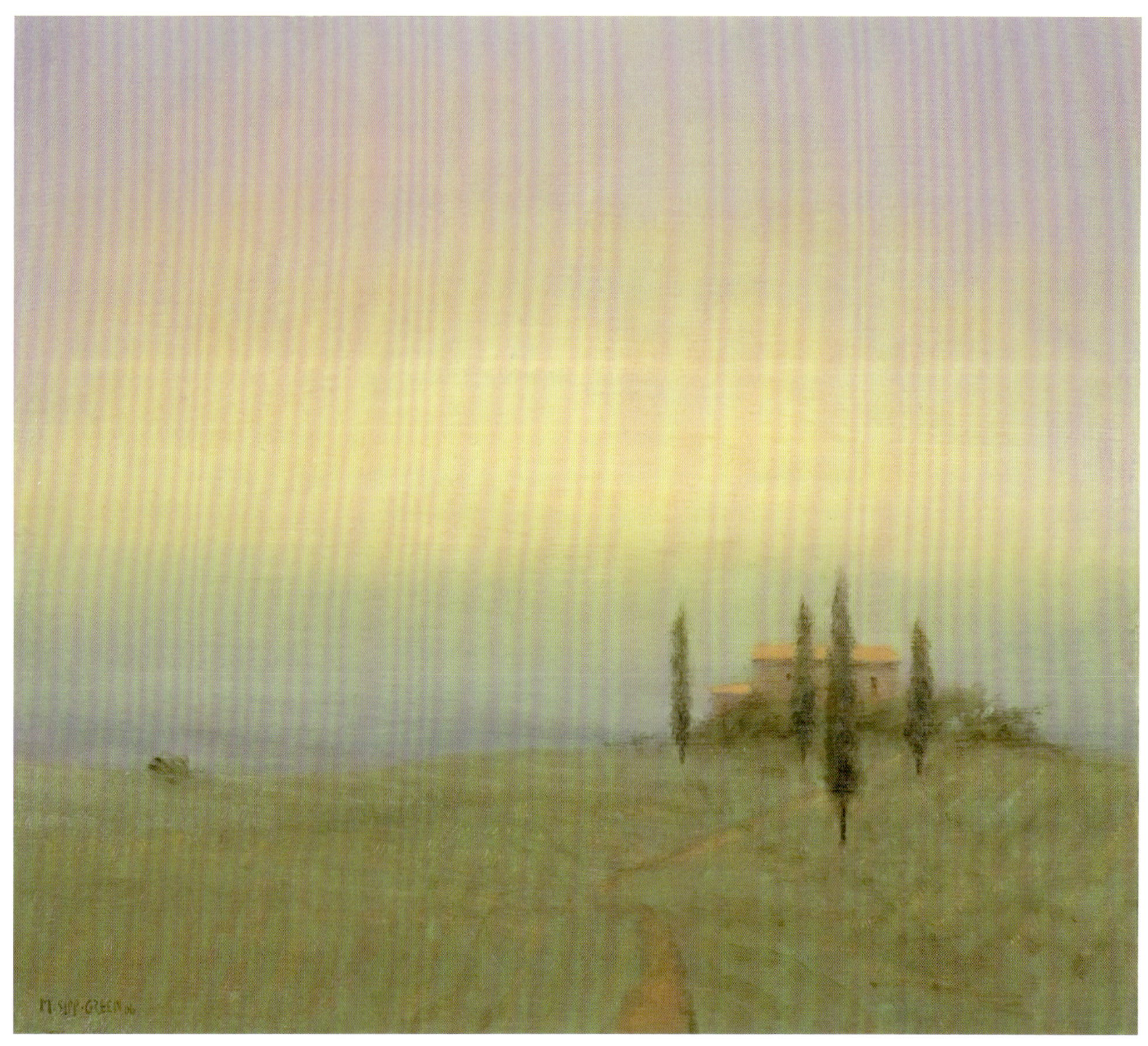

TUSCANY, 2006.
Oil on panel, 18$^{1}/_{4}$ x 16$^{1}/_{8}$ in. (46.4 x 41 cm).
Private collection.

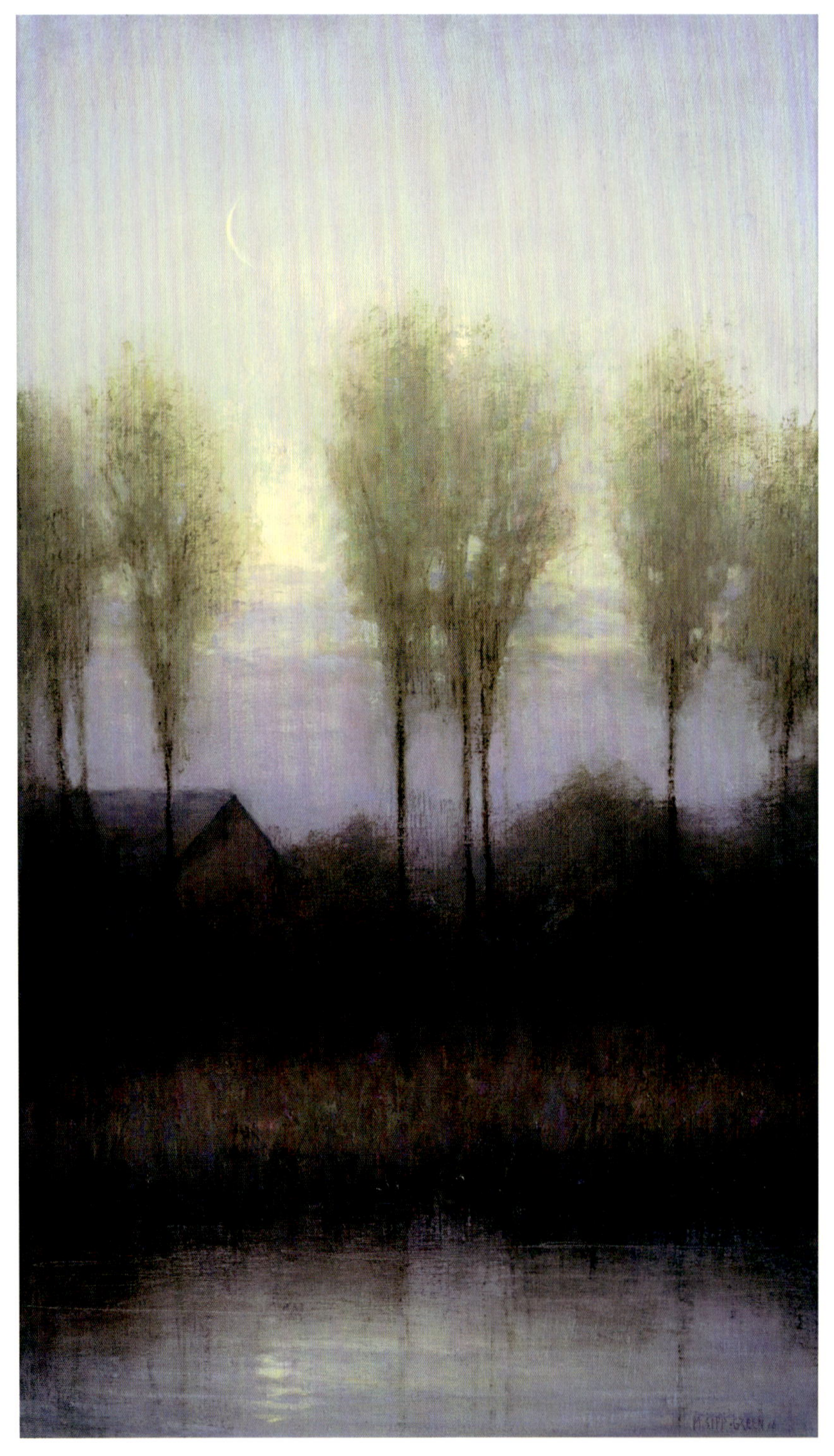

SPRINGTIME, TWILIGHT ON THE RIVER, 2006.
Oil on linen, 36 x 22 in. (91.4 x 55.9 cm).
Private collection.

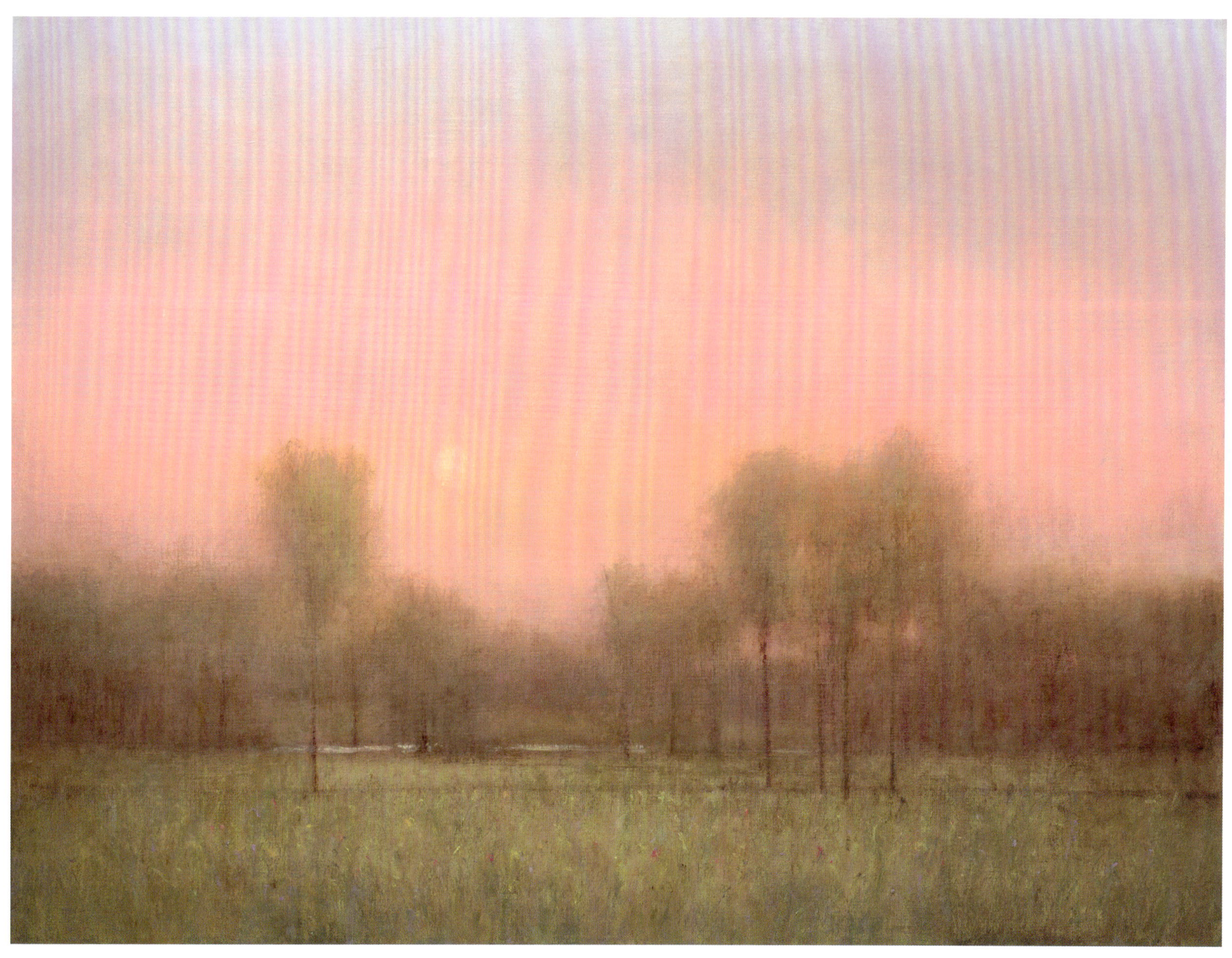

PINK MORNING, 2006.
Oil on linen, 34 x 46 in. (86.4 x 116.8 cm).
Private collection.

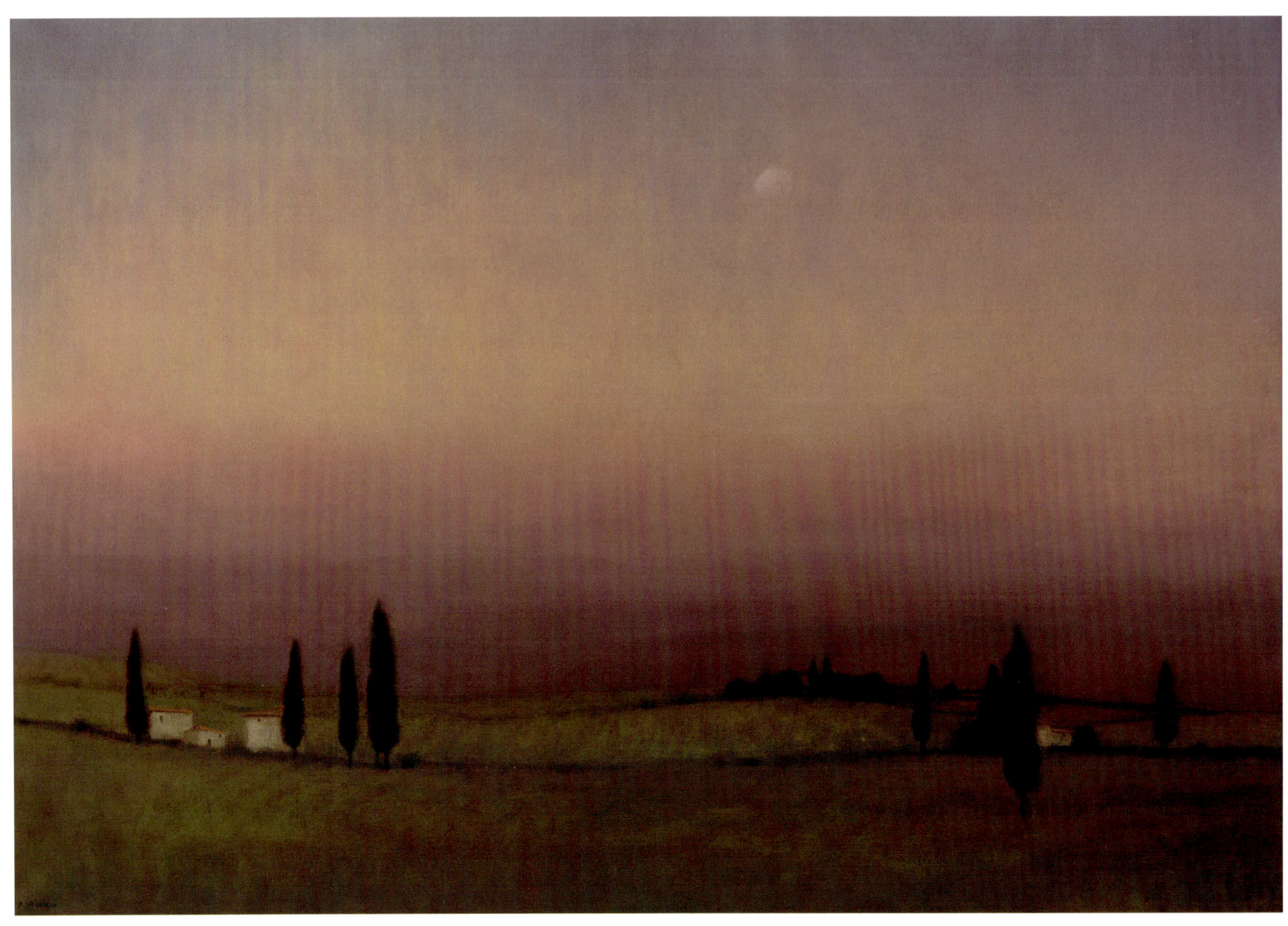

SPRINGTIME IN TUSCANY (I), 2004.

Oil on linen, 42 x 60 in. (106.7 x 152.4 cm).
Private collection.

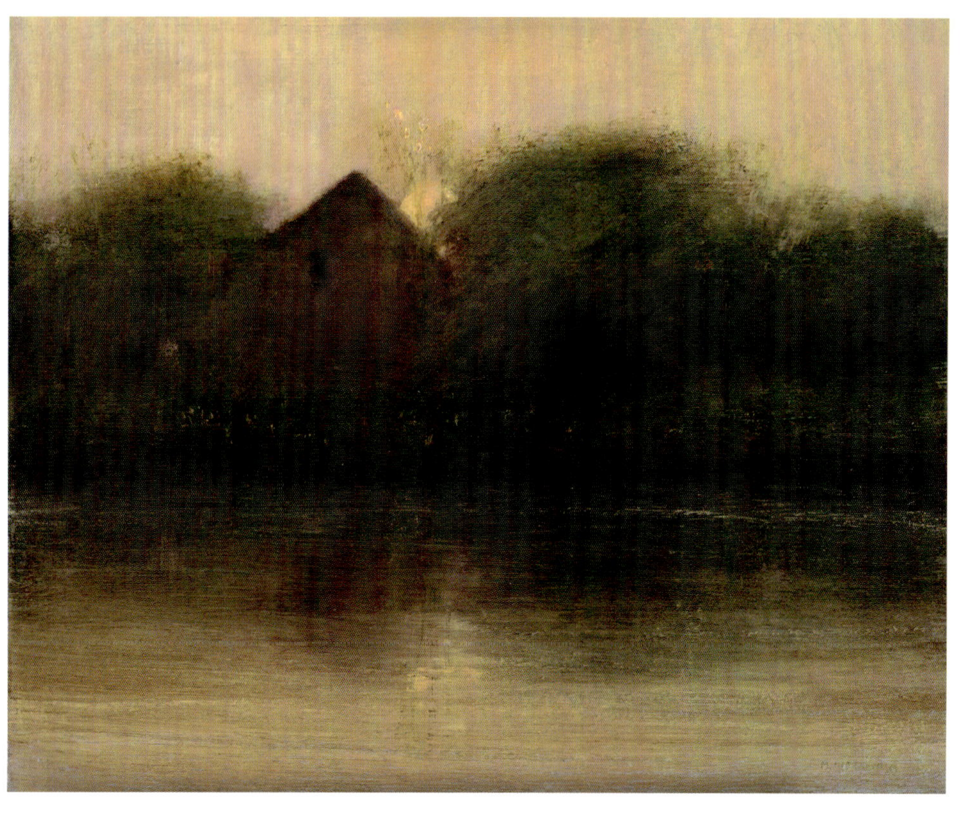

SPRING MORNING, ON RIVER, 2003.

Oil on panel, 13 x 16 in. (33x 40.6 cm).
Private collection.

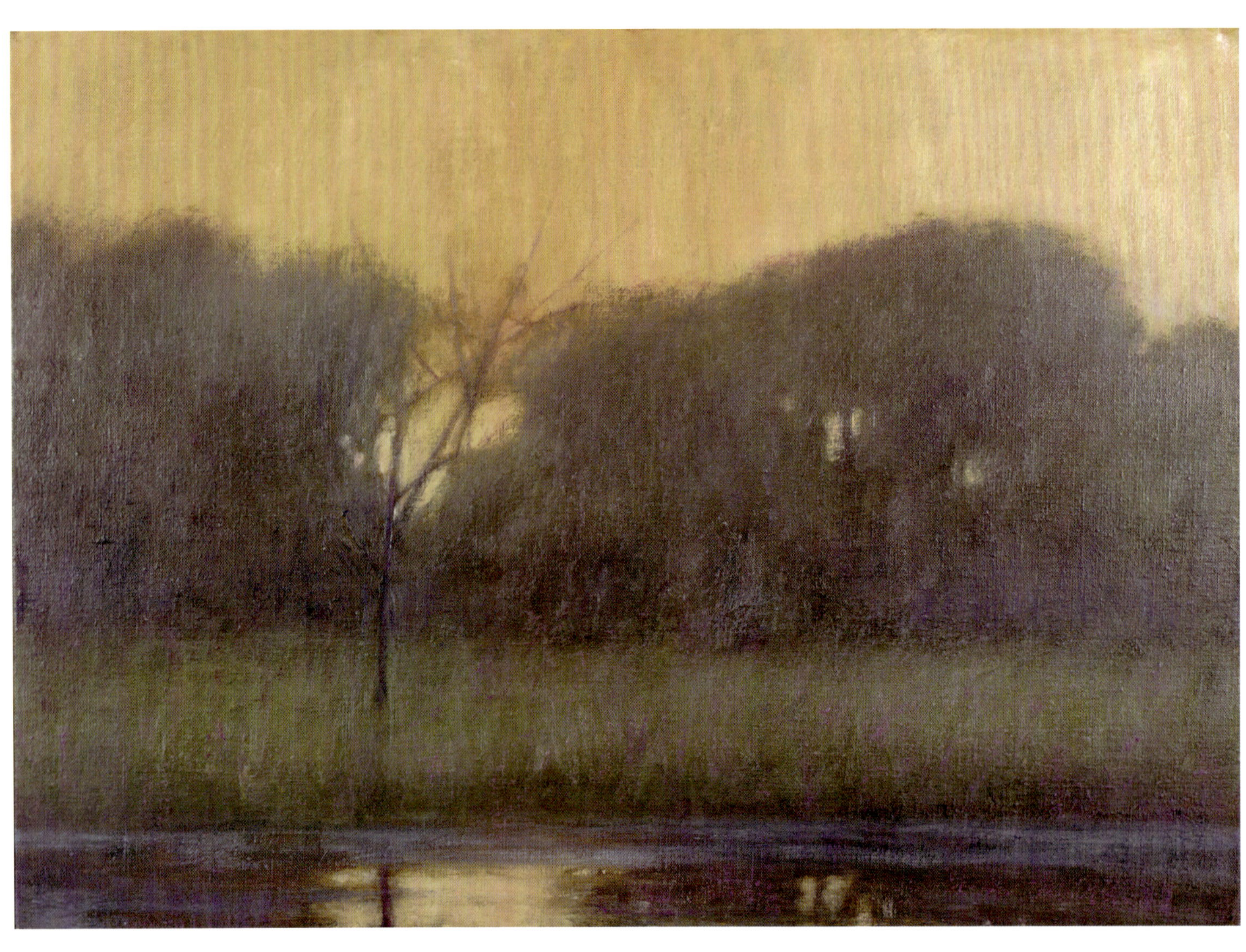

EARLY MORNING, EARLY SPRING, 1998.
Oil on linen, 20 x 28 in. (50.8 x 71.1 cm).
Private collection.

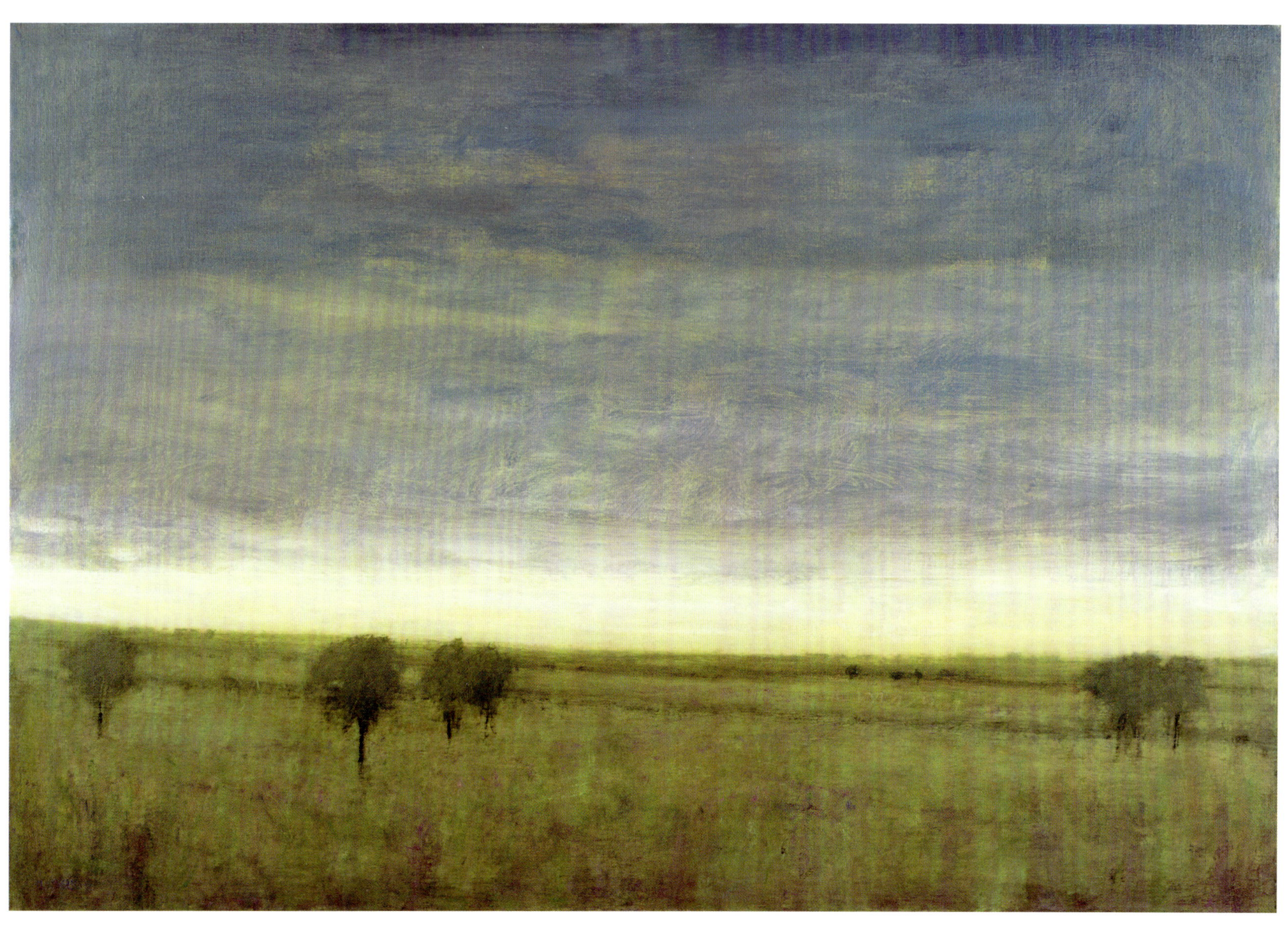

SPRING CLOUDS CLEARING, 1998.

Oil on linen, 34 x 50 in. (86.4 x 127 cm).
Private collection.

TRIO, 1997.

Oil on linen, 12 x 14 in. (30.5 x 35.6 cm).
Private collection.

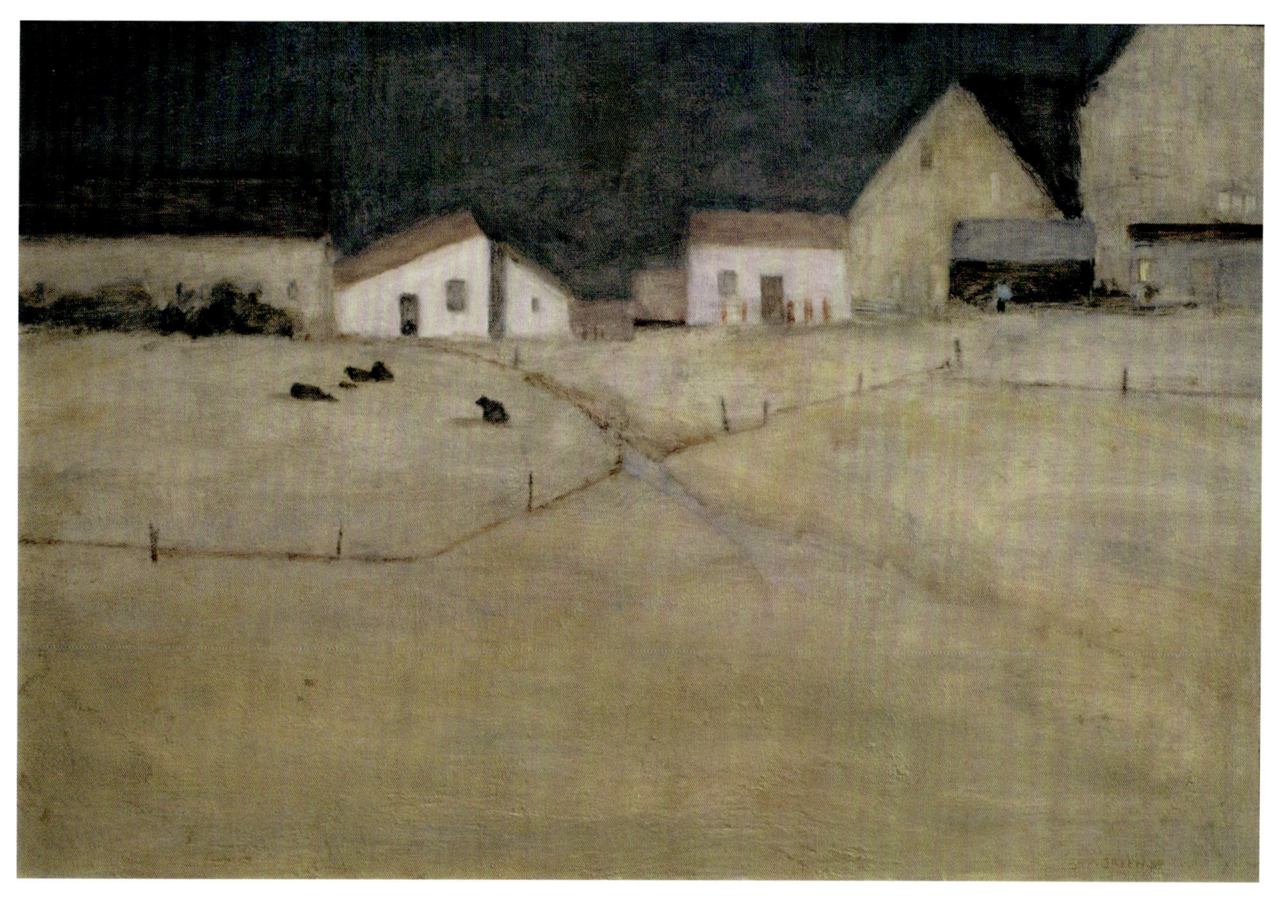

GREY DAY ON CHERRYHILL FARM, 1992.

Oil on linen, 18 x 28 in. (45.7 x 71.1 cm).
Private collection.

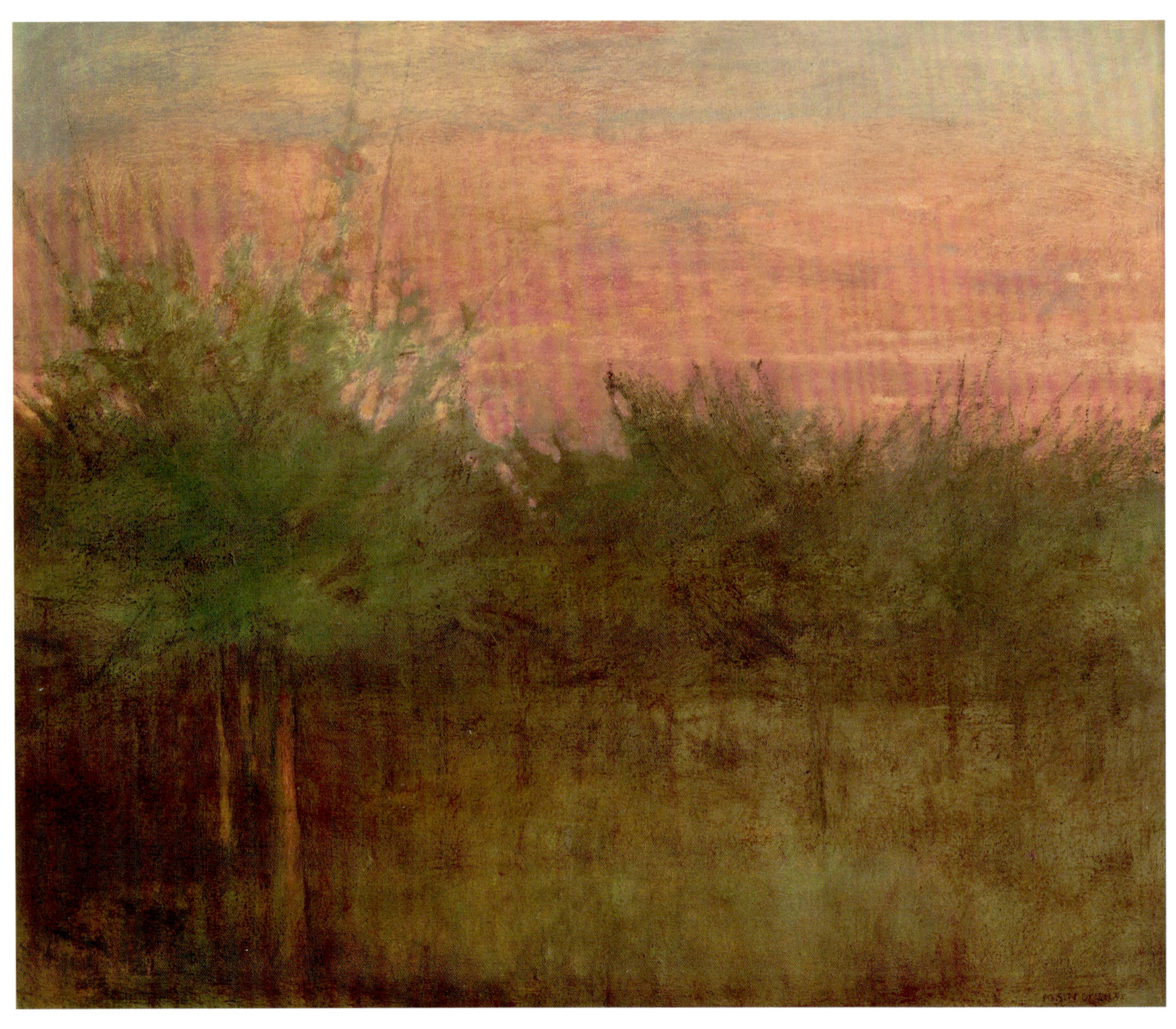

ORCHARD AT SUNSET, 1992.
Oil on linen, 34 x 42 in. (86.4 x 106.7 cm).
Private collection.

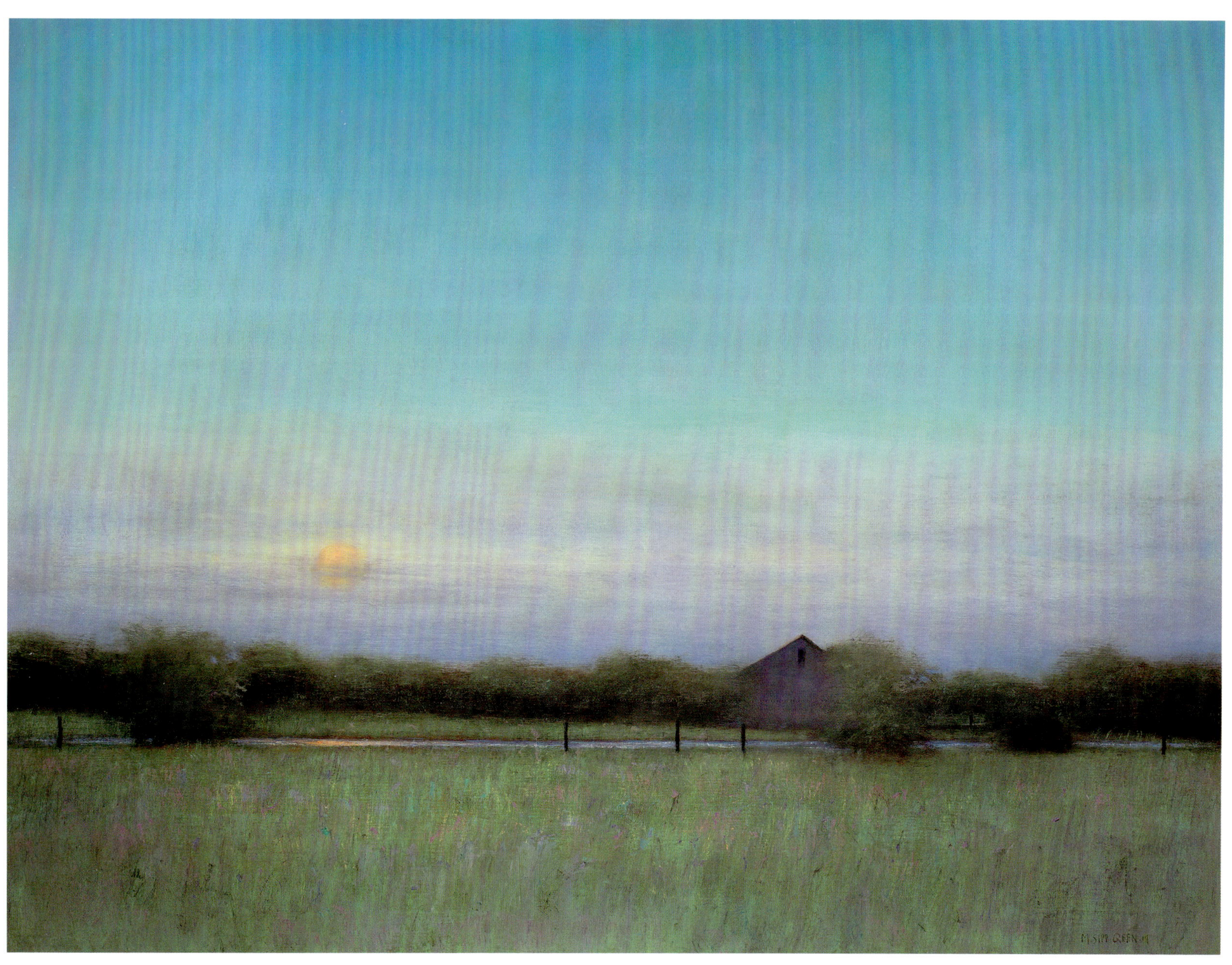

UPPER MEADOW, 2014.
Oil on linen, 38 x 56 in. (96.5 x 142.2 cm).
Private collection.

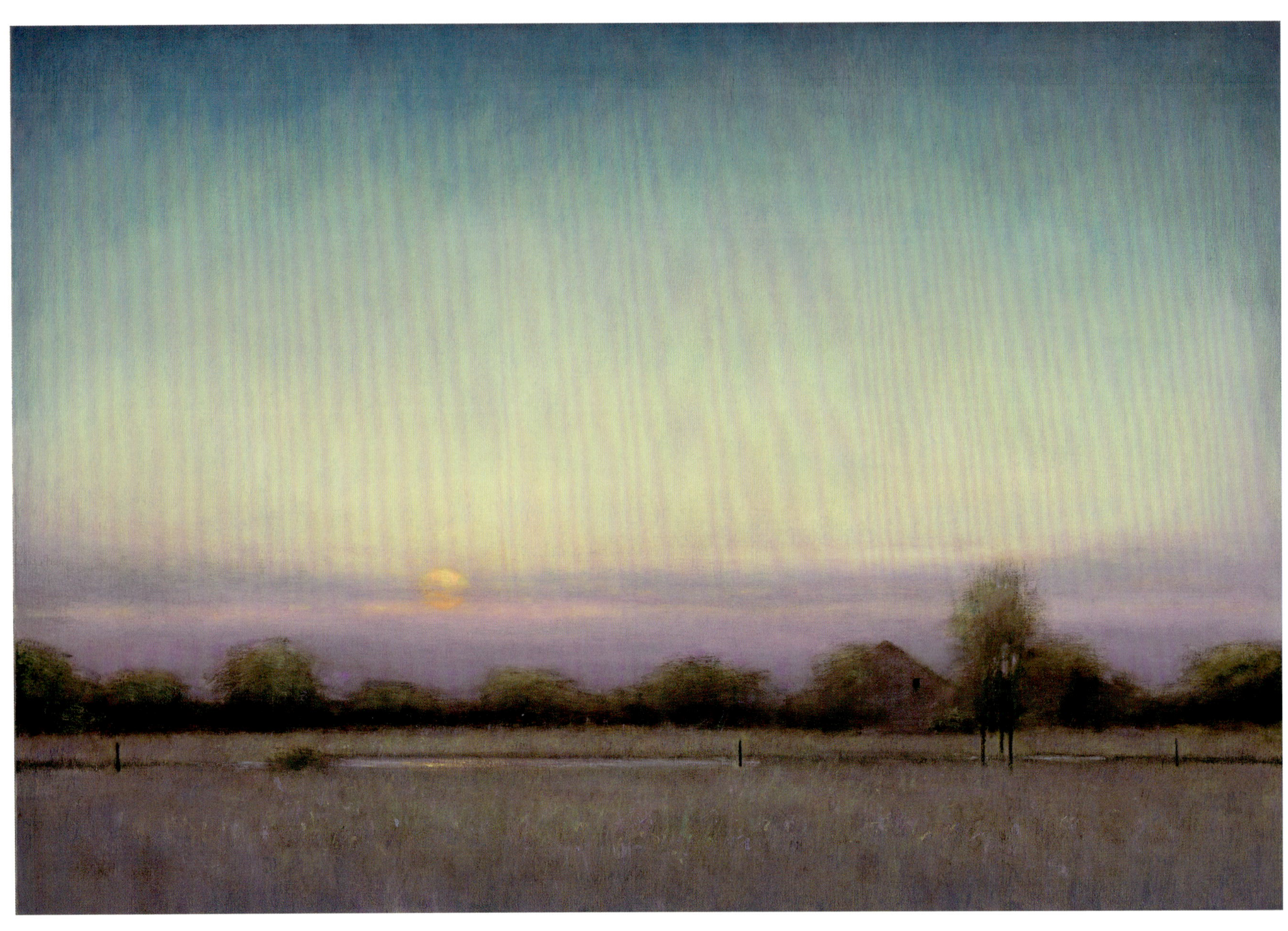

TWILIGHT FALLS, IN SOUTH COUNTY, 2013.

Oil on linen, 36 x 56 in. (91.4 x 142.2 cm).
Springfield Museum of Art, permanent collection.

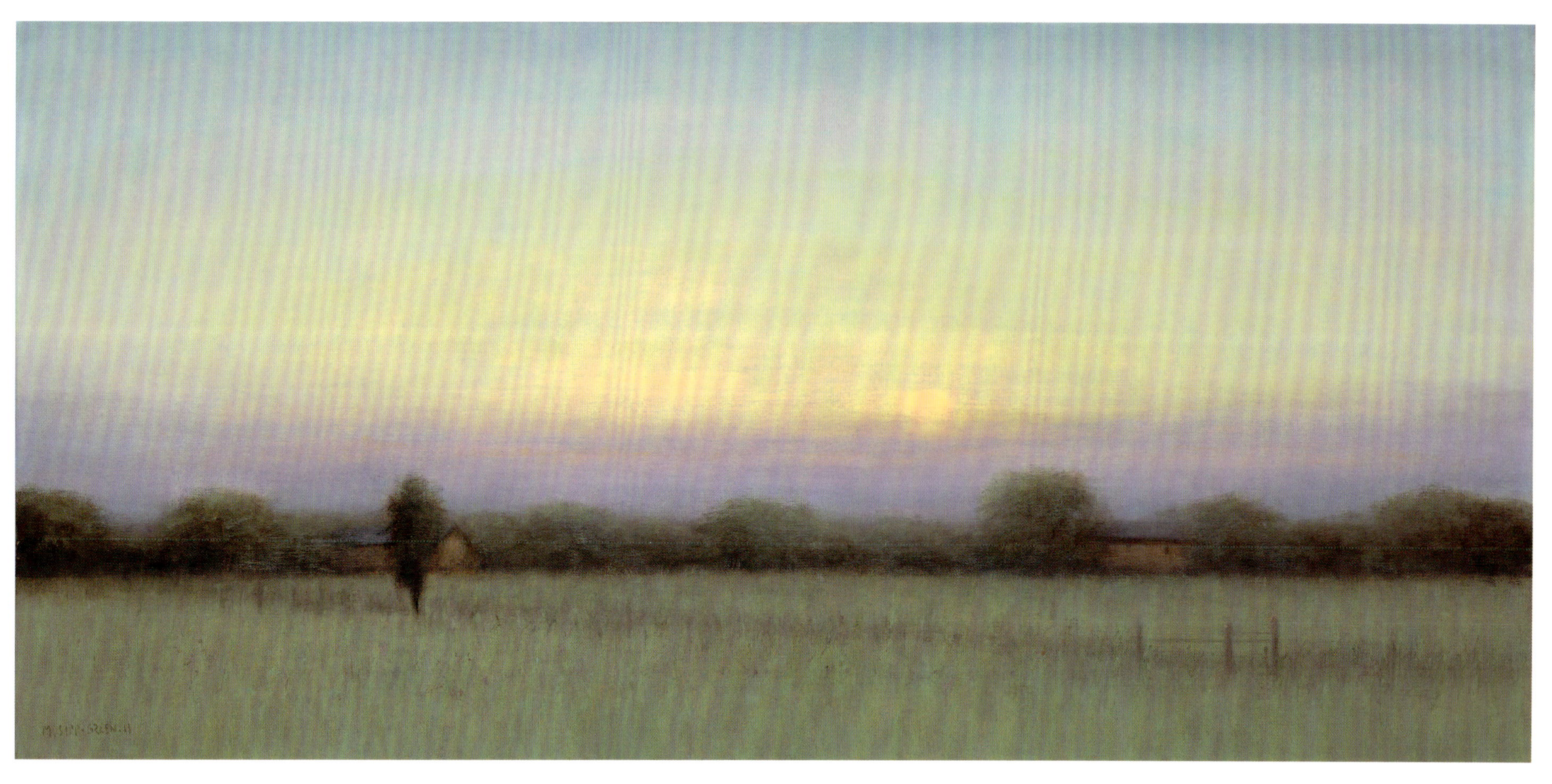

TWO BARNS, 2013.
Oil on linen, 29 x 61 in. (73.7 x 154.9 cm).
Courtesy Granary Gallery.

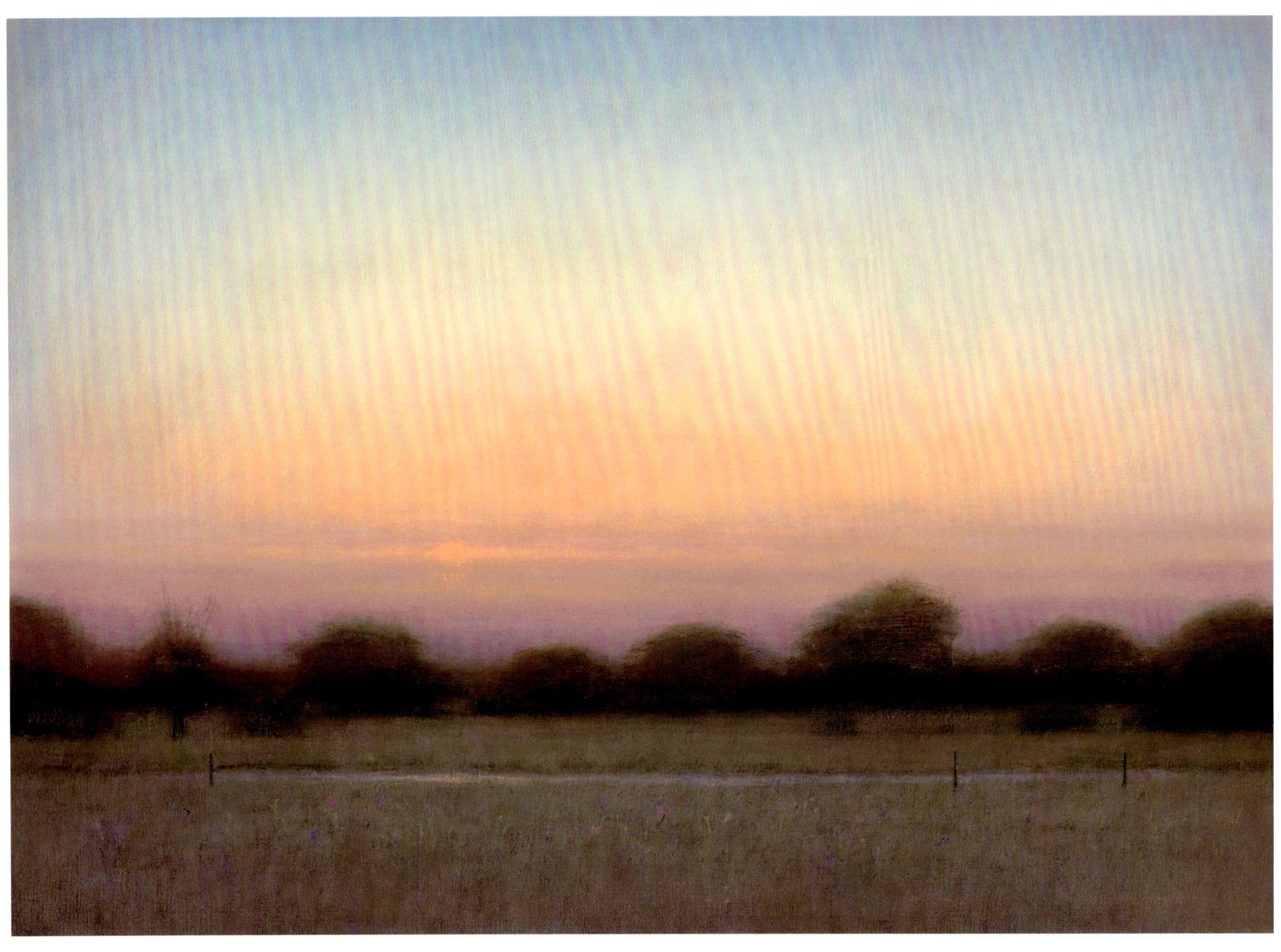

DUSK, 2013.
Oil on linen, 40 x 58 in. (101.6 x 147.3 cm).
Courtesy Granary Gallery.

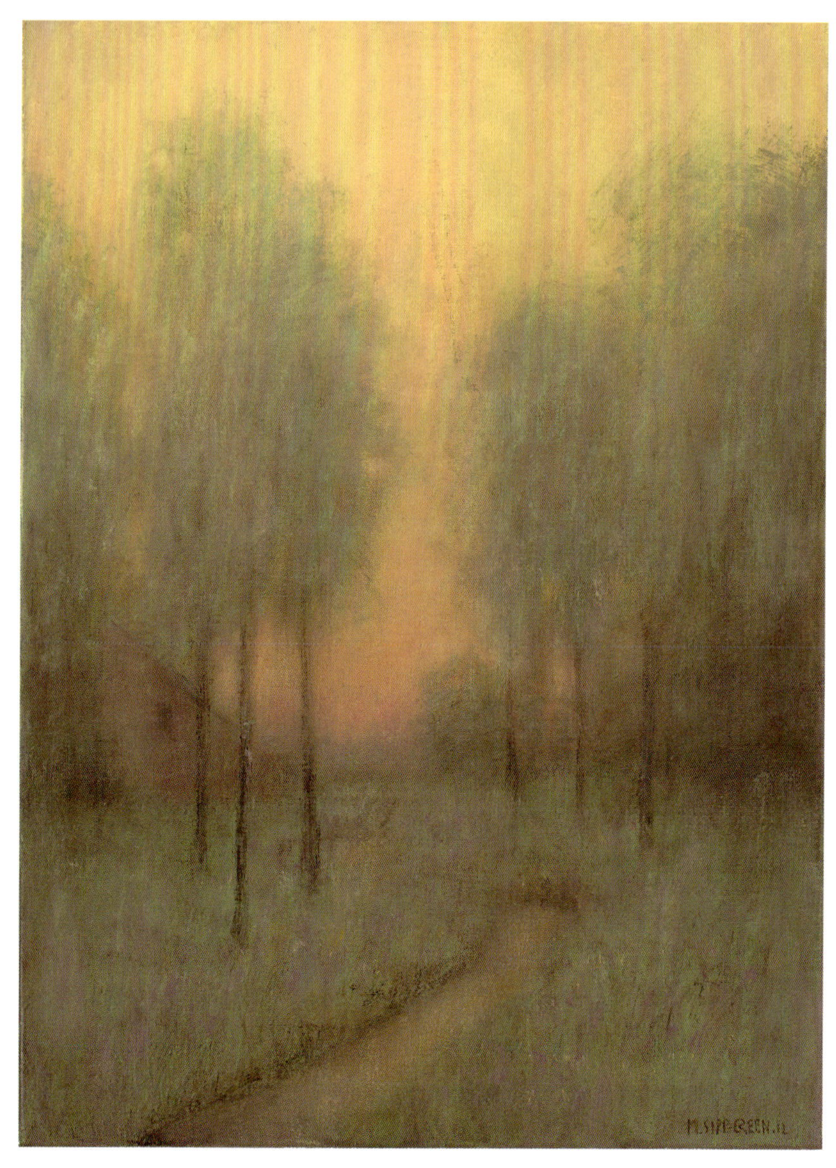

ROAD TO COTTLE COVE, 2012.
Oil on linen, 23 x 17 in. (58.4 x 43.2 cm).
Courtesy Wally Findlay Galleries International.

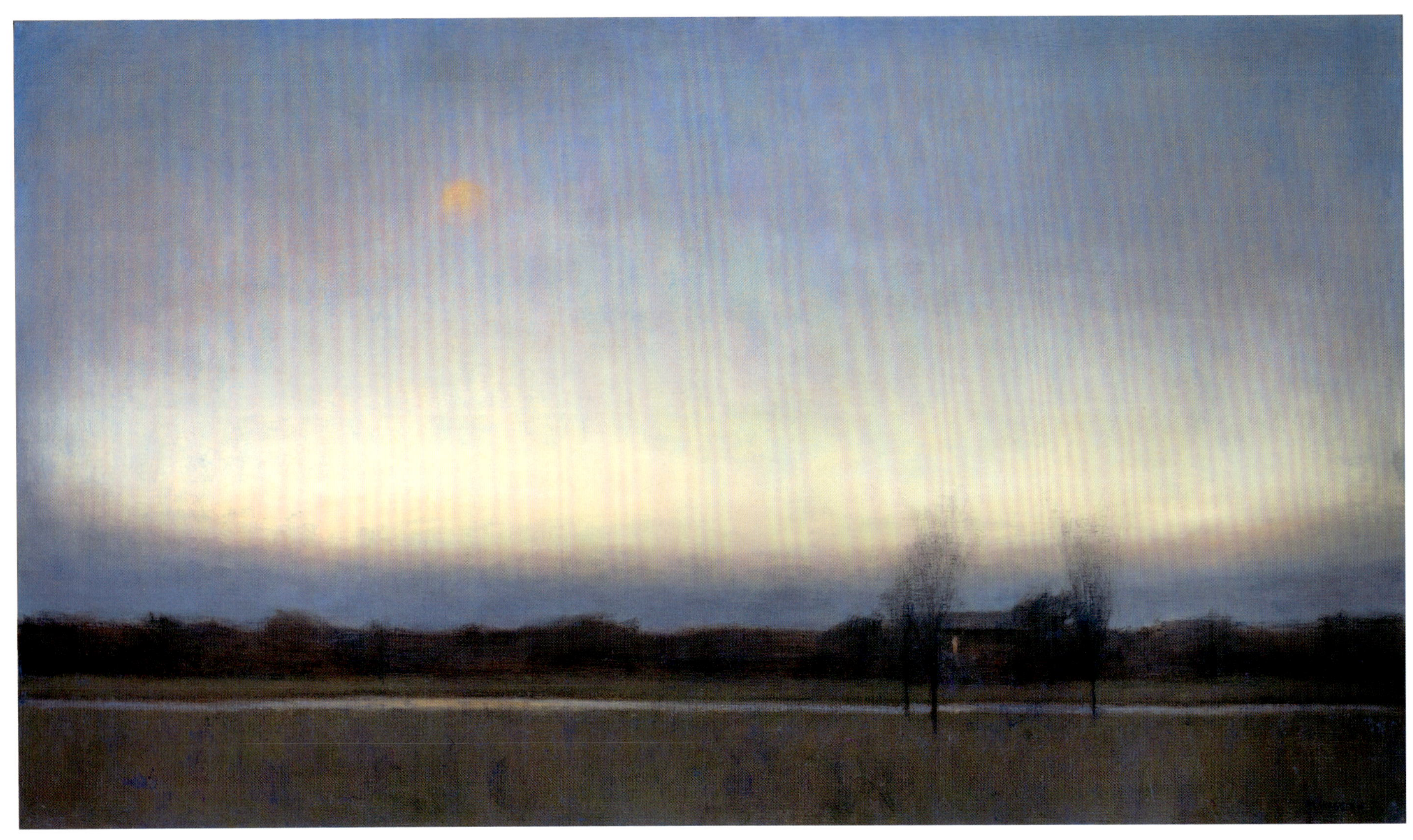

TYRINGHAM IN TWILIGHT, 2009.

Oil on linen, 34 x 60 in. (86.4 x 152.4 cm).
Private collection.

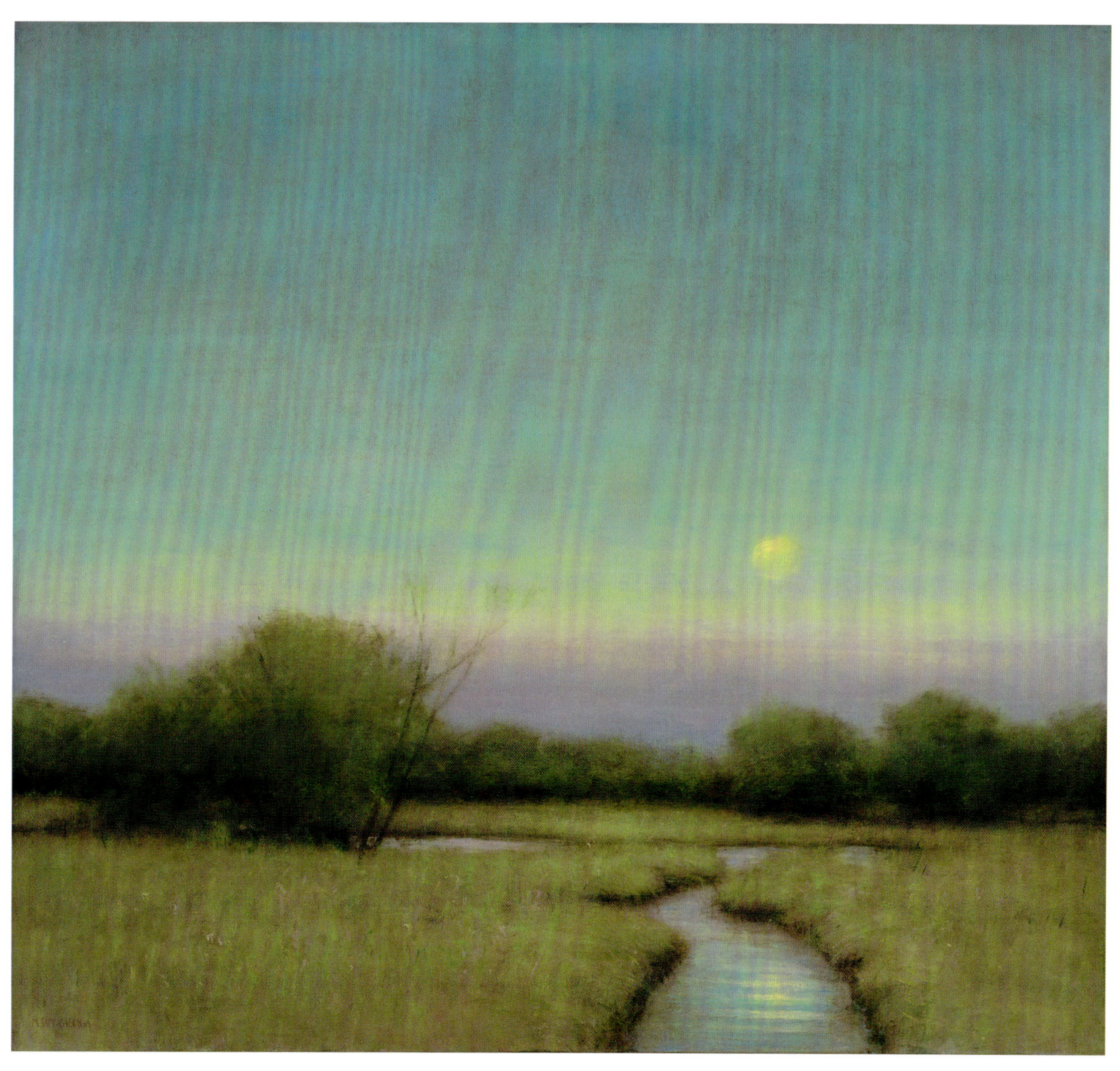

SUMMER EVENING, 2009.

Oil on linen, 38 x 42 in. (96.5 x 106.7 cm).
Courtesy Wally Findlay Galleries International.

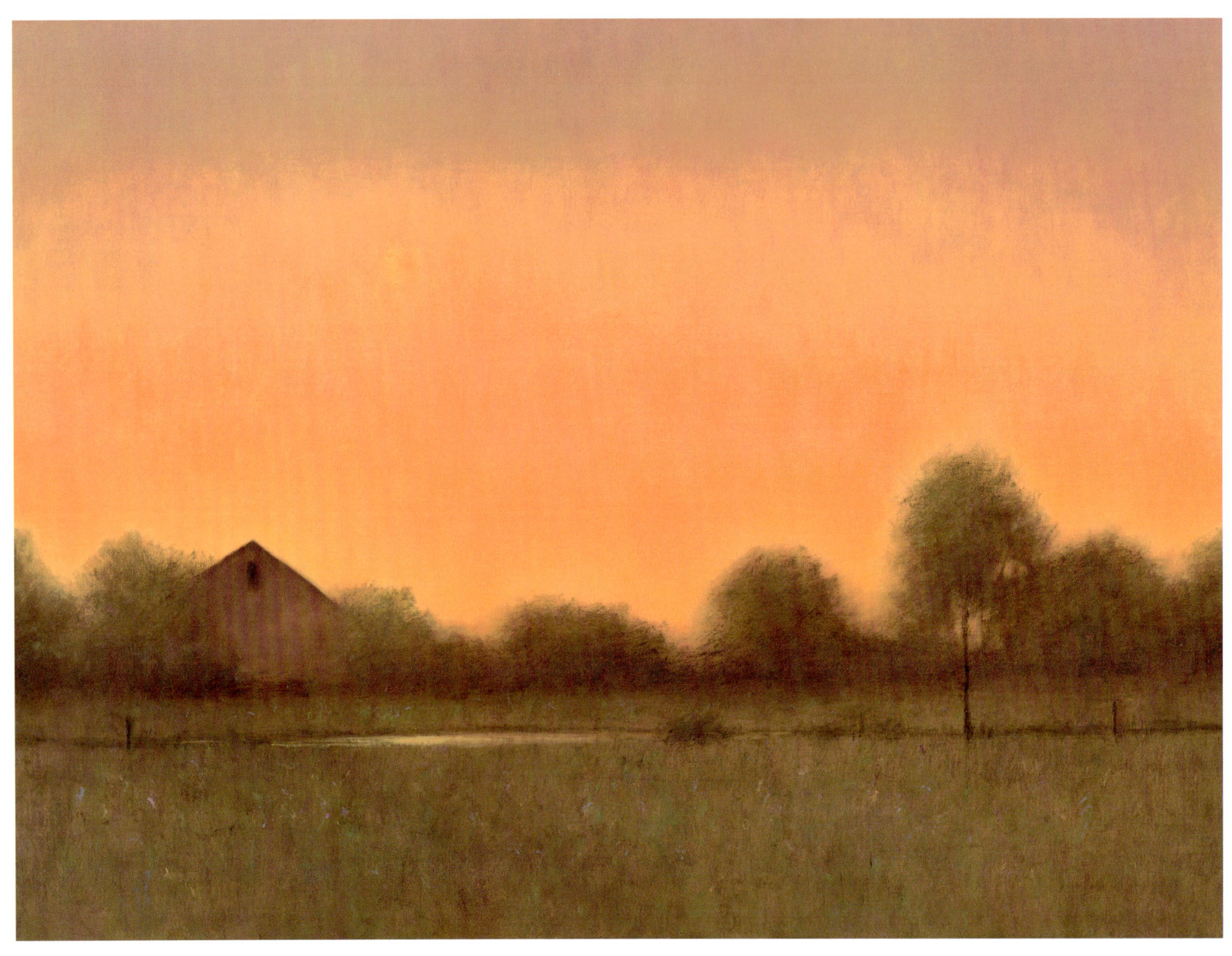

ROSY TWILIGHT, 2008.
Oil on linen, 32 x 48 in. (81.3 x 121.9 cm).
Private collection.

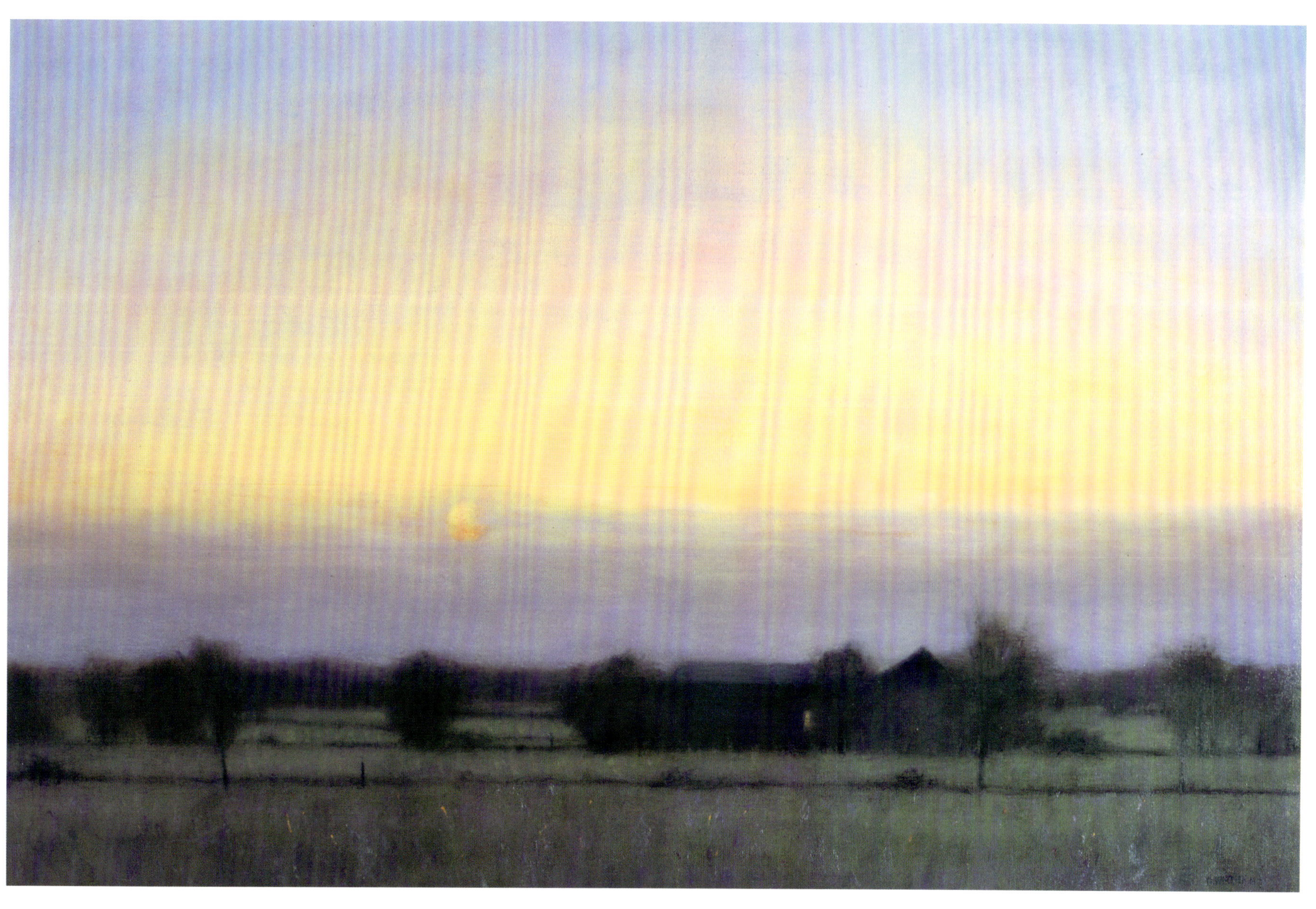

SUNSET, LATE AUGUST, 2004.
Oil on linen, 40 x 60 in. (101.6 x 152.4 cm).
Private collection.

GRAZING FIELDS, 2003.

Oil on linen, 12 x 22 in. (30.5 x 55.9 cm).
Private collection.

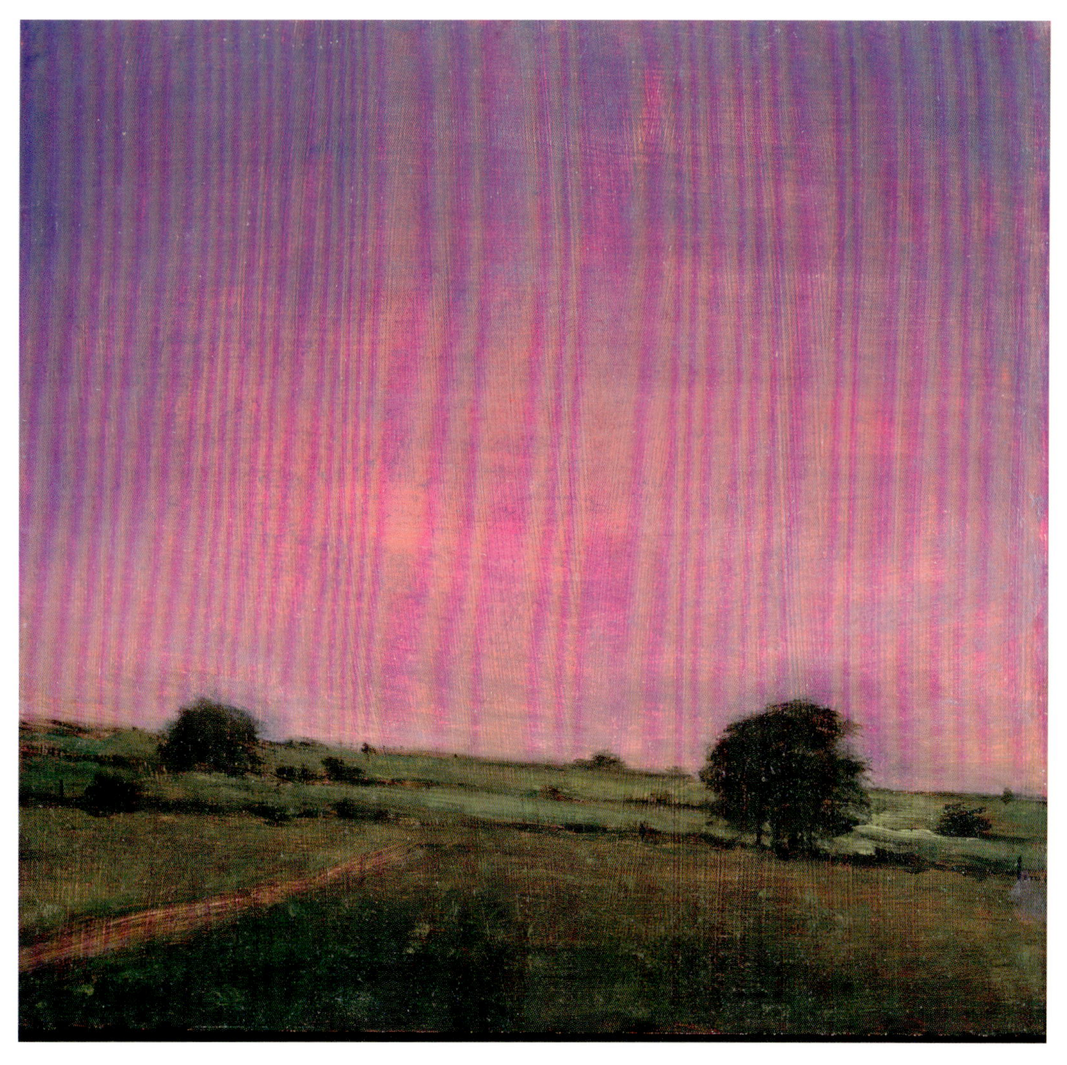

VINEYARD LIGHT, 2000.

Oil on panel, 15 x 15 in. (38.1 x 38.1 cm).
Private collection.

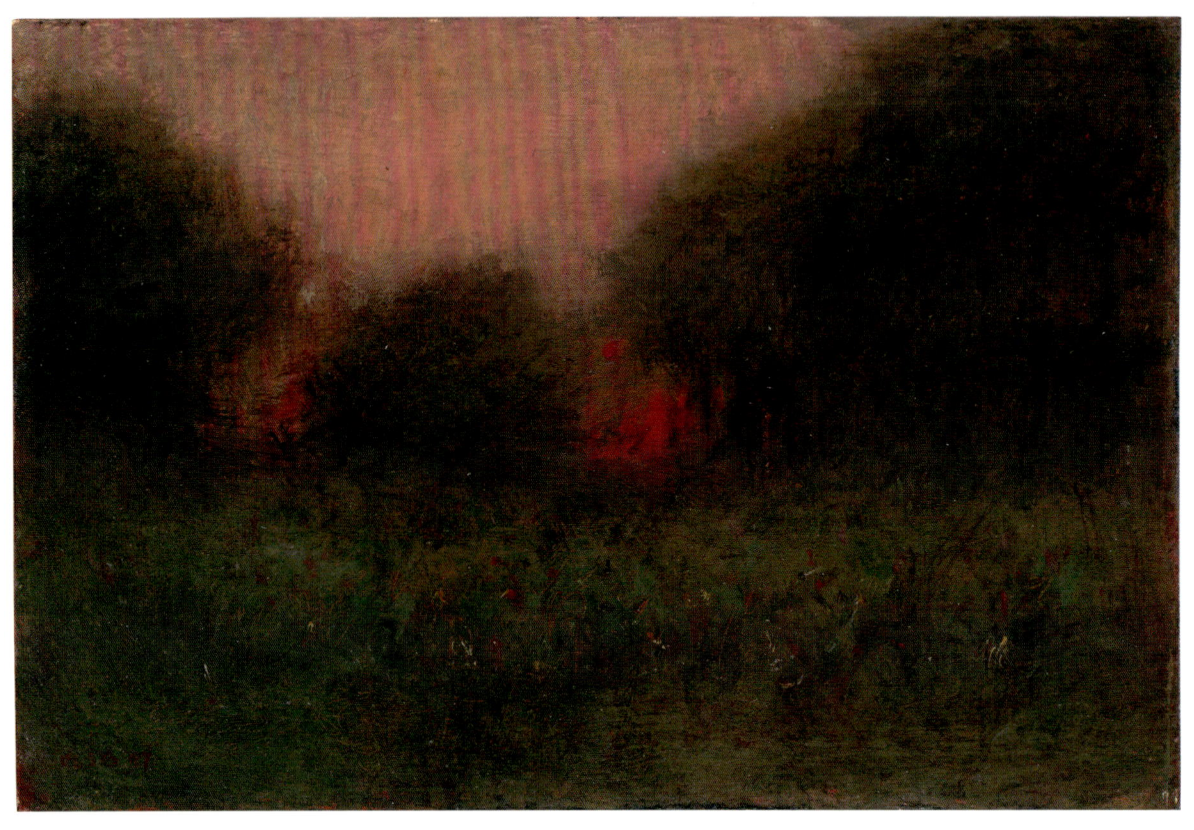

ROMANTIC TWILIGHT I, 1999.

Oil on panel, 7 x 10¼ in. (17.8 x 26 cm).
Private collection.

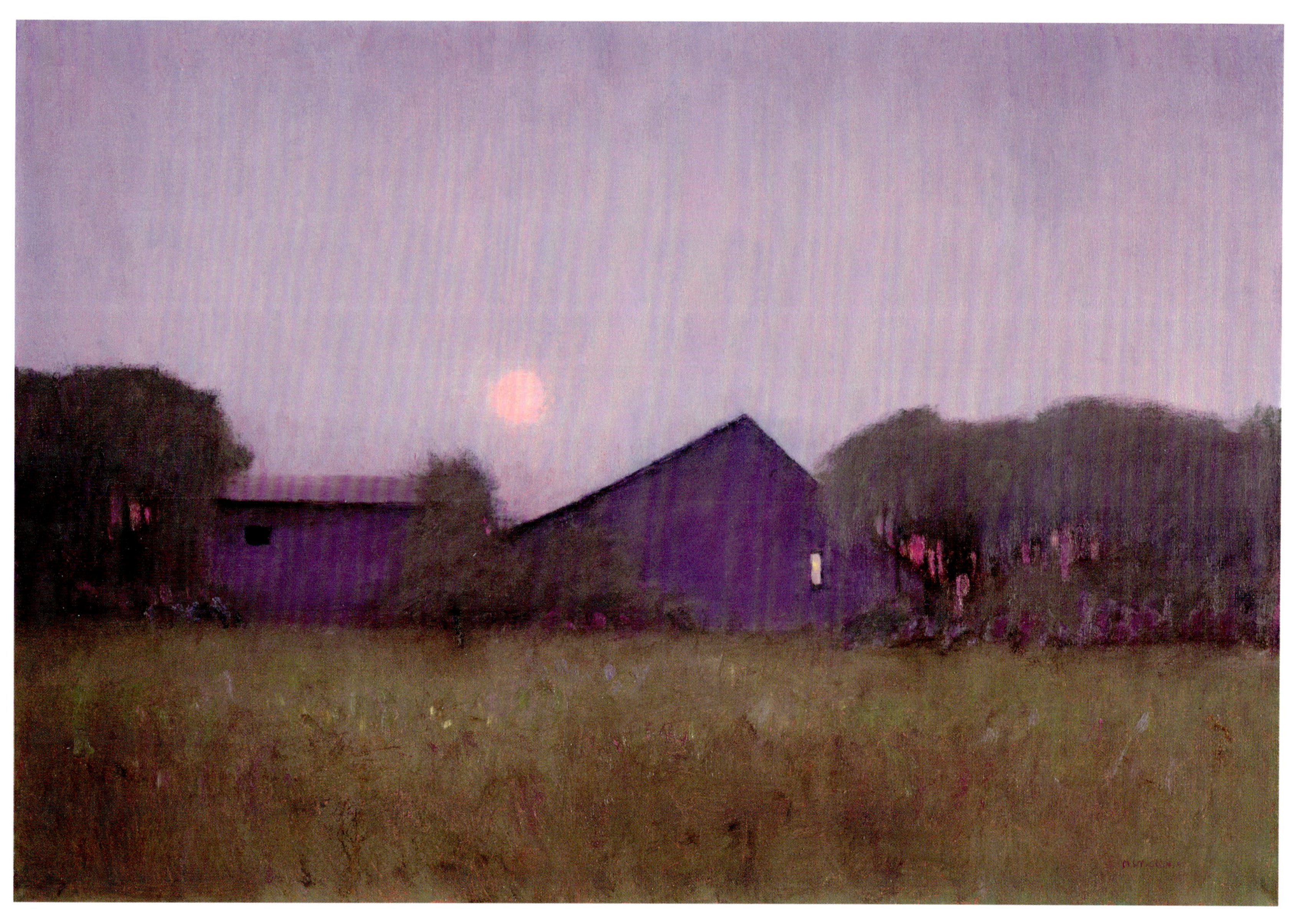

VINEYARD TWILIGHT I, 1997.
Oil on linen, 34 x 50 in. (86.4 x 127 cm).
Private collection.

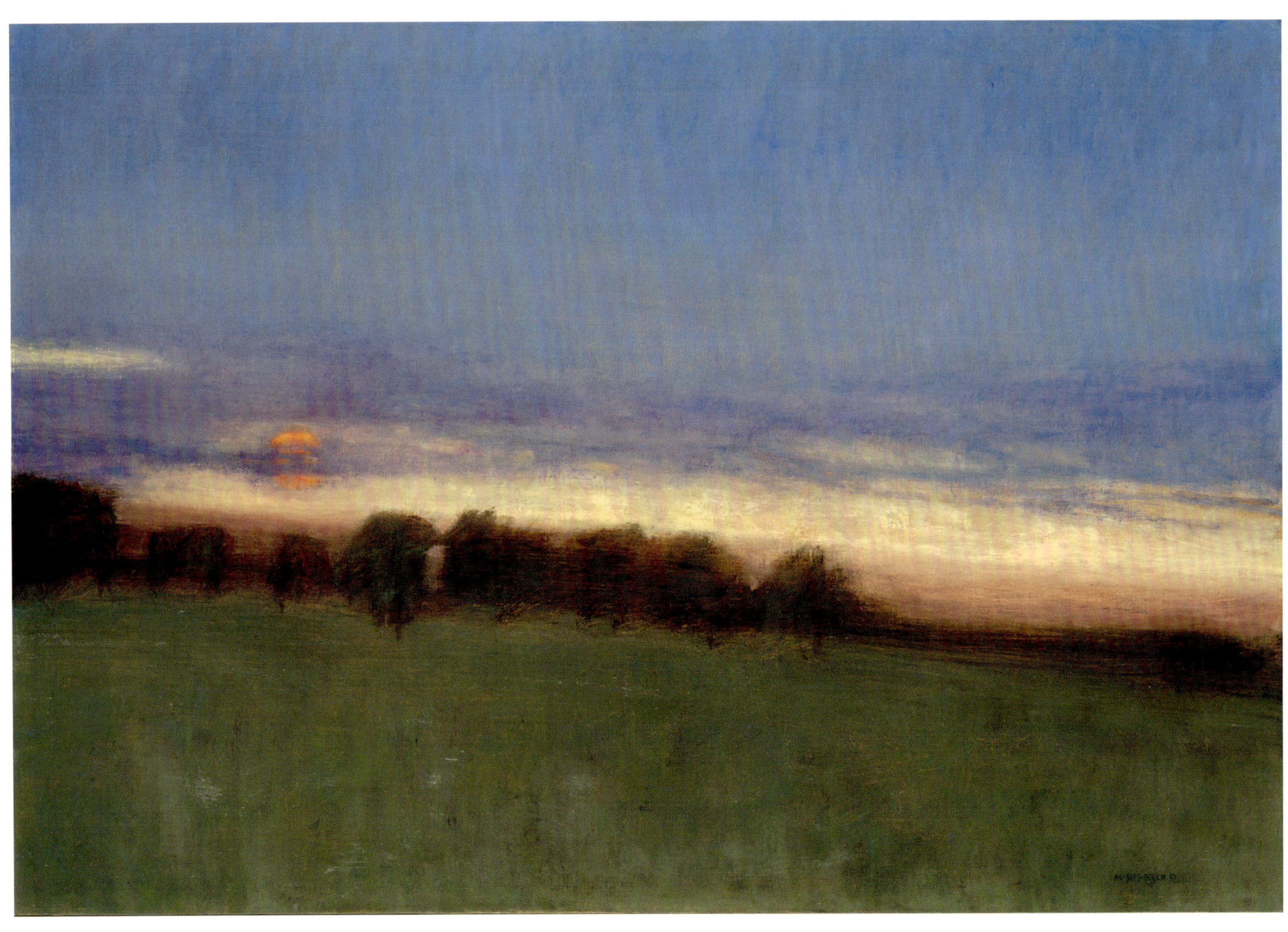

STOCKBRIDGE SUNSET, 1995.

Oil on linen, 36 x 50 in. (91.4 x 127 cm).
Private collection.

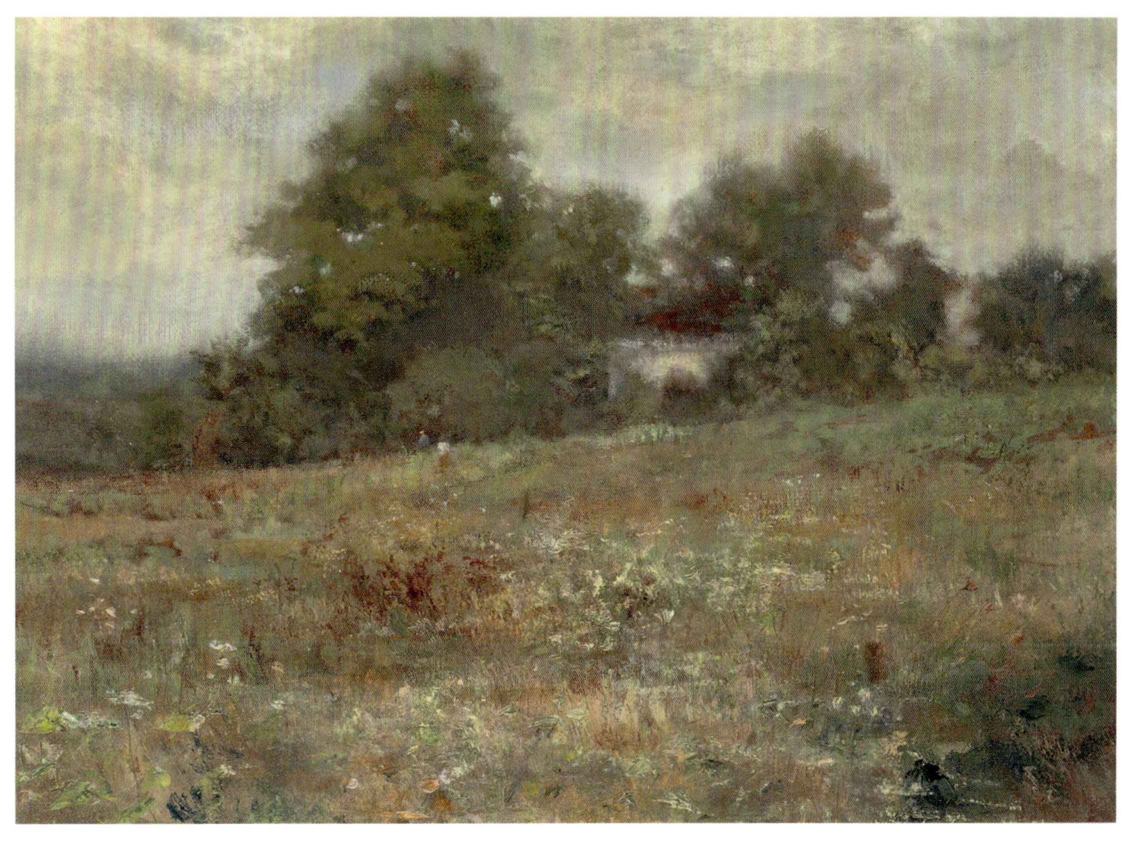

BALDWIN HILL, 1985.
Oil on linen, 13 x 18 in. (33 x 45.7 cm).
Private collection.

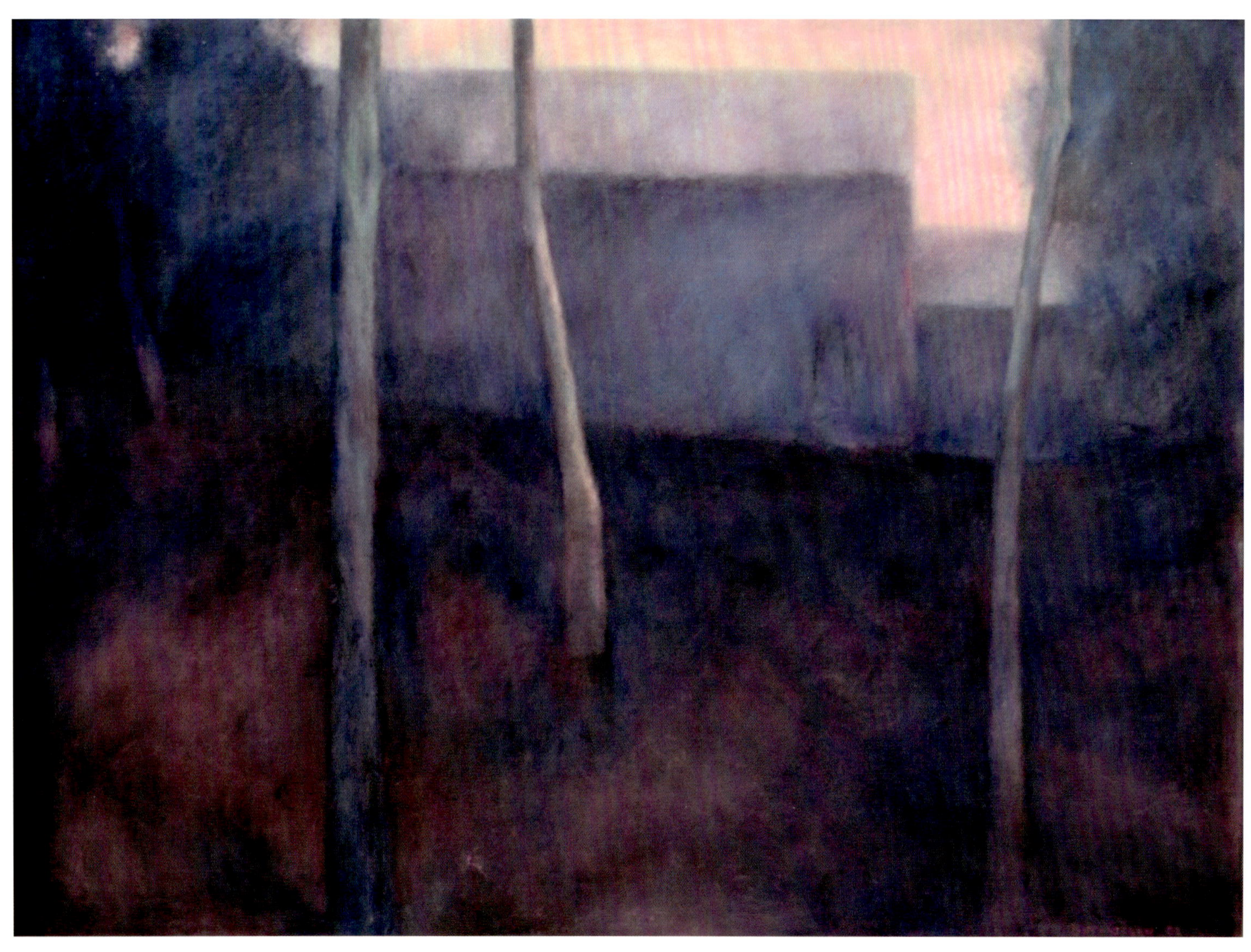

NOVEMBER HILLSIDE, 2002.
Oil on linen, 30 x 40 in. (76.2 x 101.6 cm).
Artist's collection.

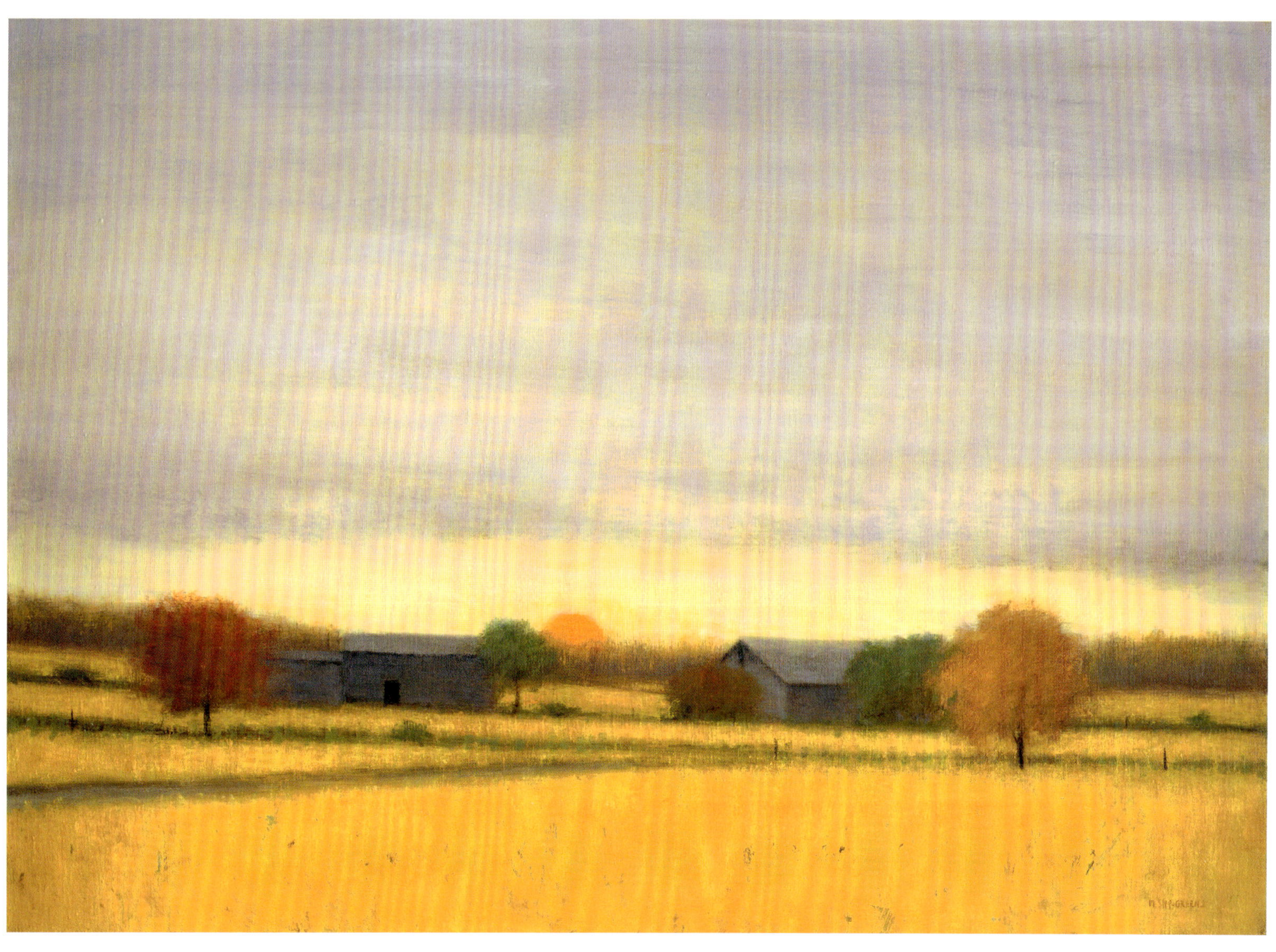

AUTUMN GOLD, 2000.

Oil on linen, 34 x 48 in. (86.4 x 121.9 cm).
Private collection.

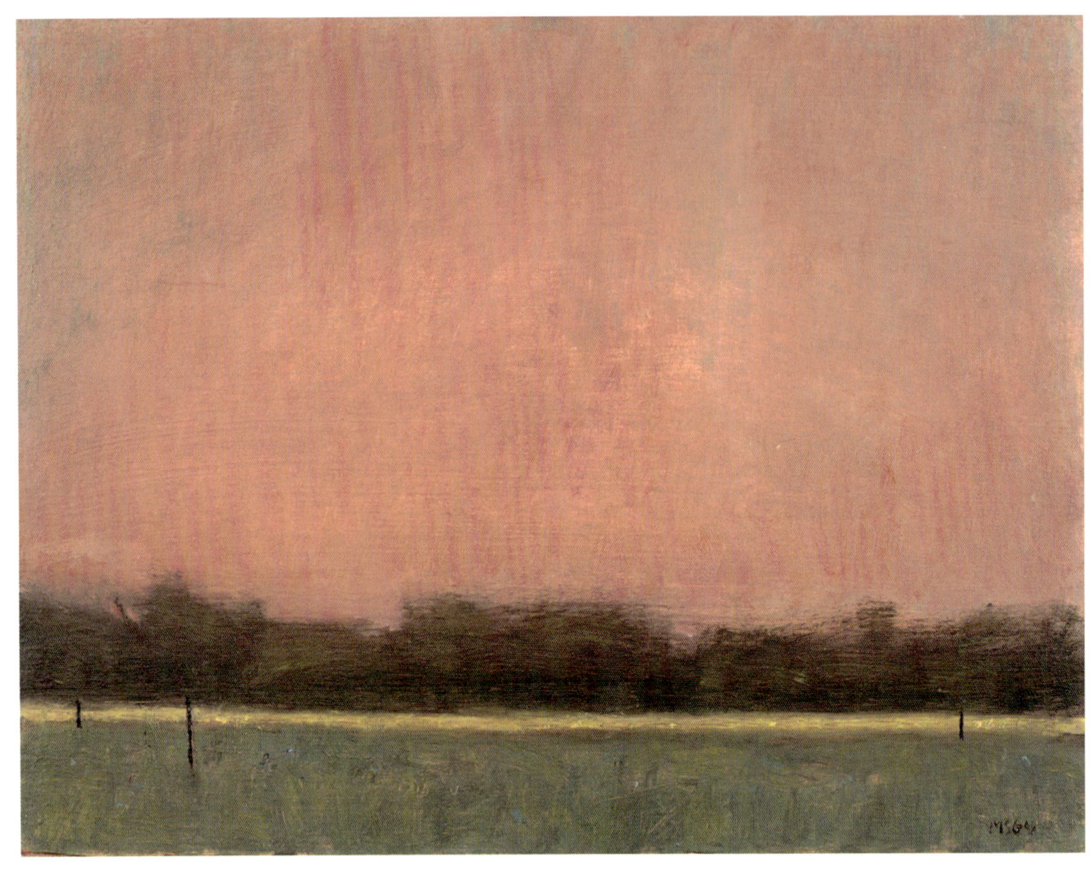

EDGE OF THE CORNFIELD, 1998.
Oil on panel, 8¹/₂ x 11¹/₄ in. (21.6 x 28.6 cm).
Private collection.

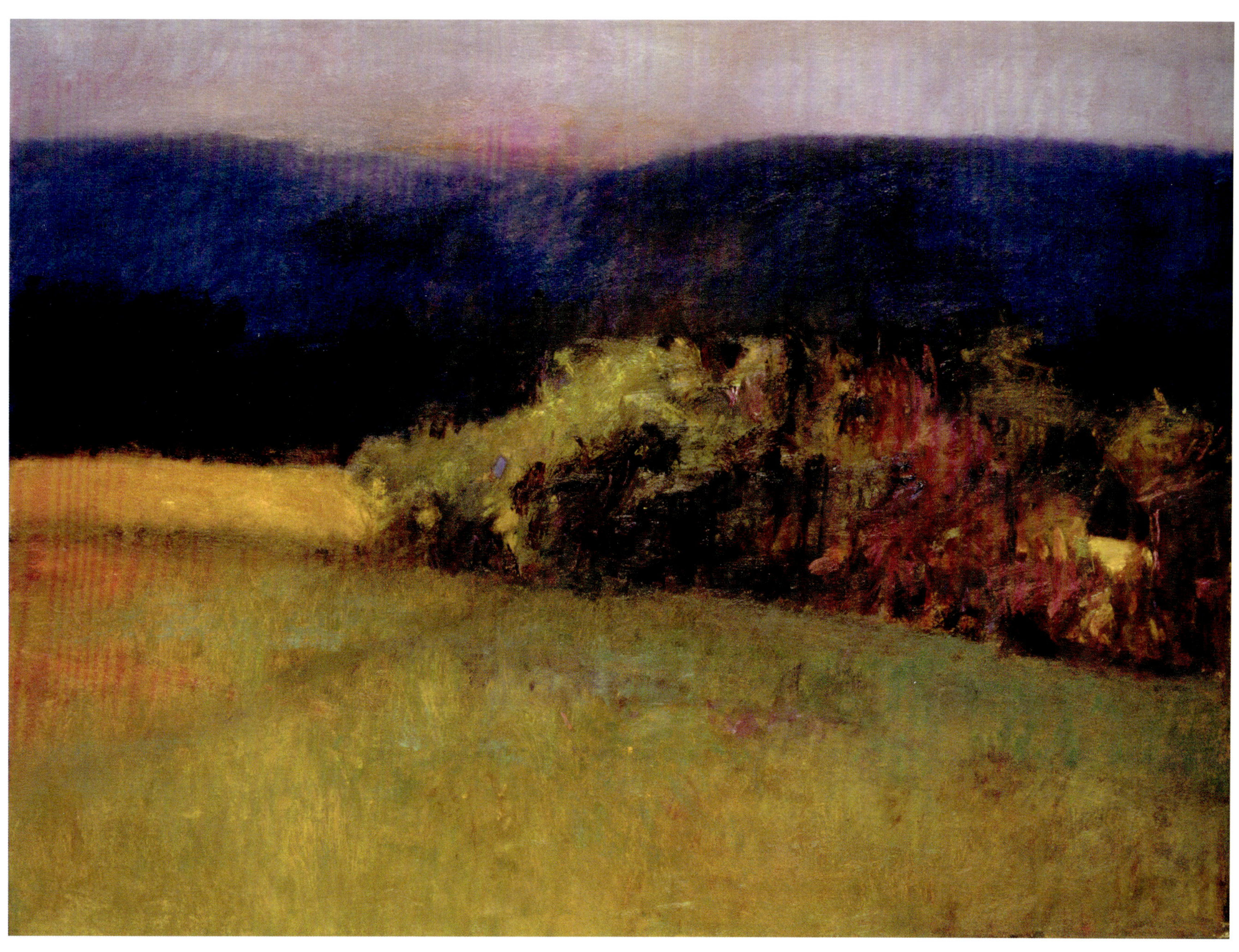

AUTUMN, END OF DAY, 1994.

Oil on linen, 38 x 50 in. (96.5 x 127 cm).
Private collection.

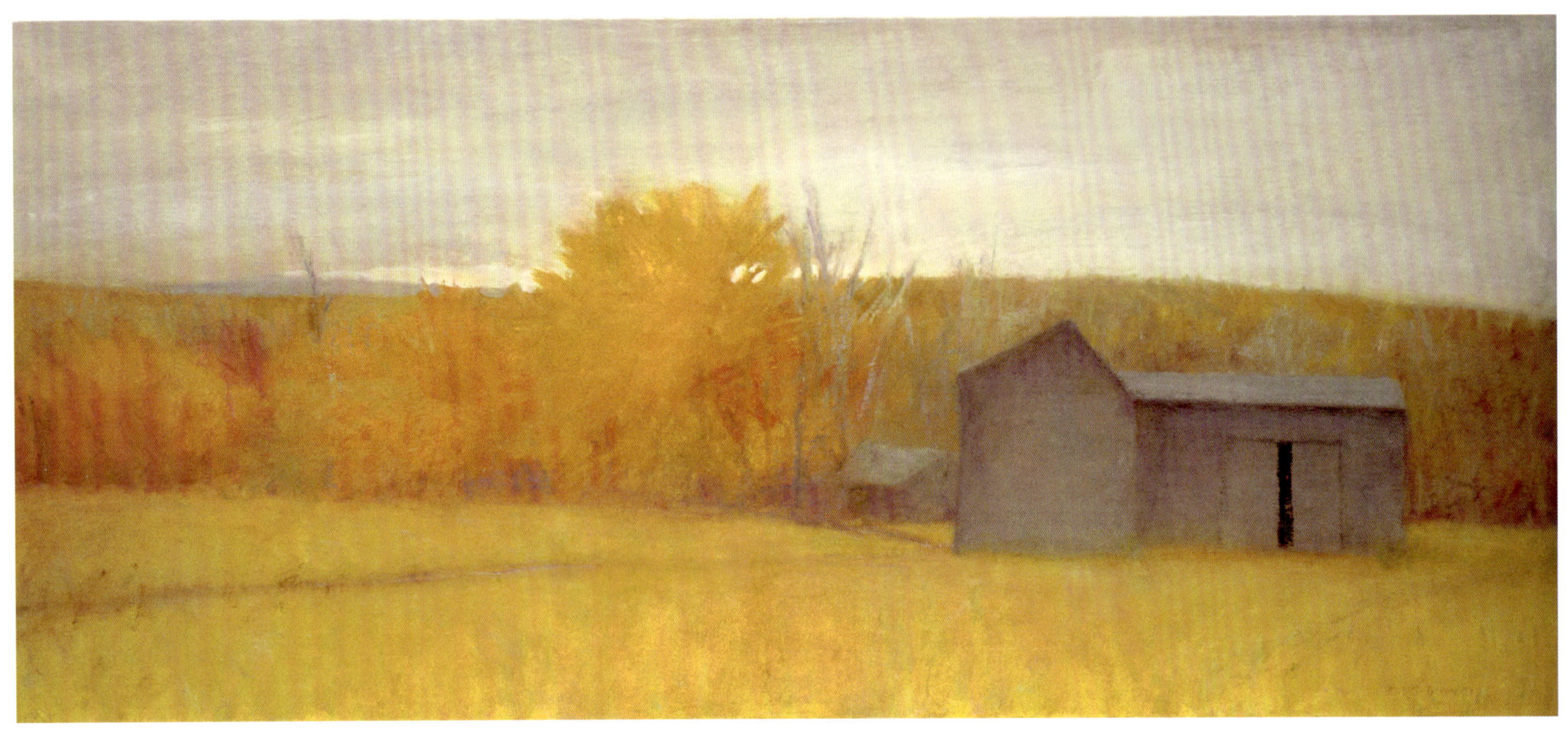

OPEN DOOR, 1994.

Oil on linen, 21 x 46 in. (53.3 x 116.8 cm).
Private collection.

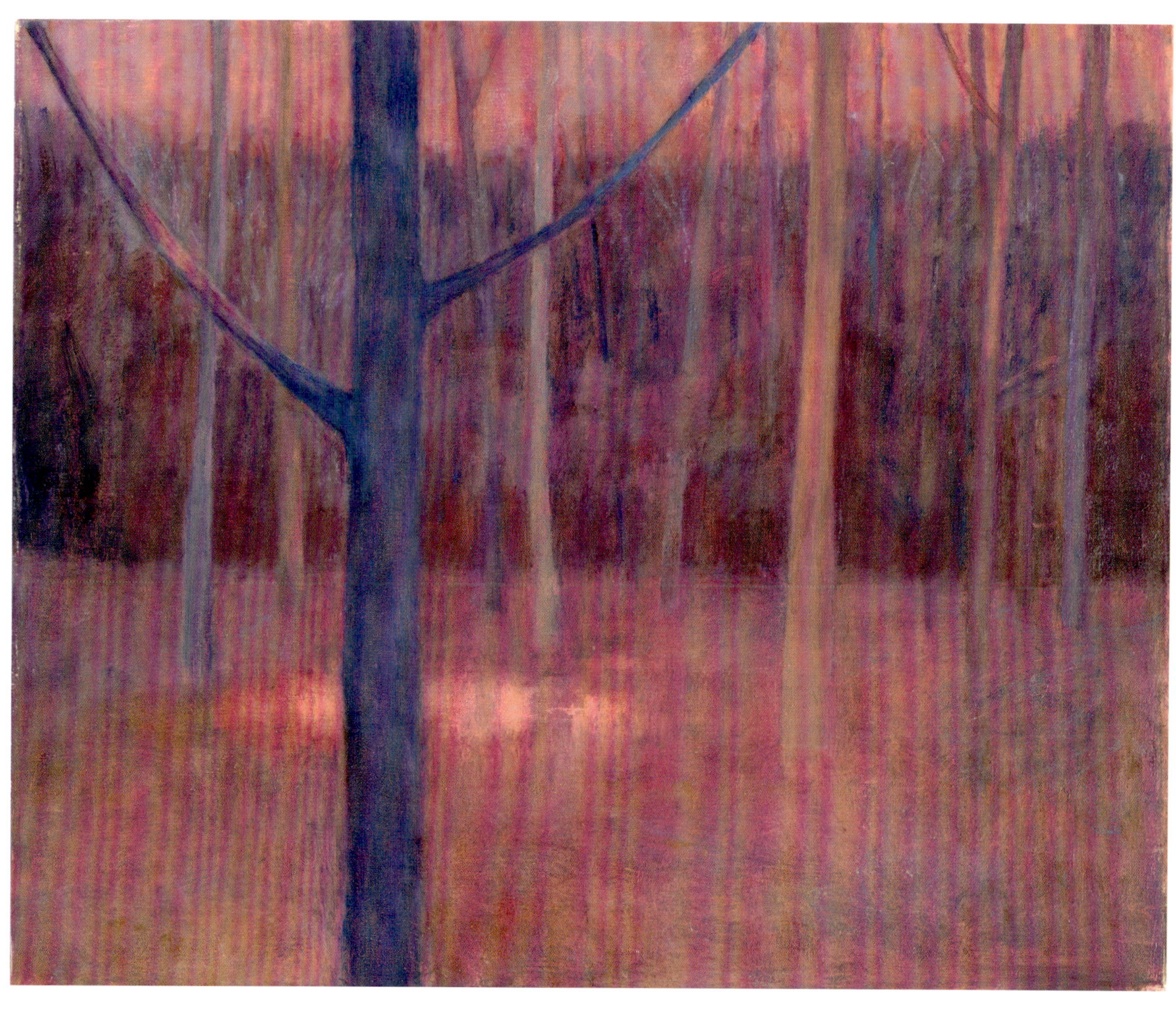

SMALL POND IN WOODS, 1992.

Oil on linen, 30 x 36 in. (76.2 x 91.4 cm).
Artist's collection.

WINTER IN STOCKBRIDGE, 2009.

Oil on panel, 23¼ x 9 in. (59.1 x 22.9 cm).
Courtesy of Wally Findlay Galleries International.

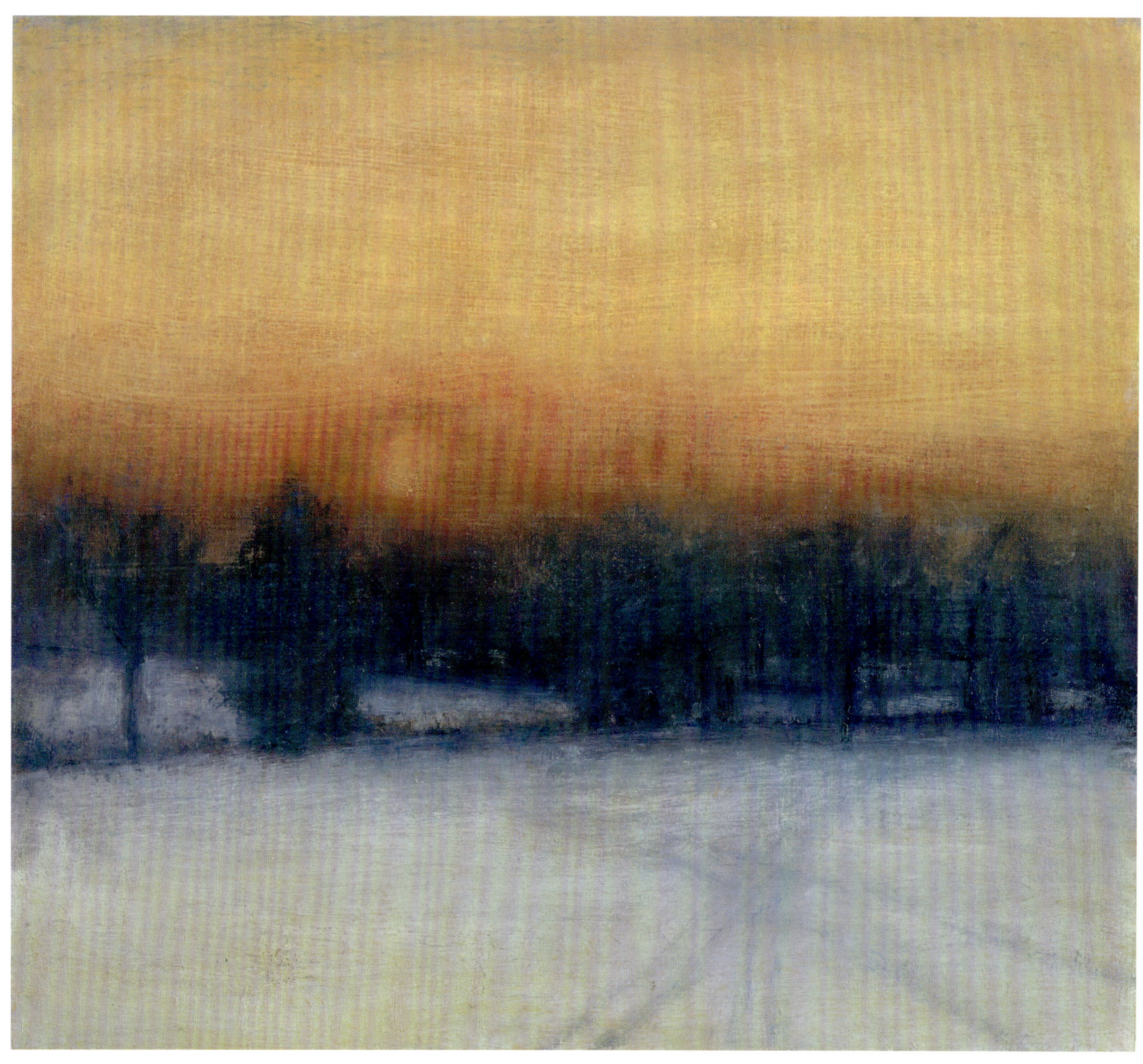

SNOWY TRACKS, 2002.

Oil on linen, 36 x 44 in. (91.4 x 111.8 cm).
Private collection.

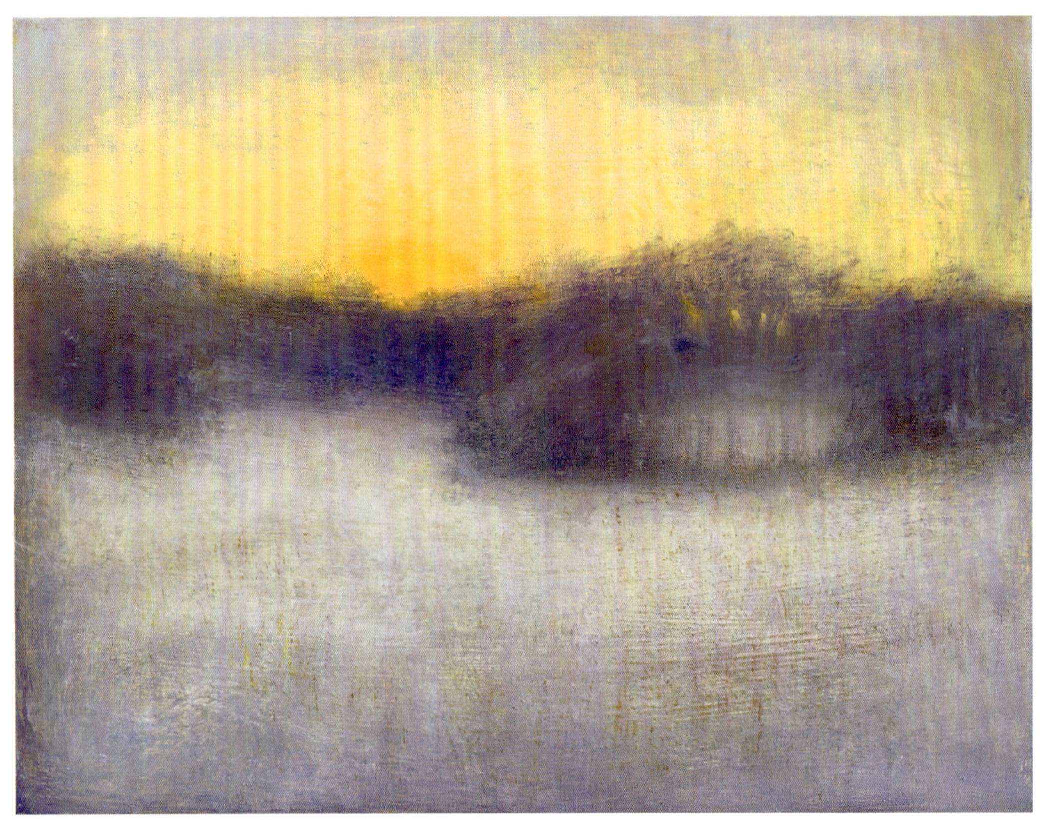

WINTER ON EDEN HILL, 2002.

Oil on panel, 8¹/₂ x 11¹/₄ in. (21.6 x 28.6 cm).
Private collection.

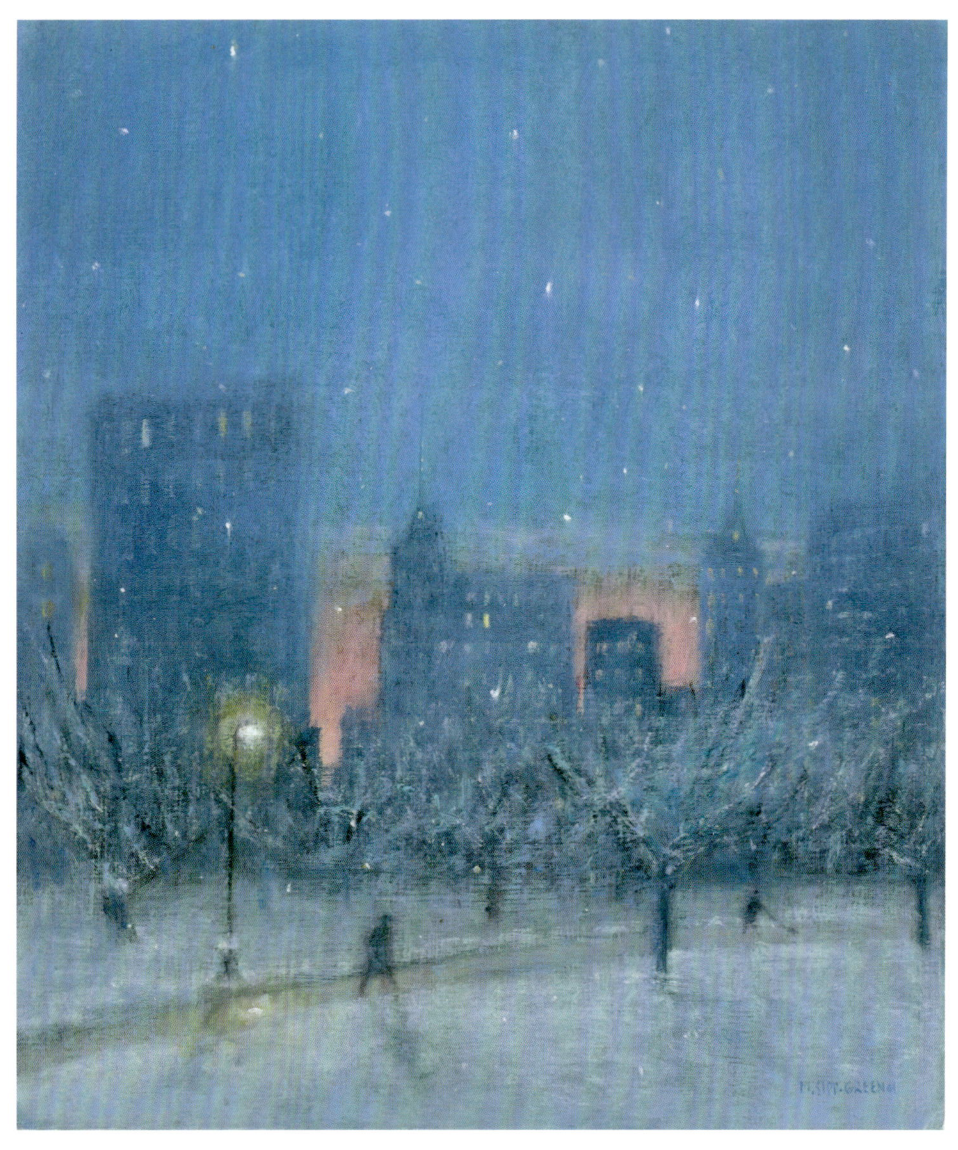

WINTER MORNING, MANHATTAN, 2001.
Oil on panel, 13 x 15 in. (33 x 38.1 cm).
Private collection.

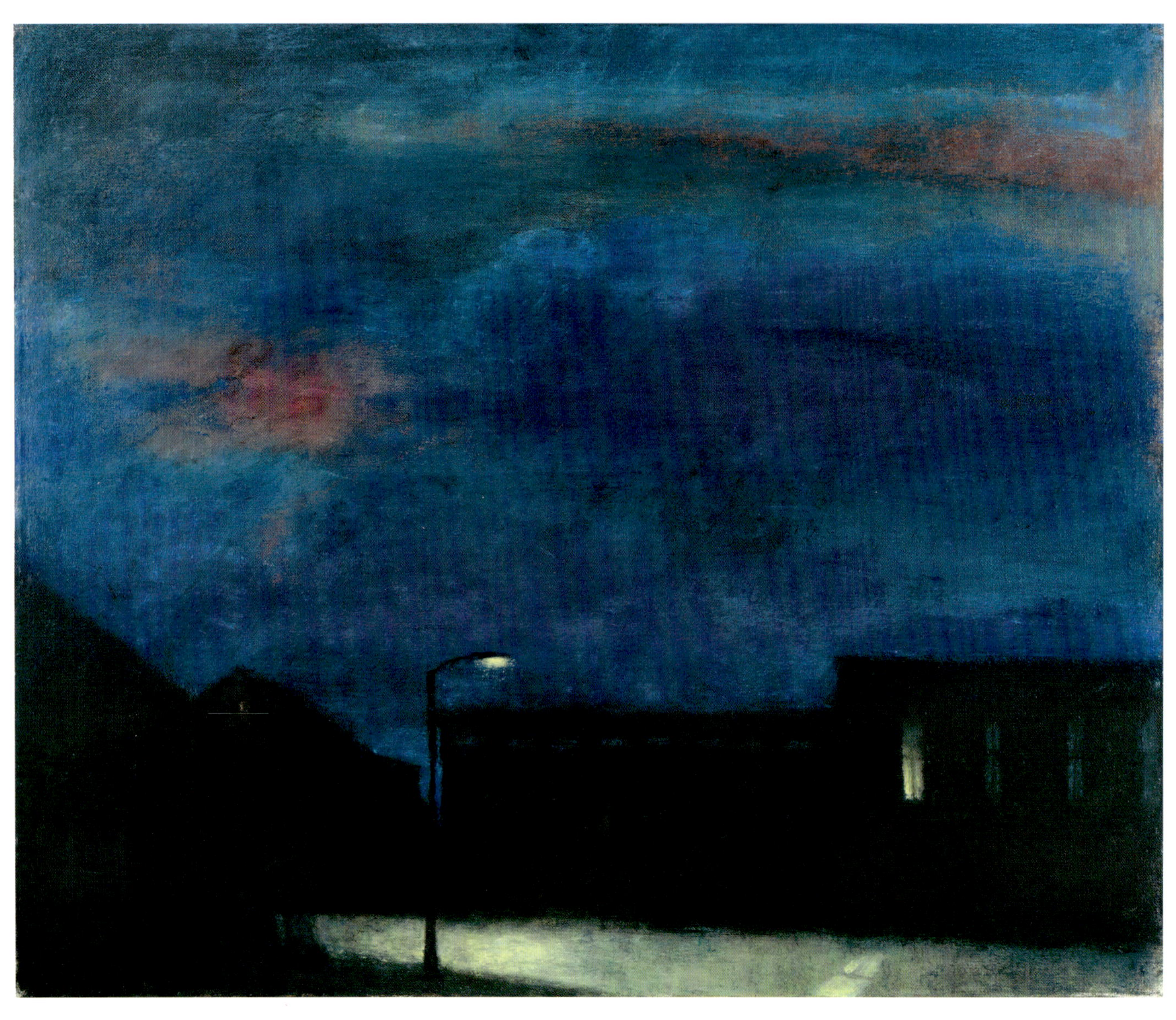

Oil on linen, 39 x 32 in. (99.1 x 81.3 cm).
Artist's collection.

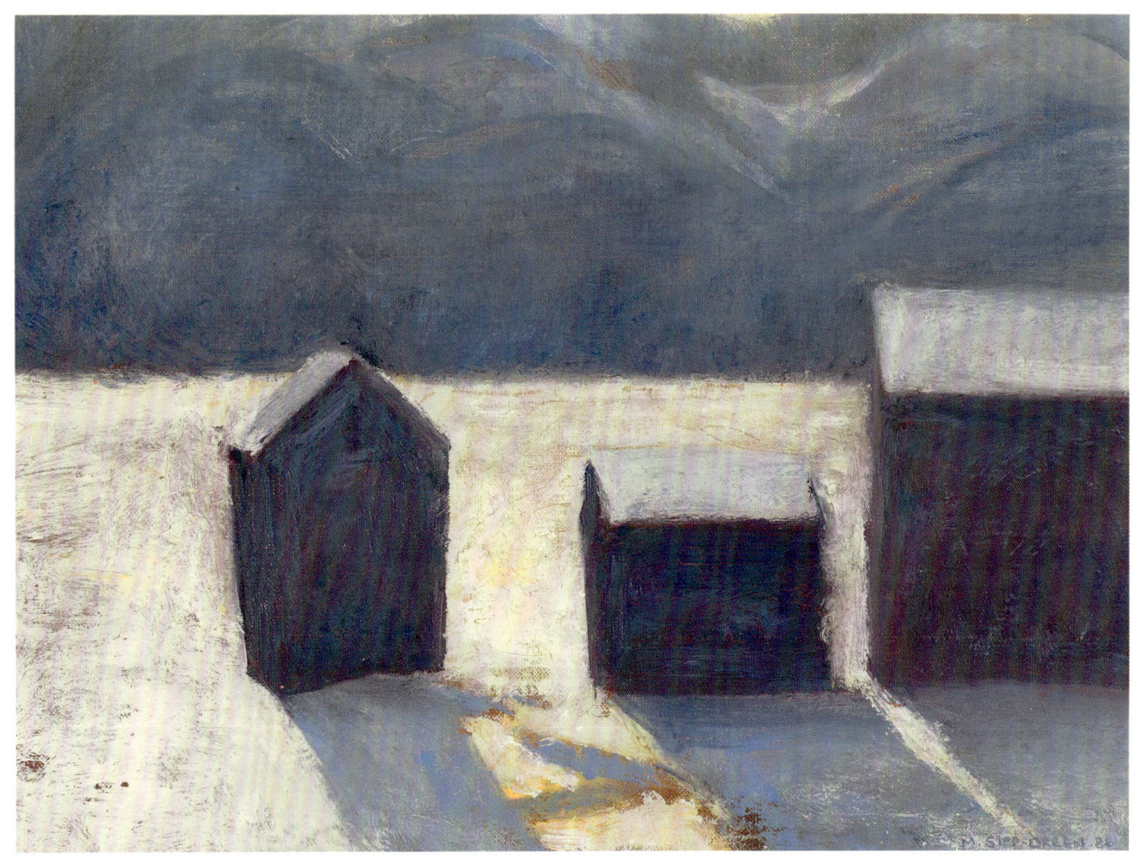

WINTER SHEDS, 1986.
Oil on linen, 11x 15 in. (27.9 x 38.1 cm).
Artist's collection.

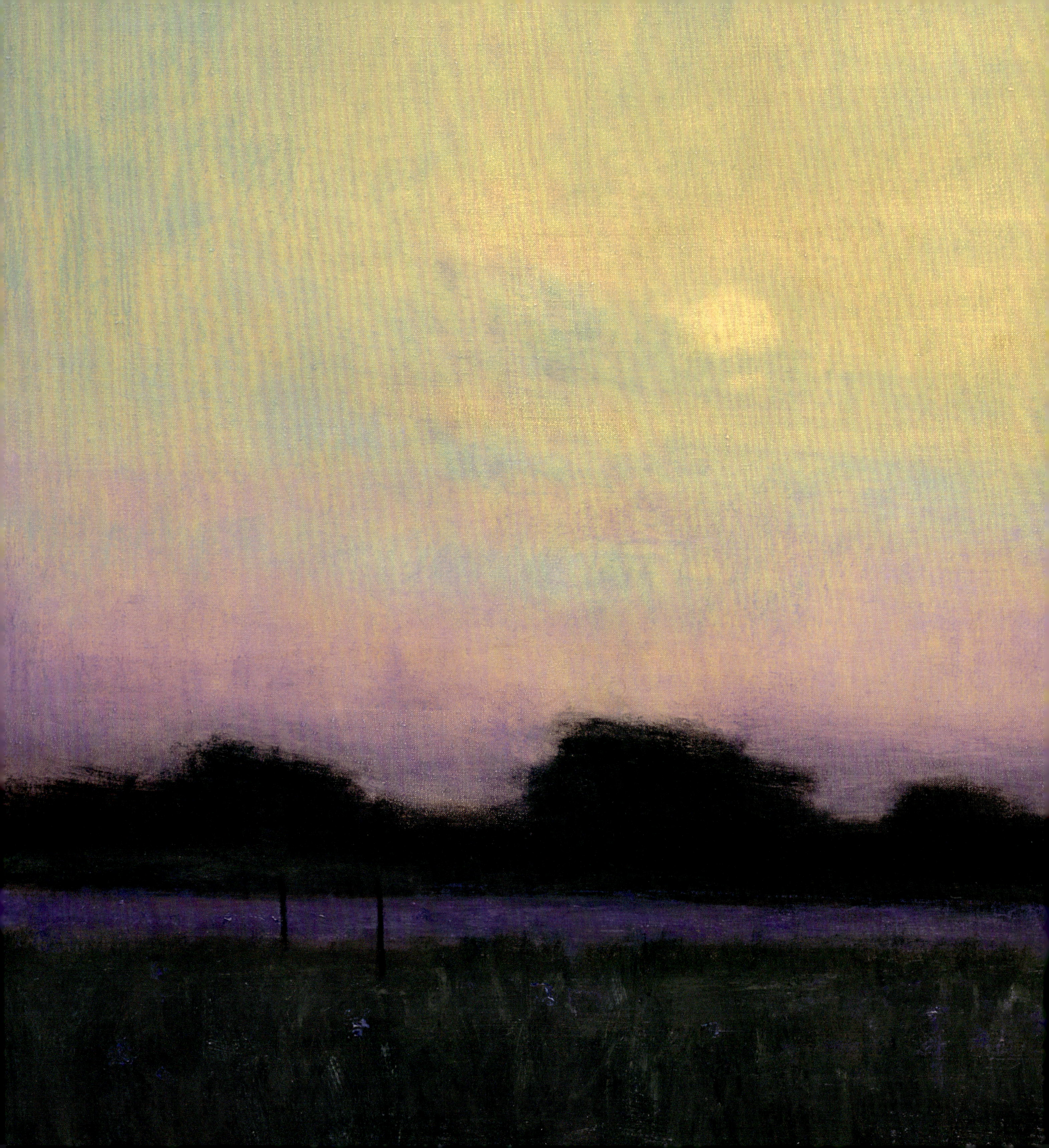

FLOWER FIELDS

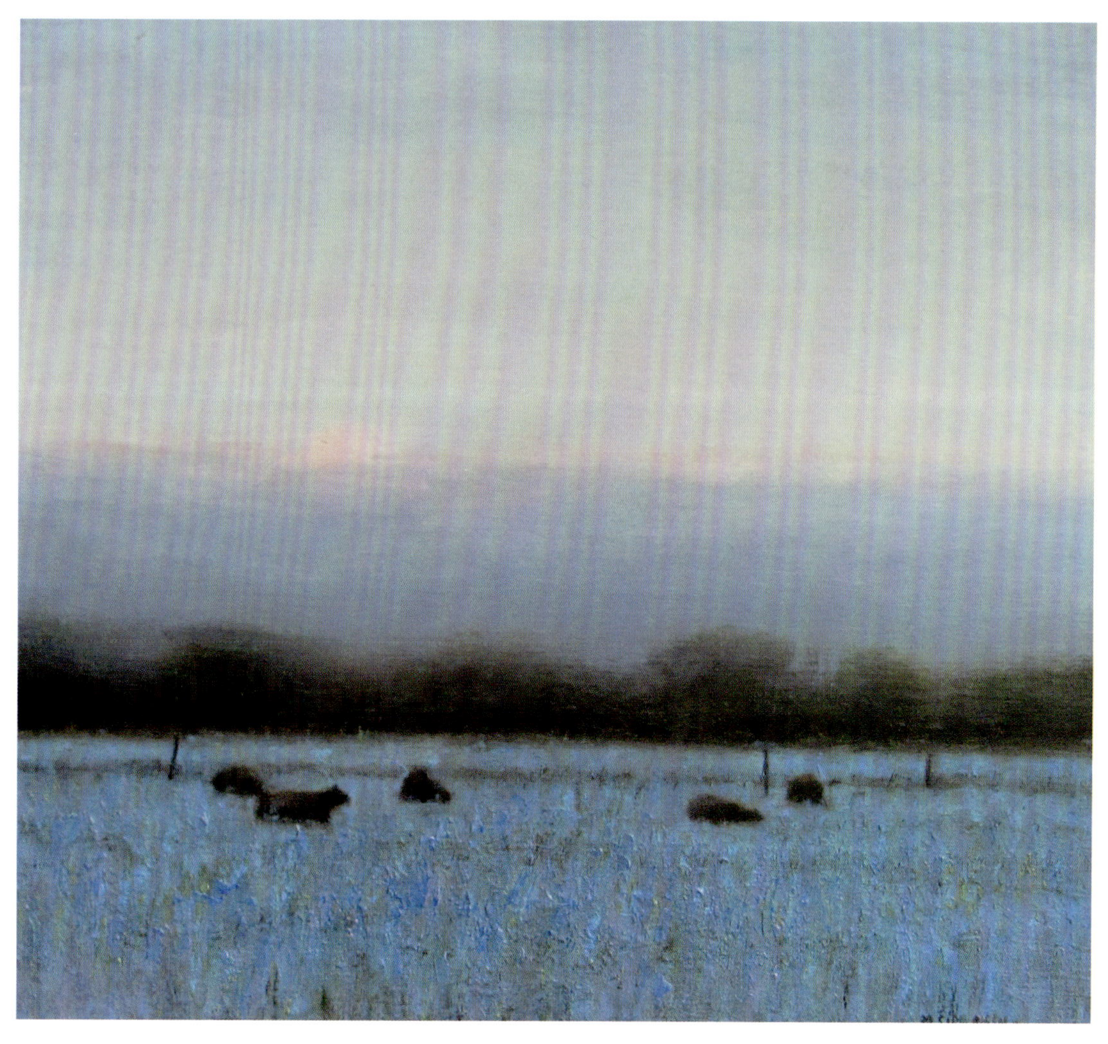

NEAR DUSK IN BLUE BONNET FIELD, 2011.

Oil on linen, 15 x 17 in. (38.1 x 43.2 cm).
Private collection.

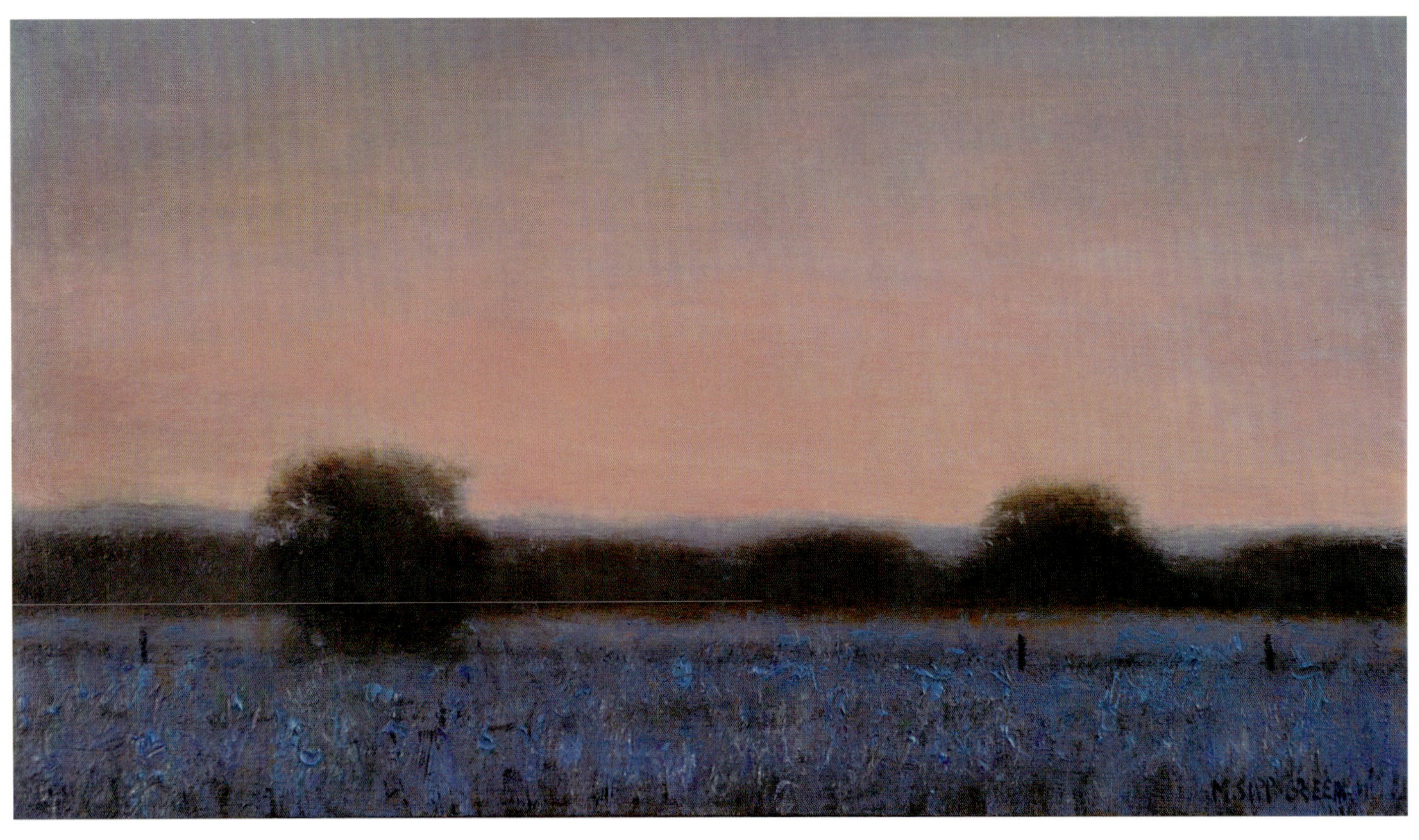

COOL TWILIGHT, 2010.

Oil on panel, 7$^{1}/_{2}$ x 13 in. (19.1 x 33 cm).
Private collection.

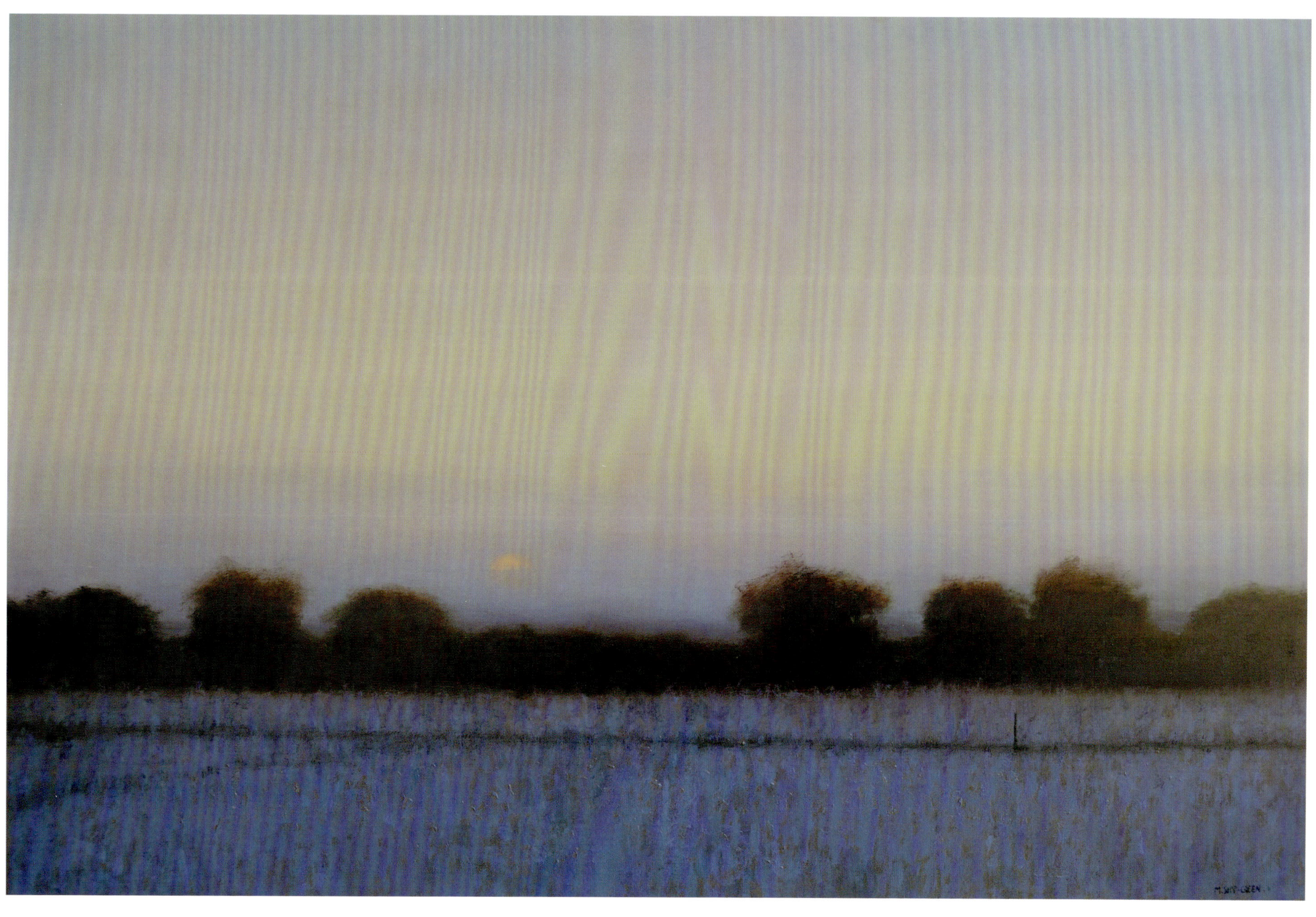

TEXAS BLUES, 2010.
Oil on linen, 40 x 60 in. (101.6 x 152.4 cm).
Private collection.

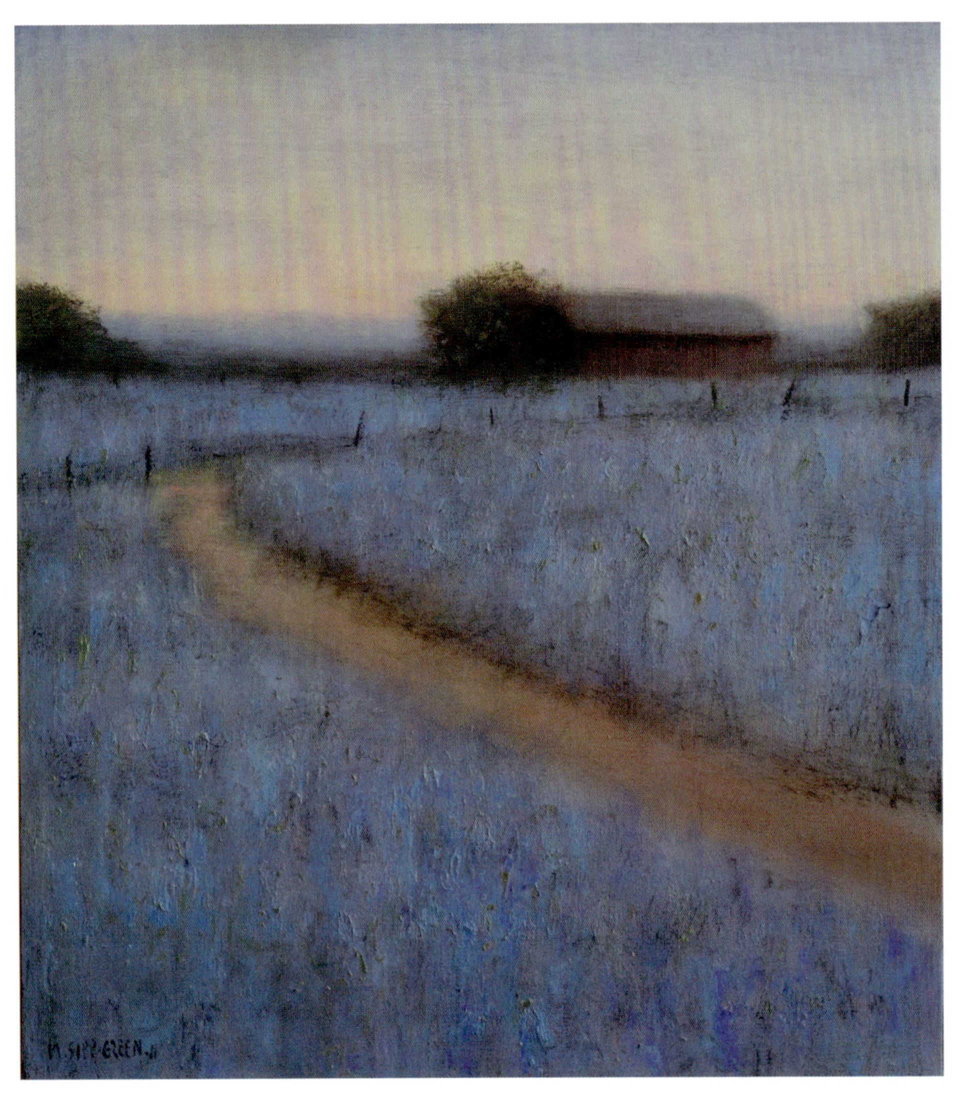

RANCH ROAD, 2010.
Oil on panel, 18 x 16 in. (45.7 x 40.6 cm).
Private collection.

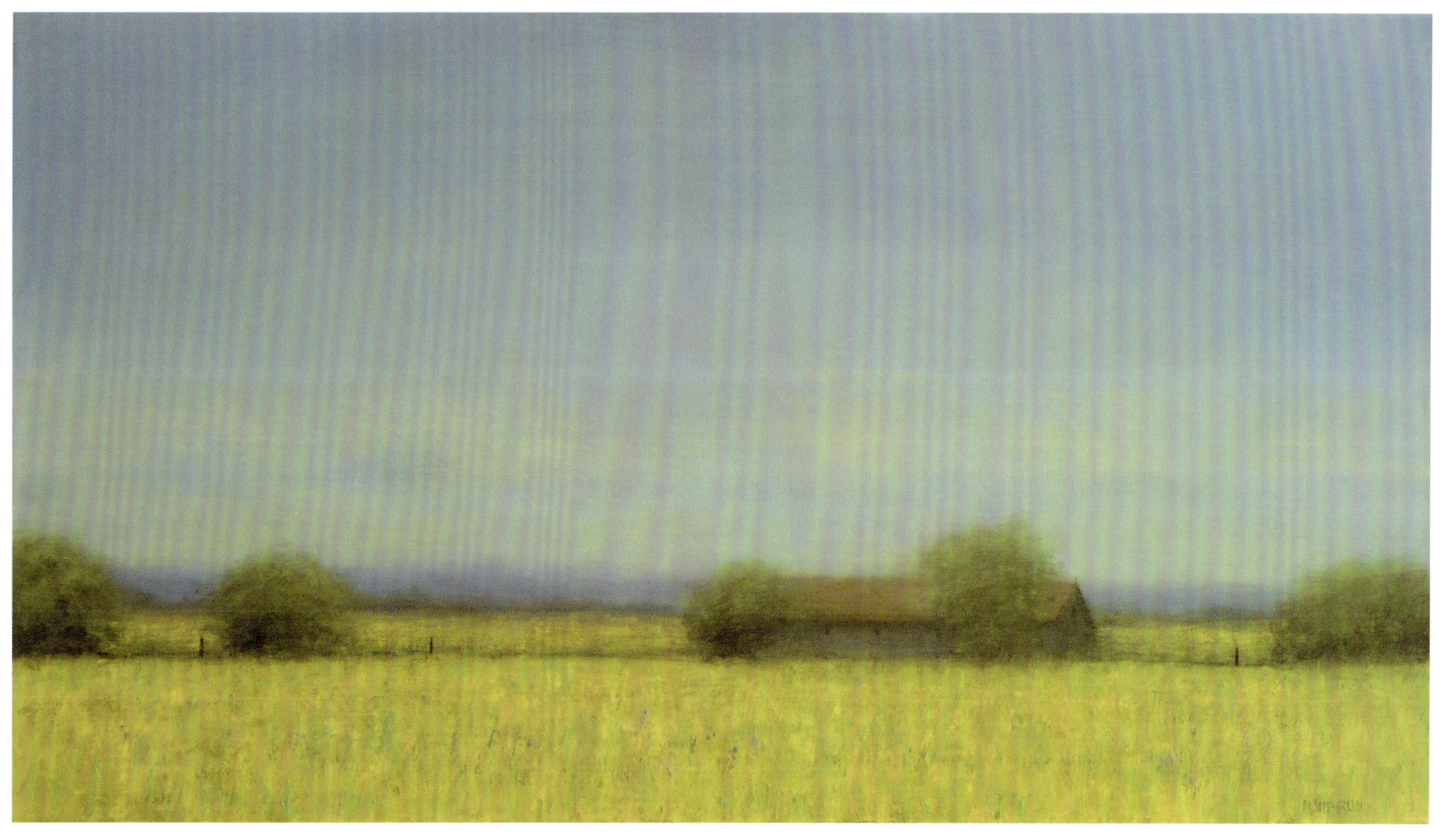

LONG BARN IN YELLOW FIELD, 2010.

Oil on linen, 20 x 36 in. (50.8 x 91.4 cm).
Courtesy Wally Findlay Galleries International.

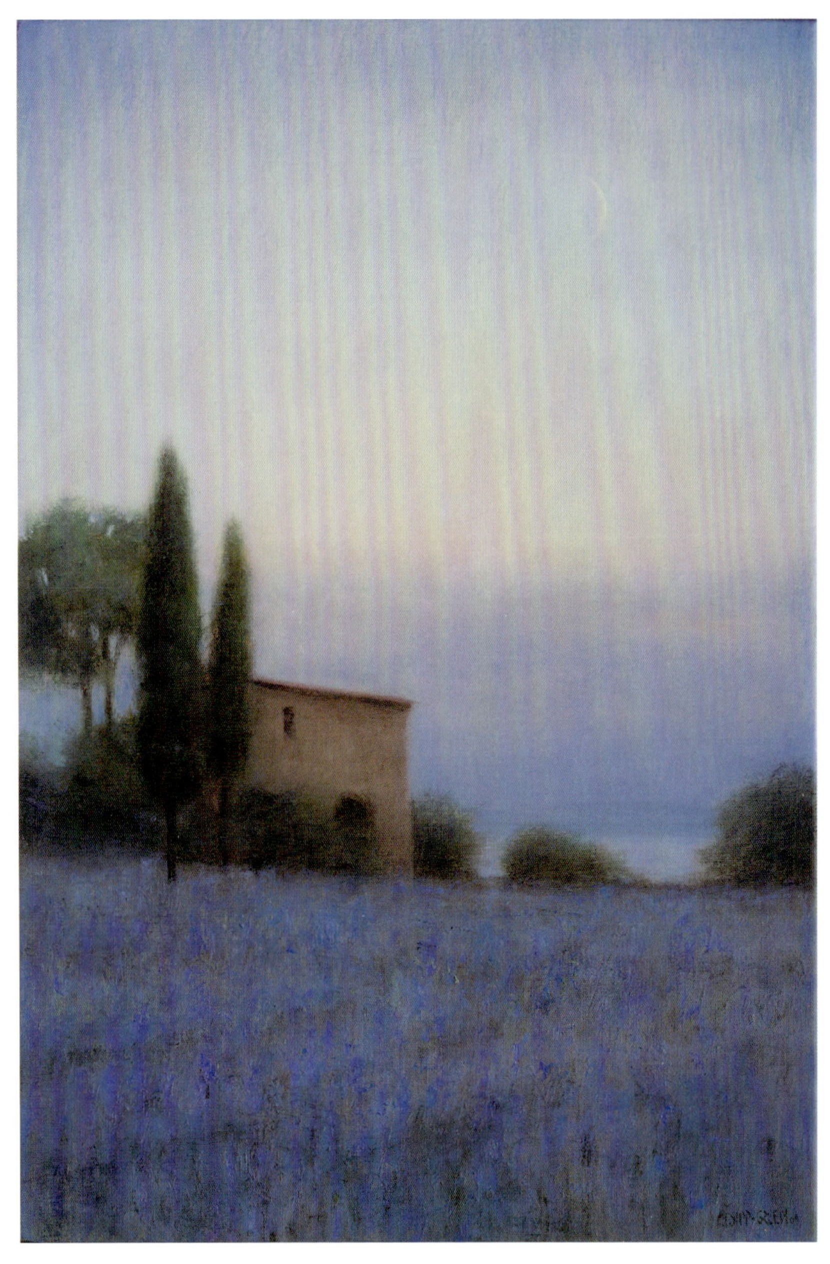

BLUE FIELDS NEAR LAKE TRASIMENO, 2009.

Oil on linen, 29 x 19 in. (73.7 x 48.3 cm).
Artist's collection.

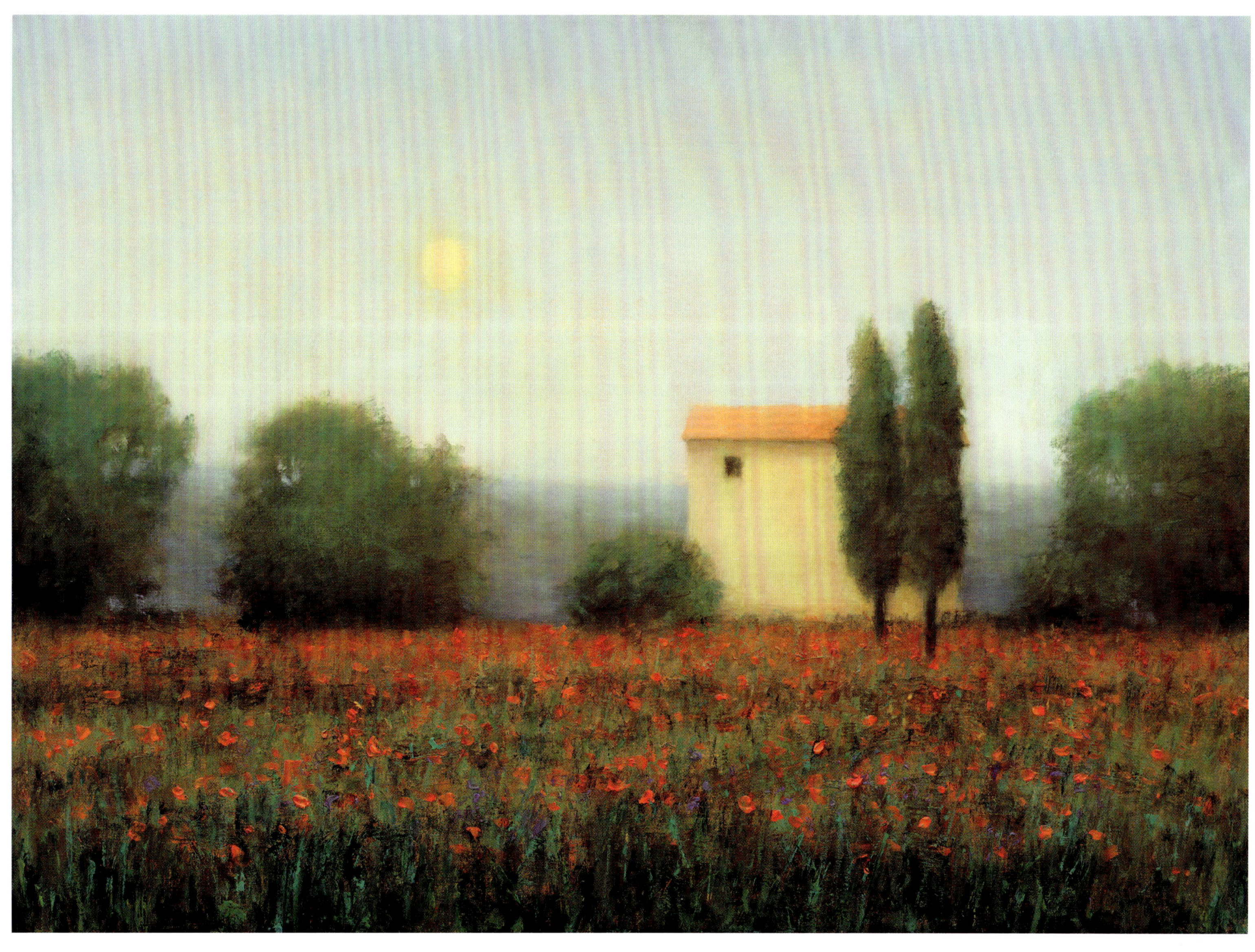

POPPY FIELD IN BETTOLE, 2009.
Oil on linen, 26 x 36 in. (66 x 91.4 cm).
Private collection.

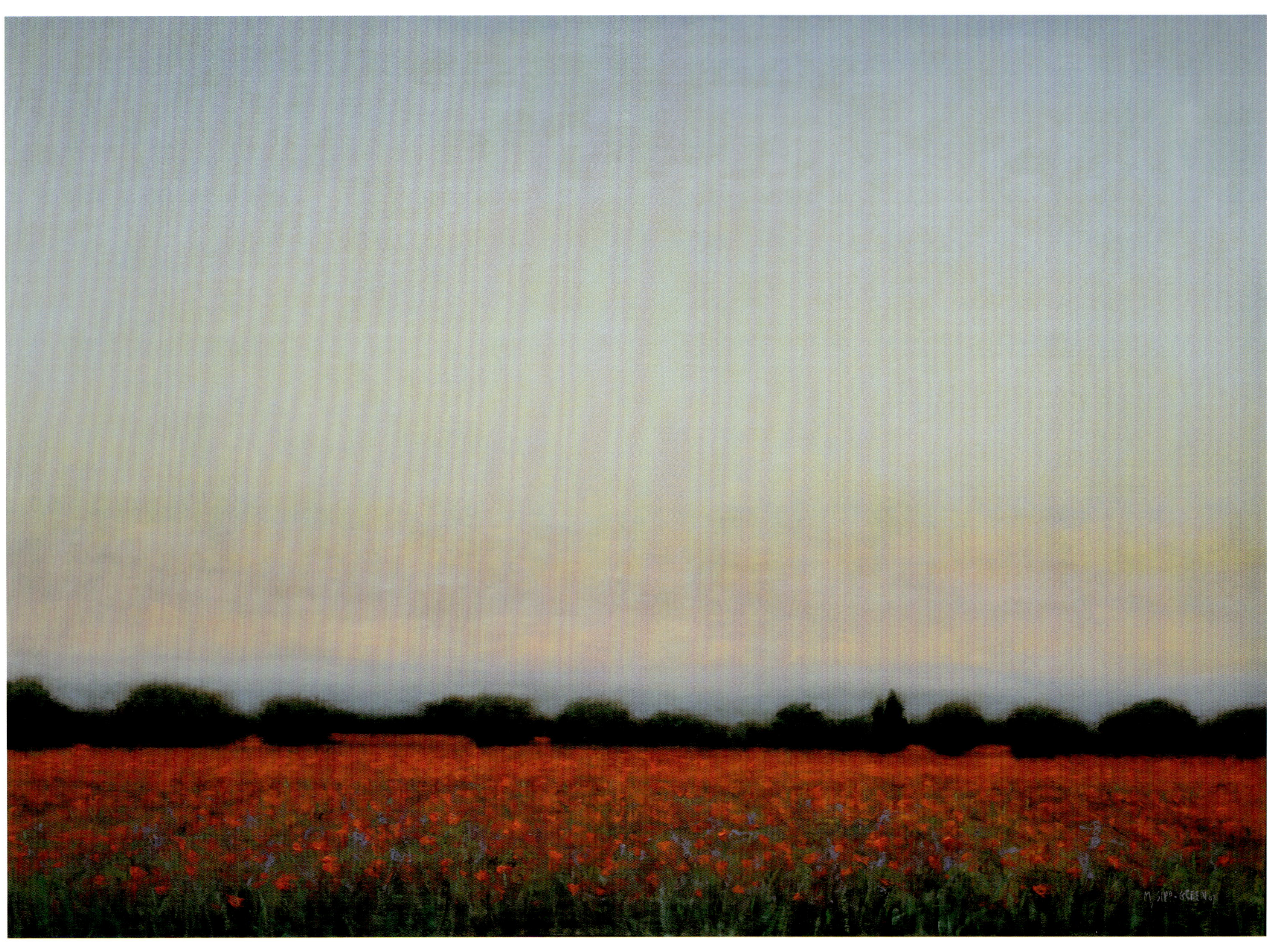

POPPY FIELDS, TUSCANY, 2007.

Oil on linen, 50 x 70 in. (127 x 177.8 cm).
Private collection.

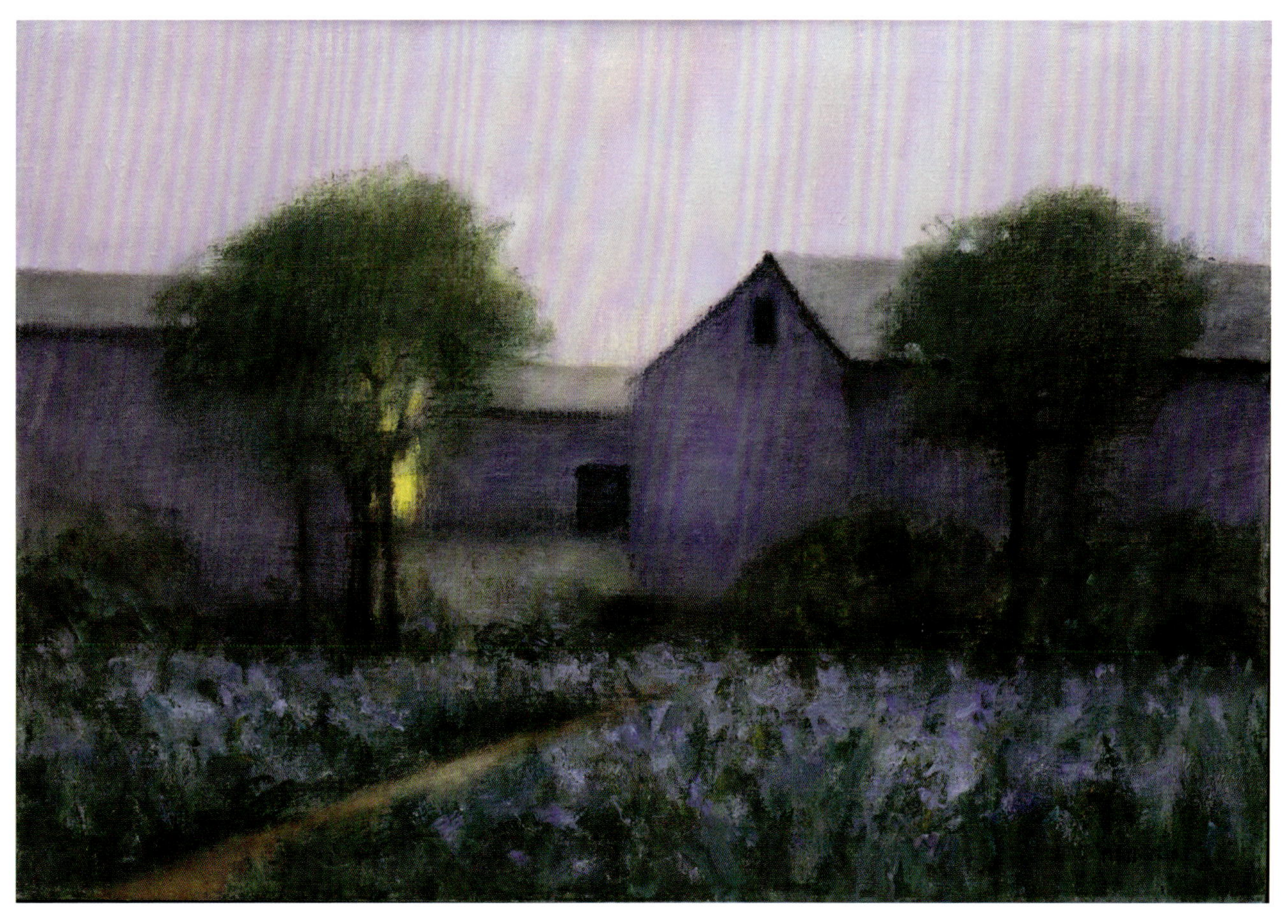

BARNS IN BLUE FLAG, 2000.
Oil on linen, 18 x 26 in. (45.7 x 66 cm).
Private collection.

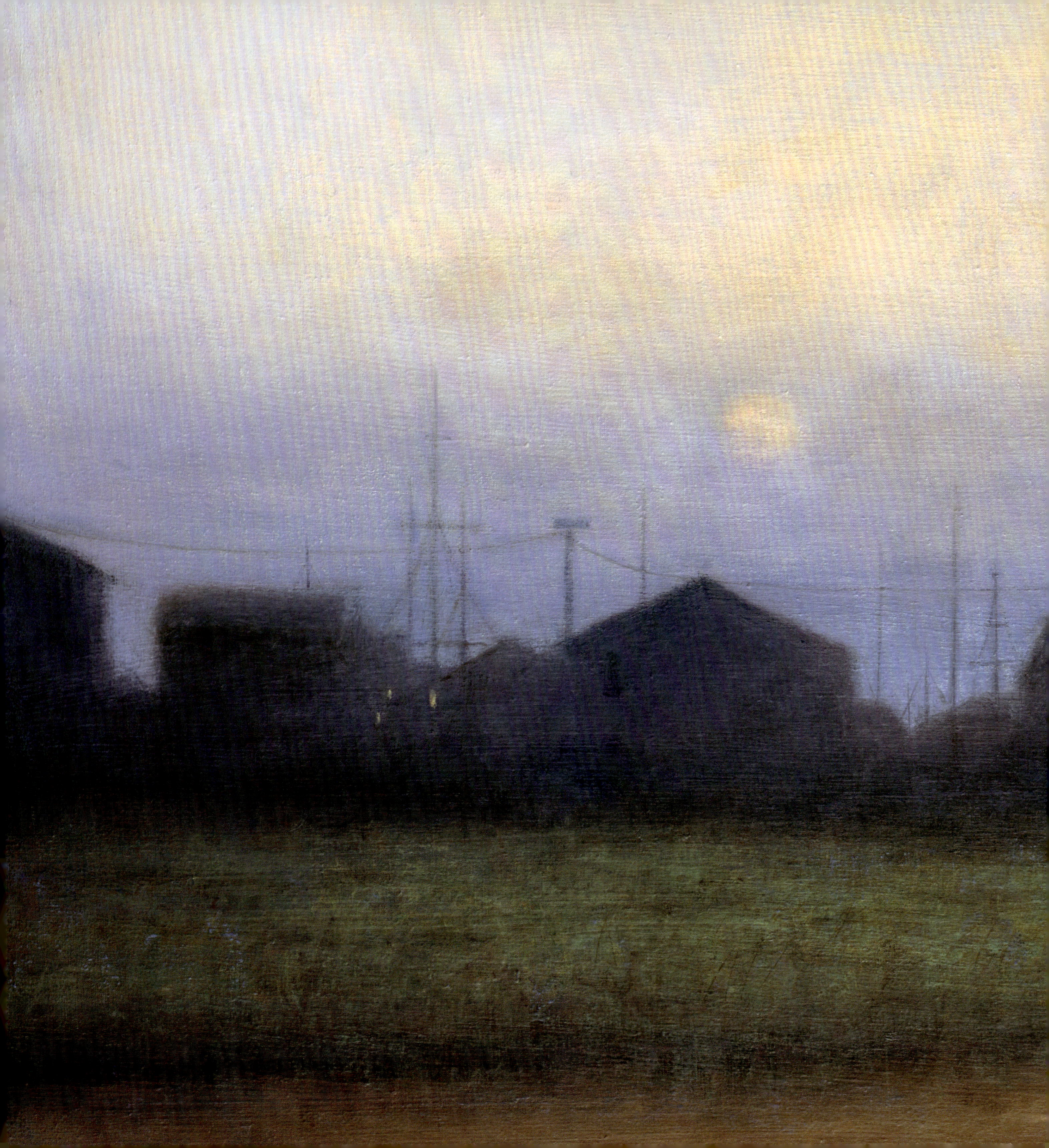

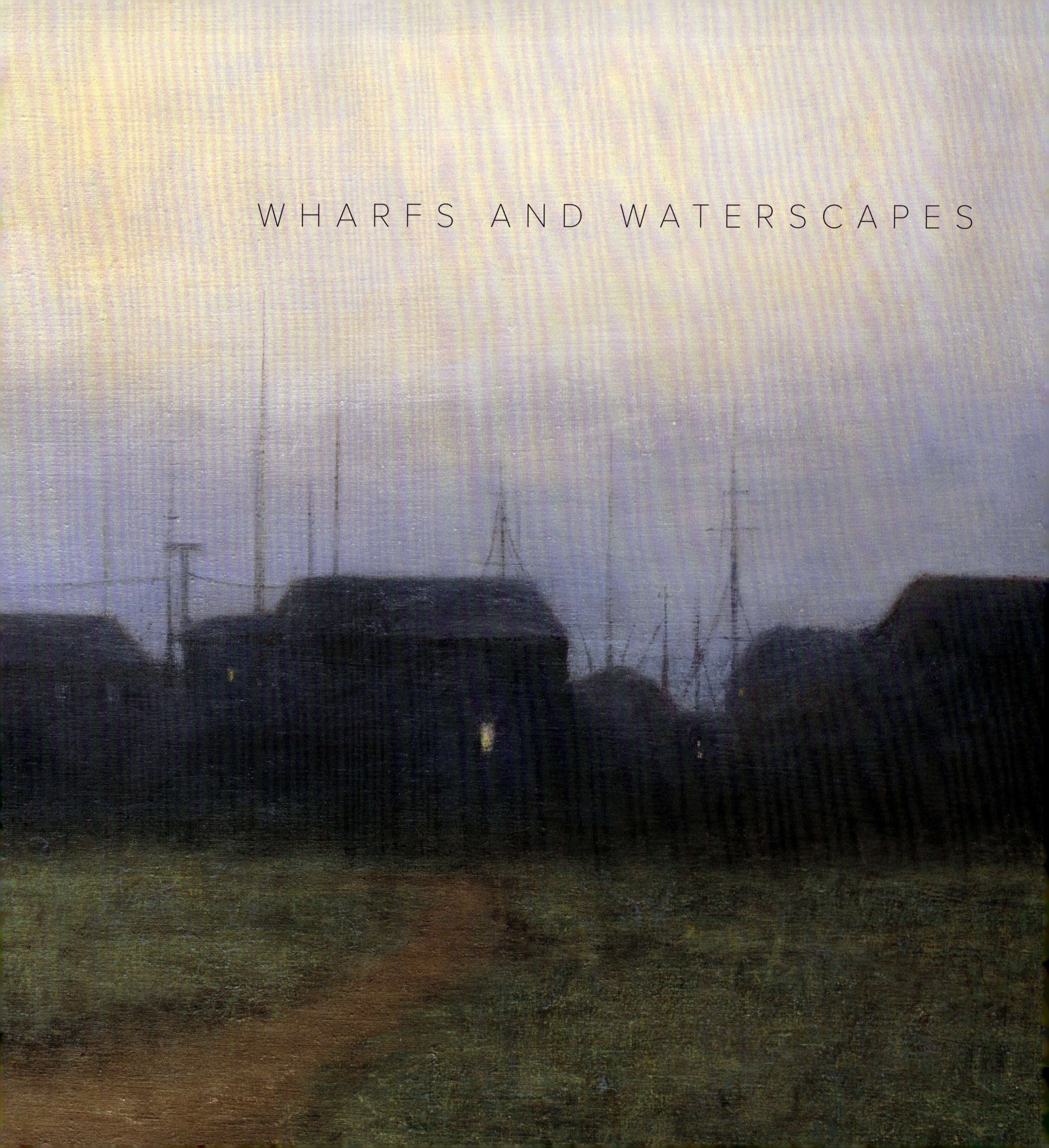

WHARFS AND WATERSCAPES

GREY DAY ON CHAPPY, 2003.
Oil on linen, 22 x 26 in. (55.9 x 66 cm).
Private collection.

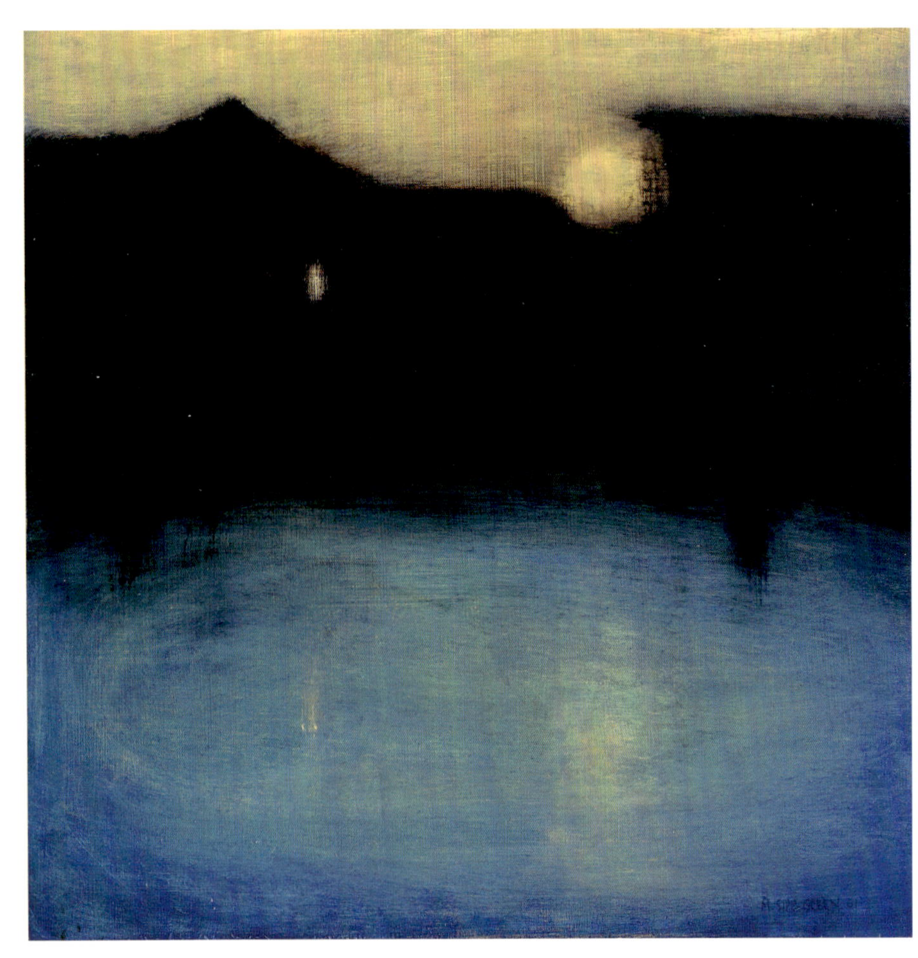

SUNRISE, ST. MARY'S, 2001.

Oil on panel, 14¹/₂ x 14¹/₂ in. (36.8 x 36.8 cm).
Private collection.

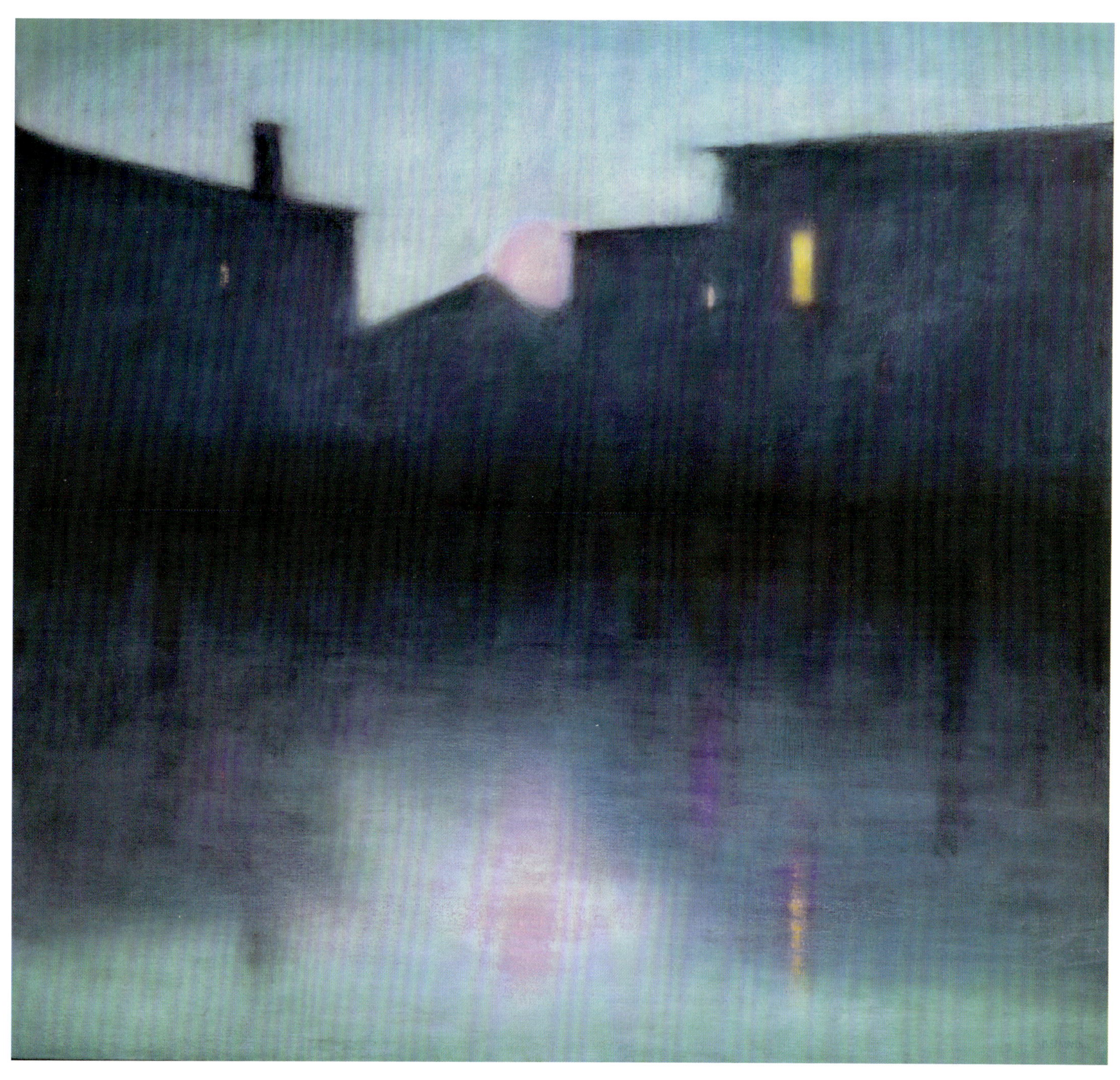

QUIET DAWN, 2001.

Oil on linen, 44 x 48 in. (111.8 x 121.9 cm).
Artist's collection.

MORNING, MARTHA'S VINEYARD, 2000.
Oil on panel, 9½ x 12½ in. (24.1 x 31.8 cm).
Artist's collection.

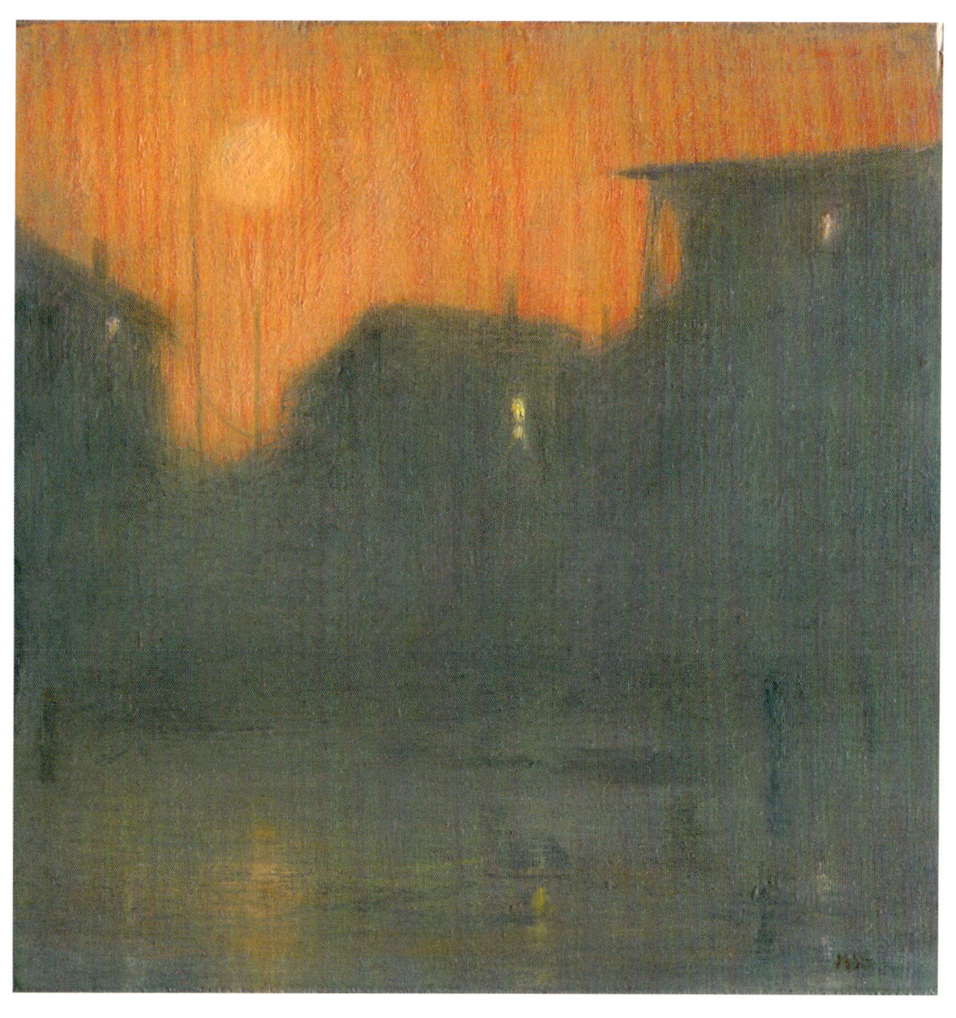

MISTY MENEMSHA, 1999.
Oil on panel, 8⅝ x 8⅝ in. (21.9 x 21.9 cm).
Private collection.

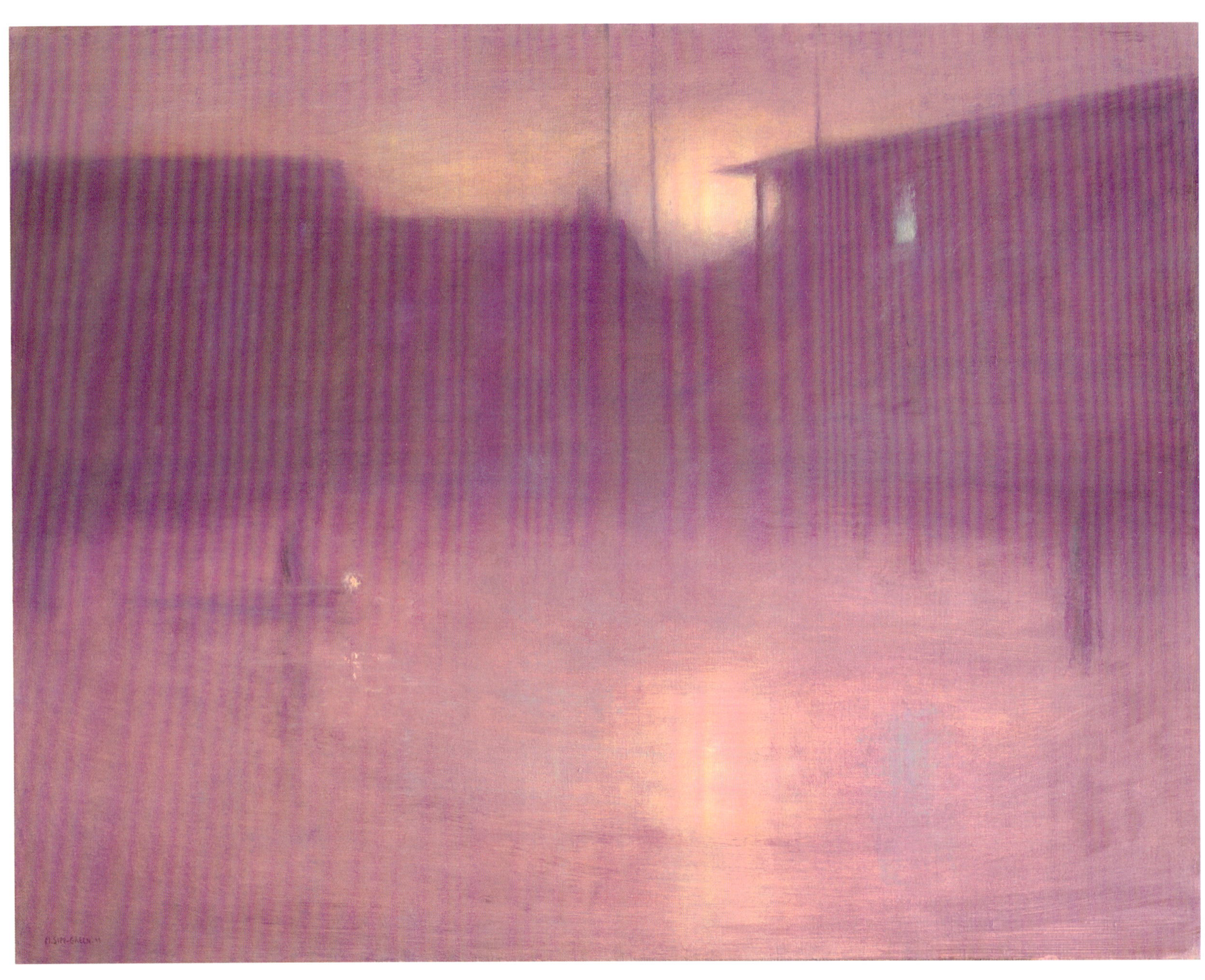

VINEYARD MORNING, MIST AND FOG, 1999.

Oil on linen, 40 x 52 in. (101.6 x 132.1 cm).
Artist's collection.

SUN RENDERING THROUGH FOG, 1992.

Oil on linen, 40 x 28 in. (101.6 x 71.1 cm).
Private collection.

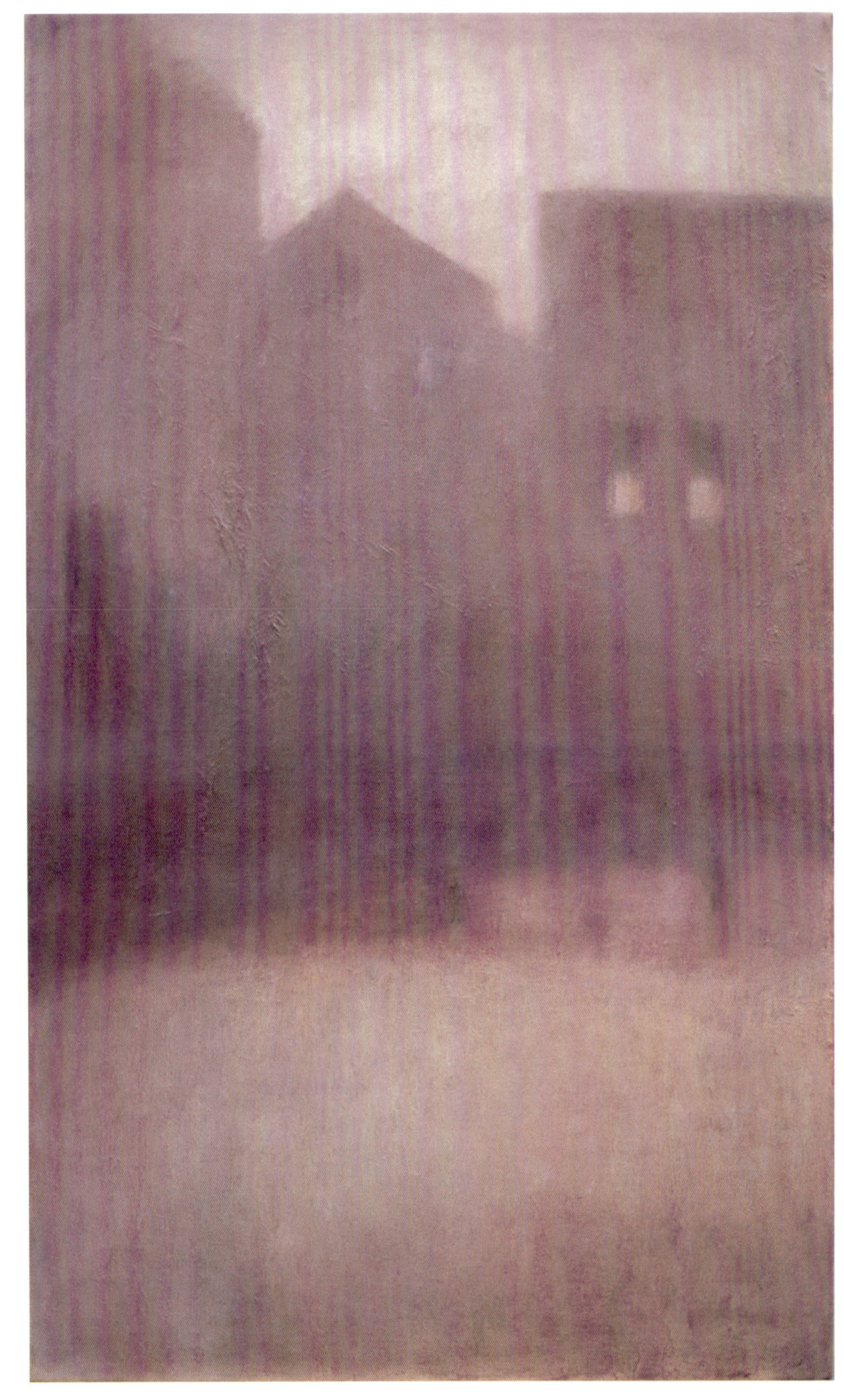

FOG ON DUTCHER DOCK, 1988.

Oil on linen, 40 x 24 in. (101.6 x 61 cm).
Private collection.

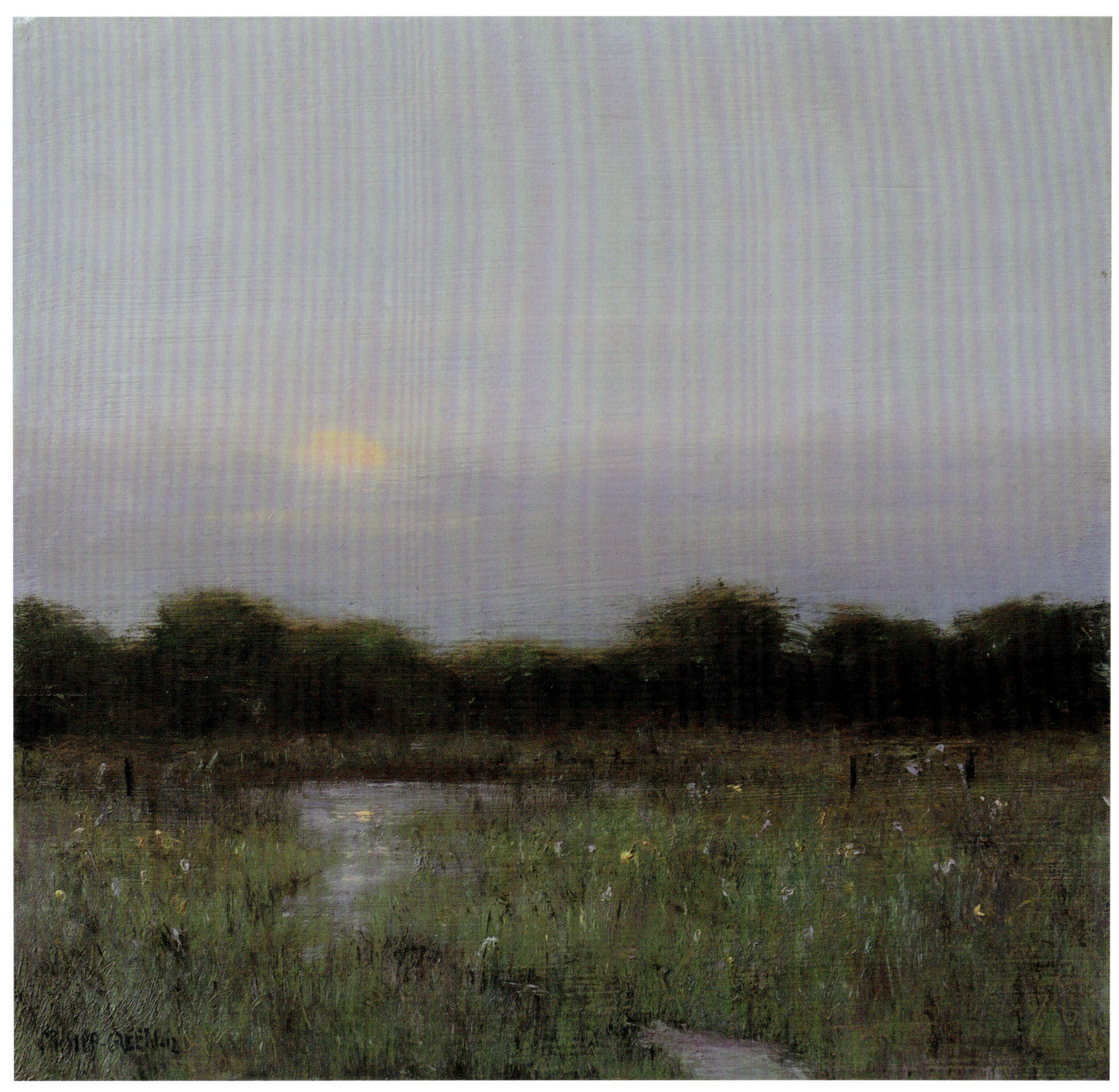

SALT MEADOW, CAPE POGE, 2012.

Oil on linen, 48 x 46 in. (121.9 x 116.8 cm).
Courtesy Granary Gallery.

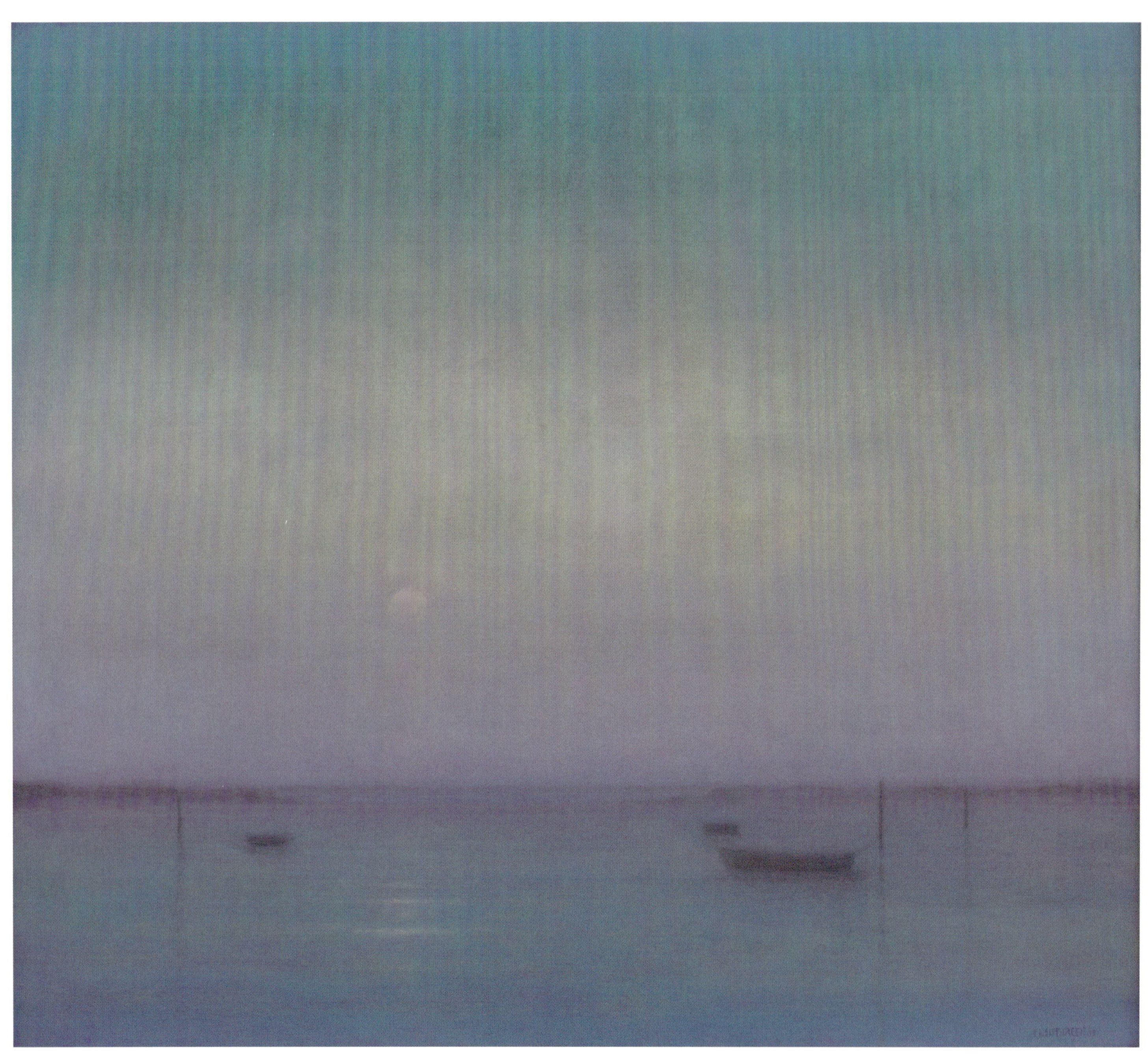

EARLY MORNING, CAPE POGE BAY, 2010.

Oil on linen, 44 x 50 in. (111.8 x 127 cm).
Private collection.

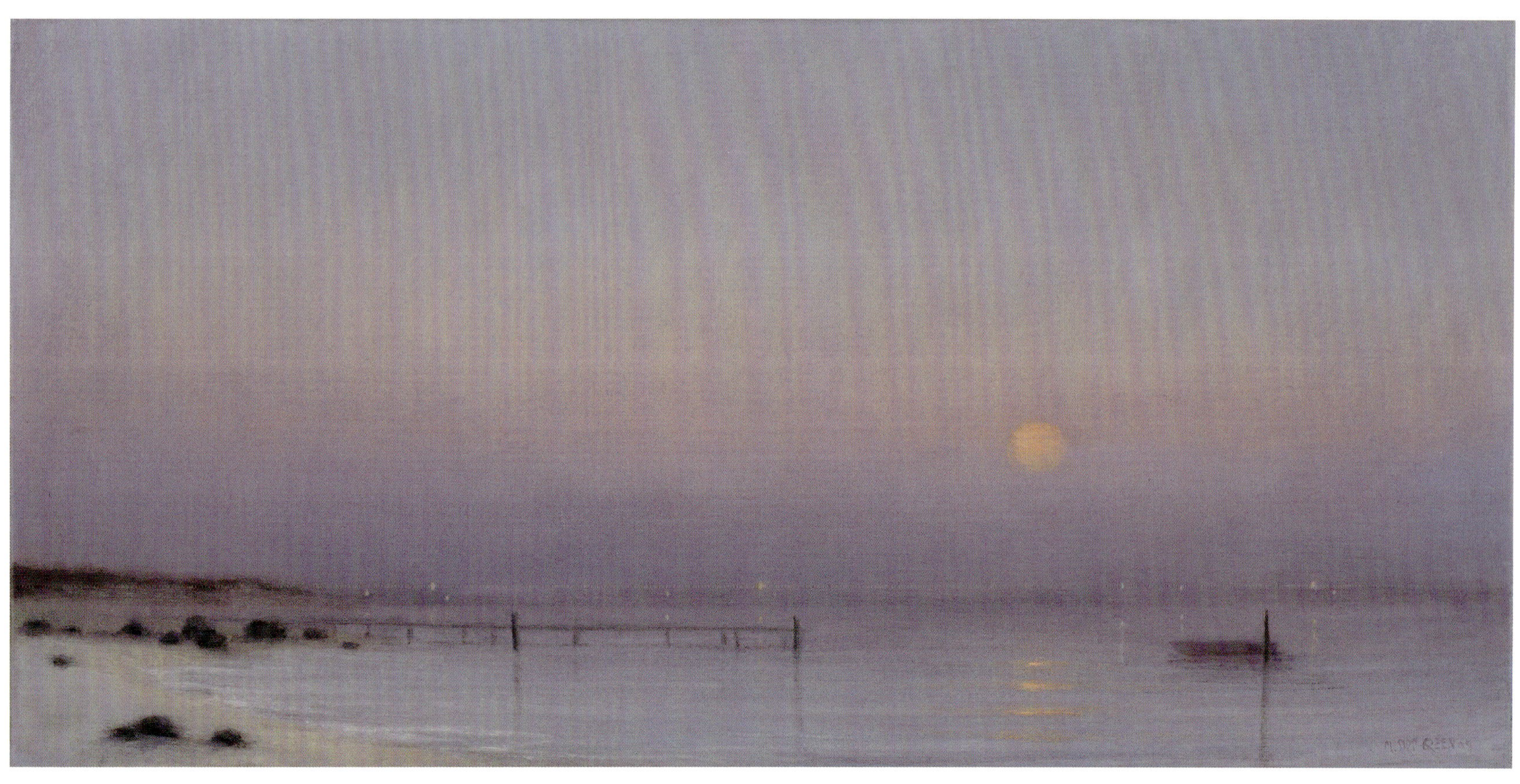

MISTY SUNSET, GREY'S BEACH, 2009.

Oil on linen, 12 x 24 in. (30.5 x 61 cm).
Private collection.

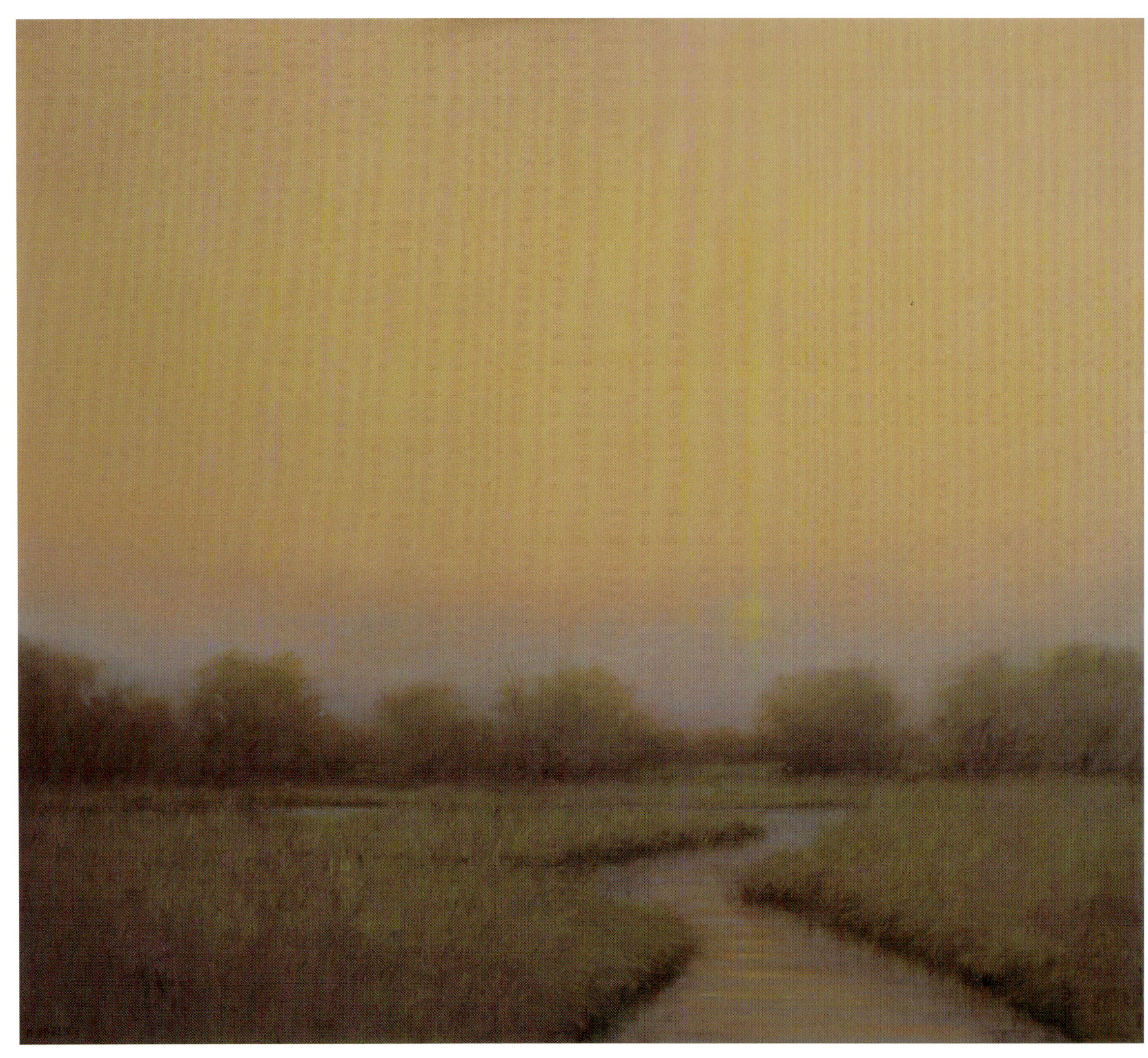

MORNING, 2008.
Oil on linen, 44 x 50 in. (111.8 x 127 cm).
Private collection.

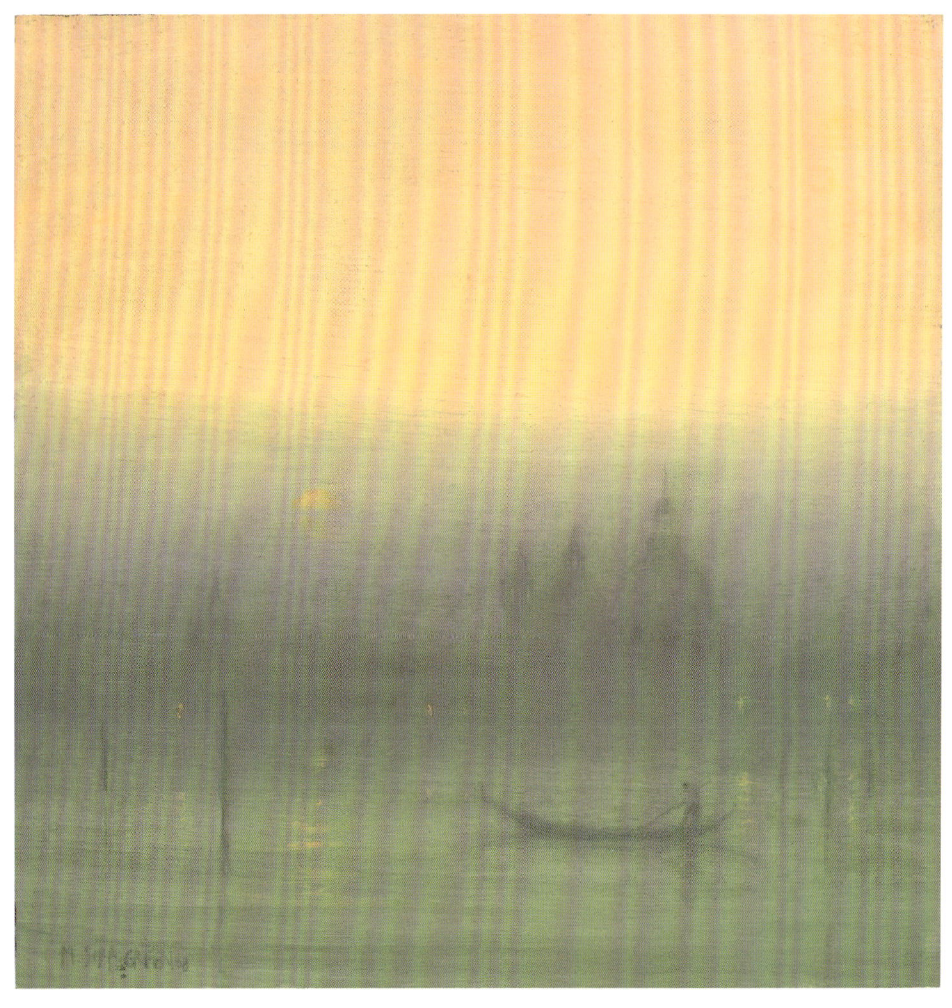

VENICE ON THE LAGOON, 2008.

Oil on panel, 9 x 8³/₄ in. (22.9 x 22.2 cm).
Private collection.

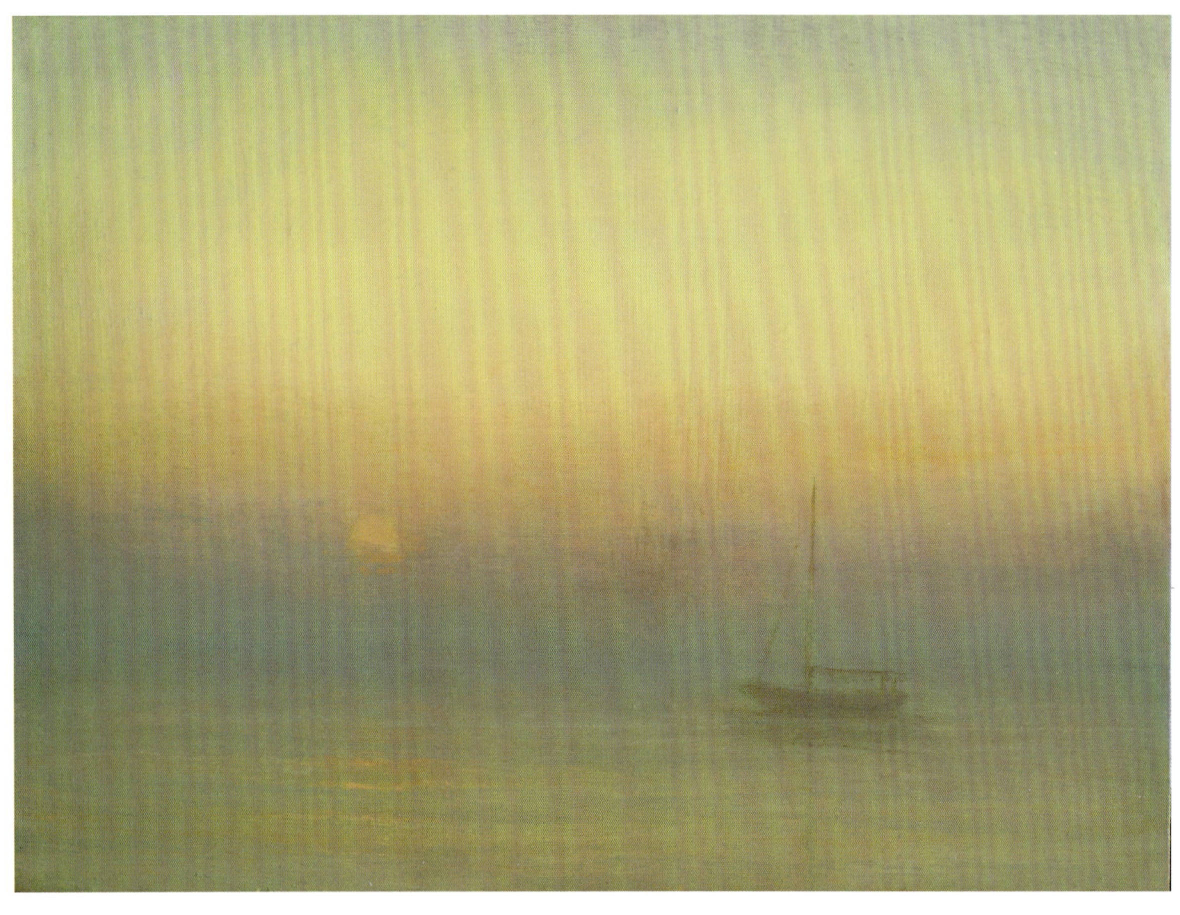

BAY OF NAPLES, 2007.
Oil on linen, 12 x 16 in. (30.5 x 40.6 cm).
Private collection.

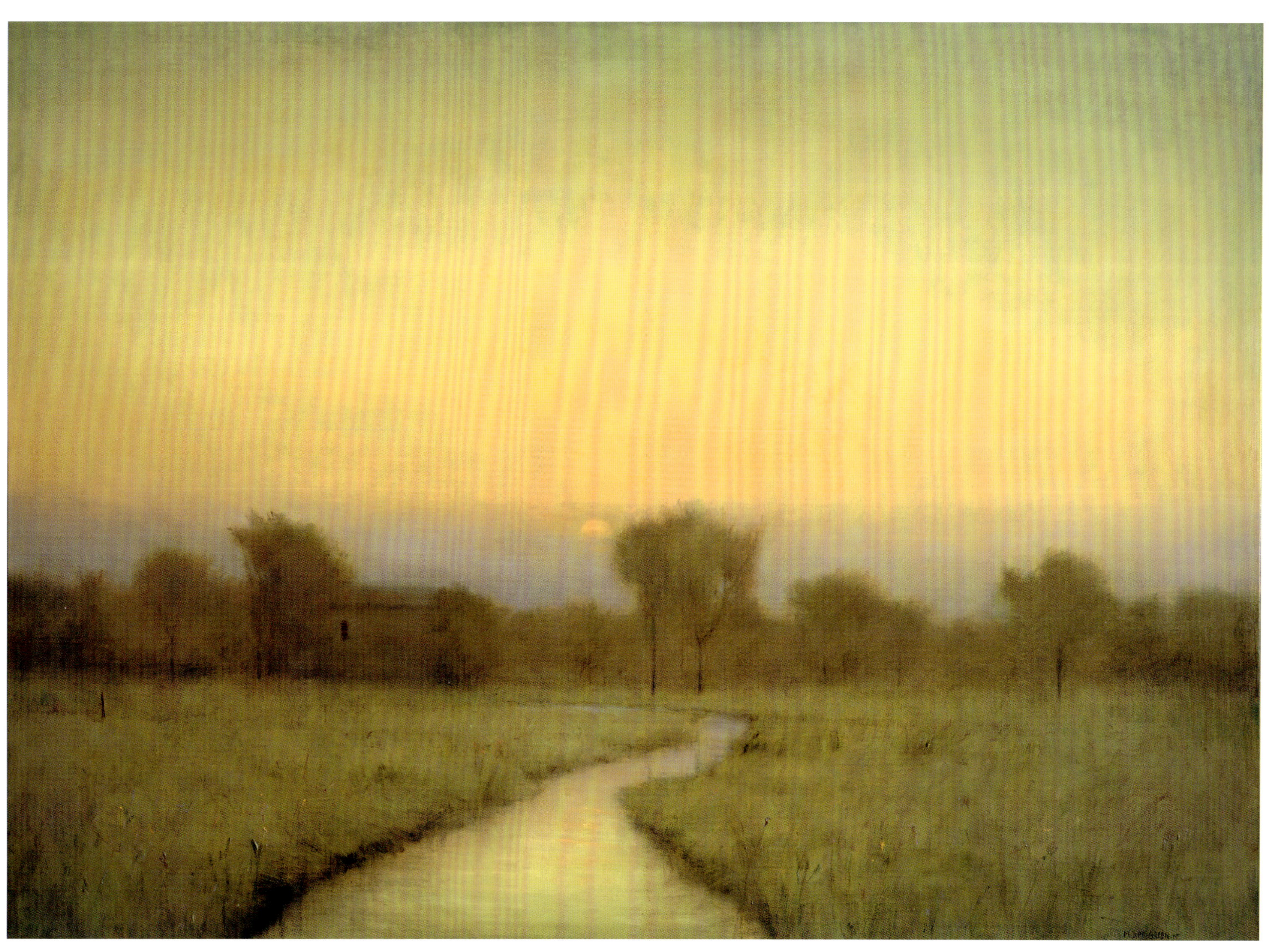

SUNRISE, 2005.
Oil on linen, 52 x 72 in. (132.1 x 182.9 cm).
Private collection.

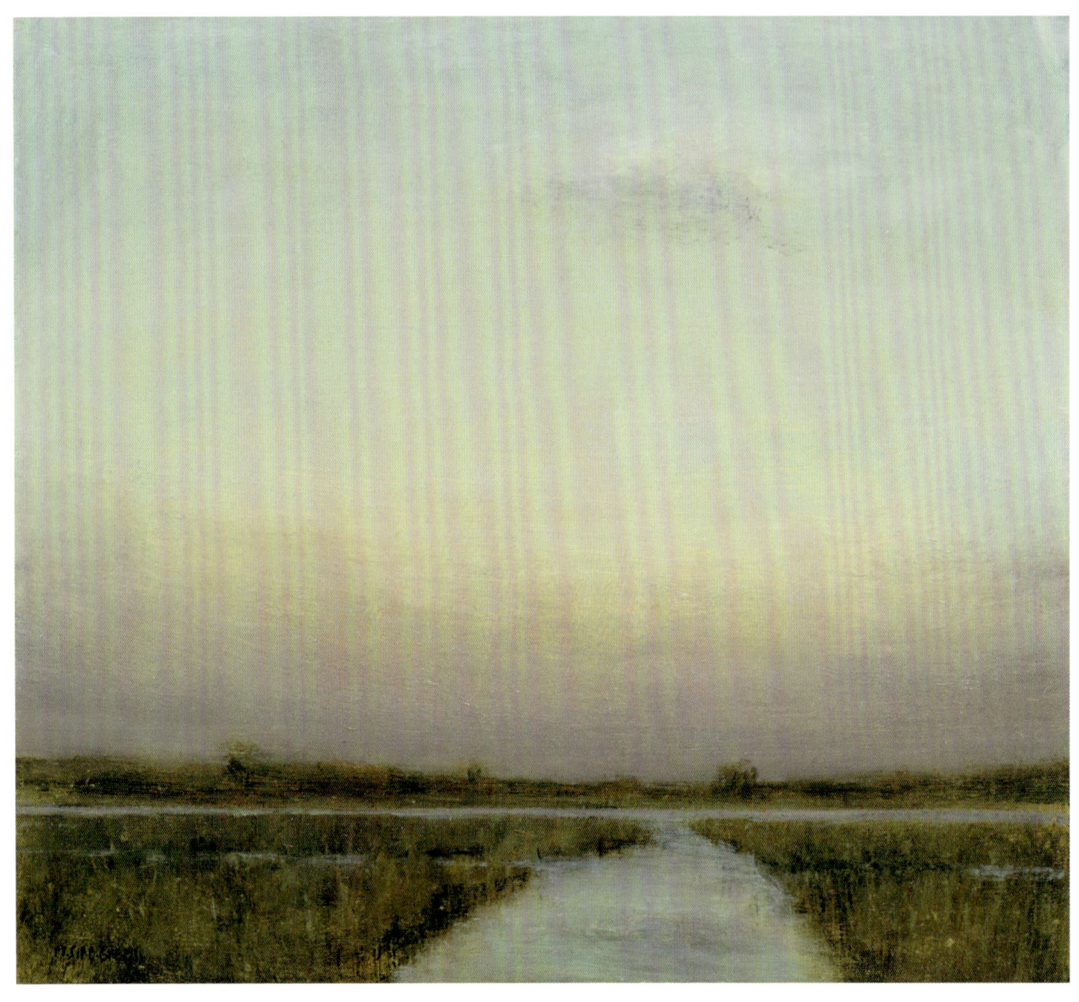

MORNING CLOUD, 2004.

Oil on linen, 13 x 14⅝ in. (33 x 37.2 cm).
Artist's collection.

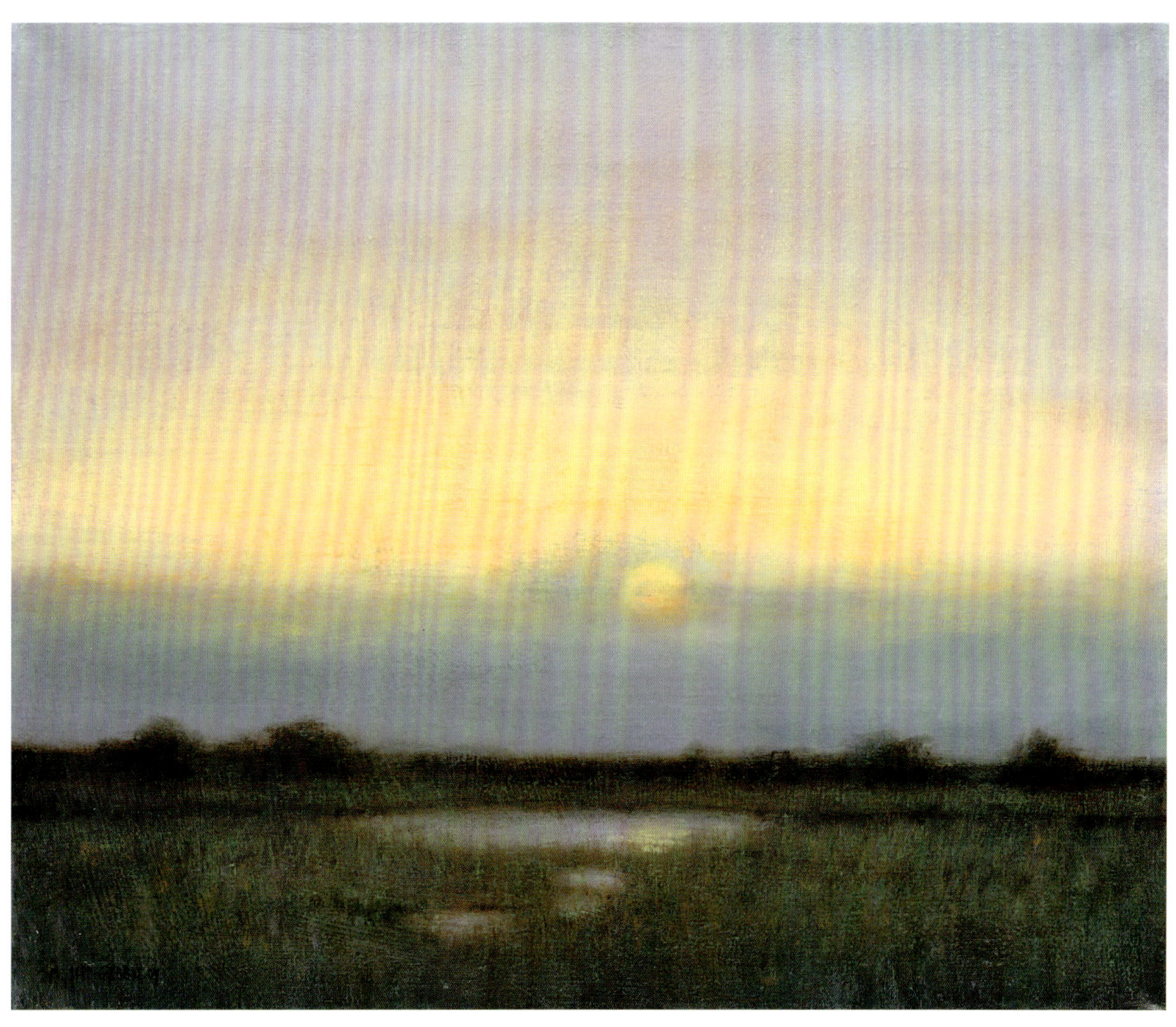

SALT PONDS, CAPE POGE, 2004.
Oil on linen, 20 x 24 in. (50.8 x 61 cm).
Private collection.

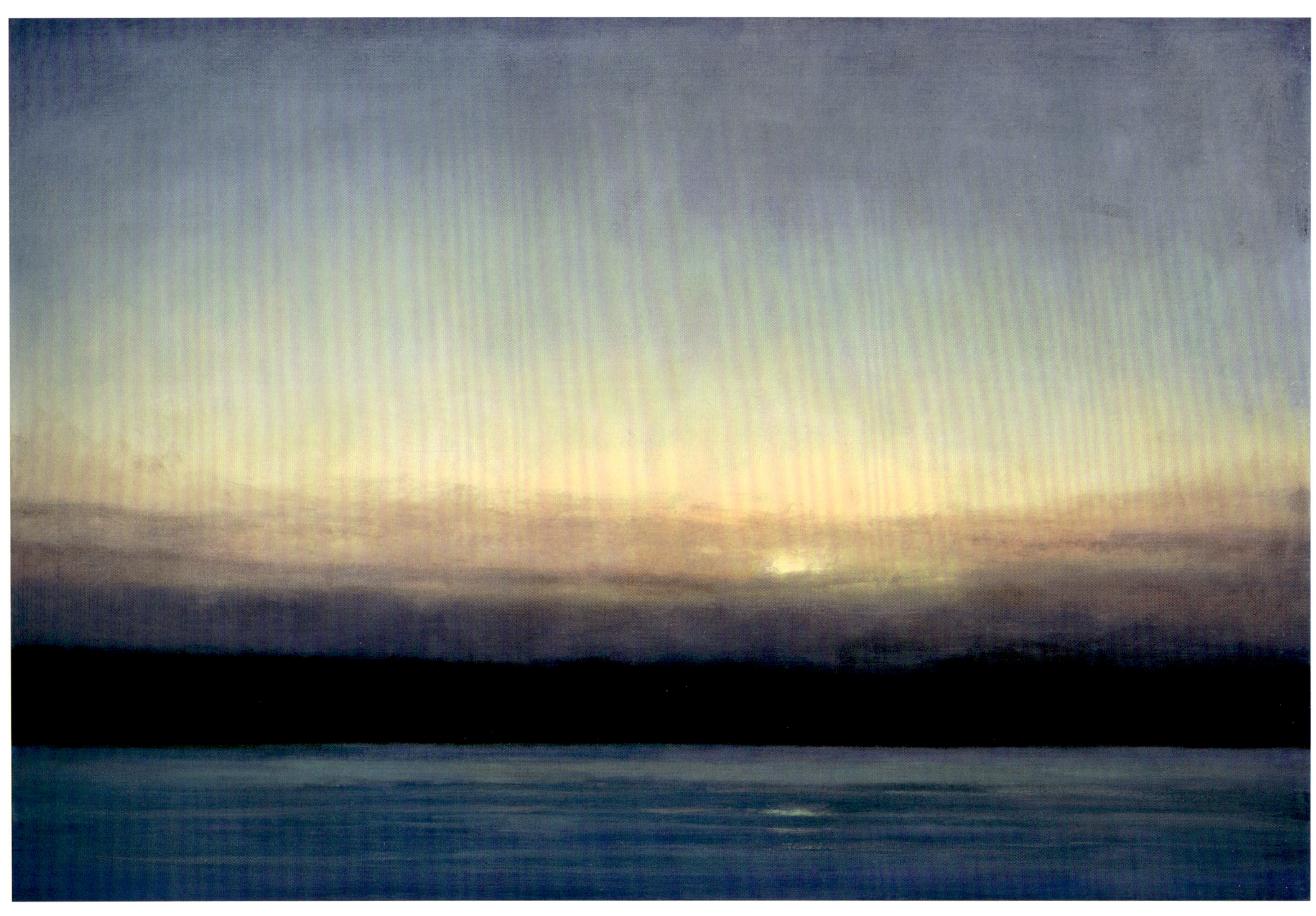

SUNSET OVER SENGEKONTACKET, 2003.
Oil on linen, 40 x 60 in. (101.6 x 152.4 cm).
Private collection.

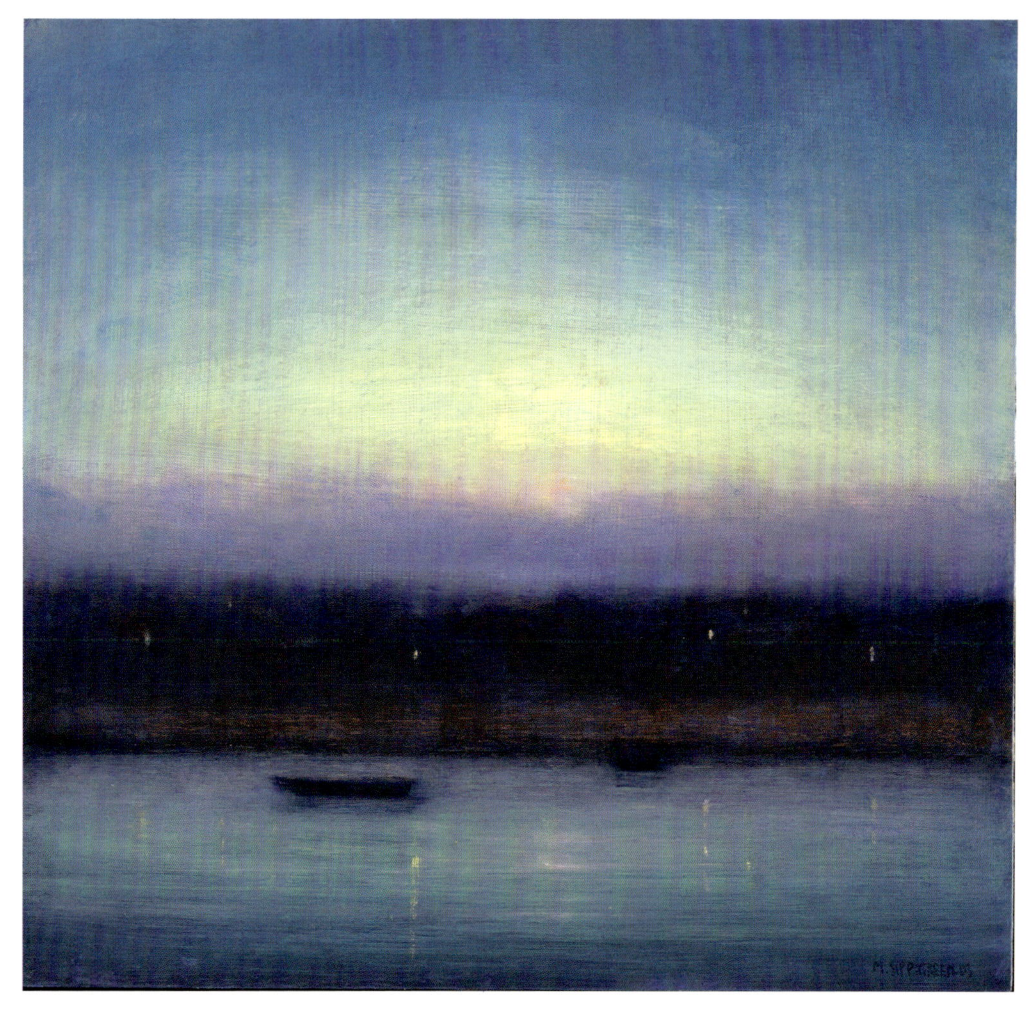

TWO BOATS, 2003.
Oil on panel, 14½ x 15¼ in. (36.8 x 38.7 cm).
Private collection.

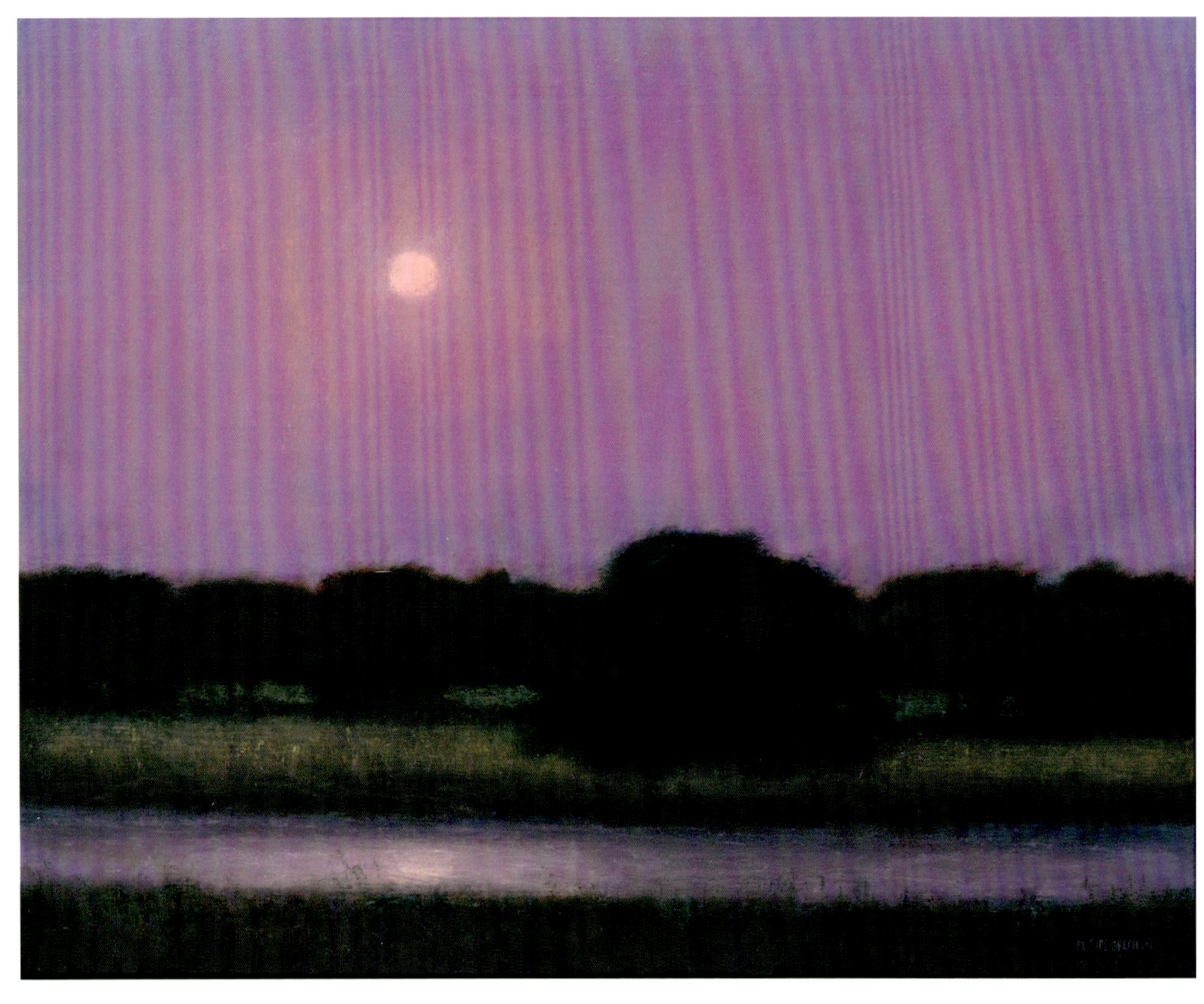

MOON RIVER, 2002.
Oil on linen, 36 x 45 in. (91.4 x 114.3 cm).
Private collection.

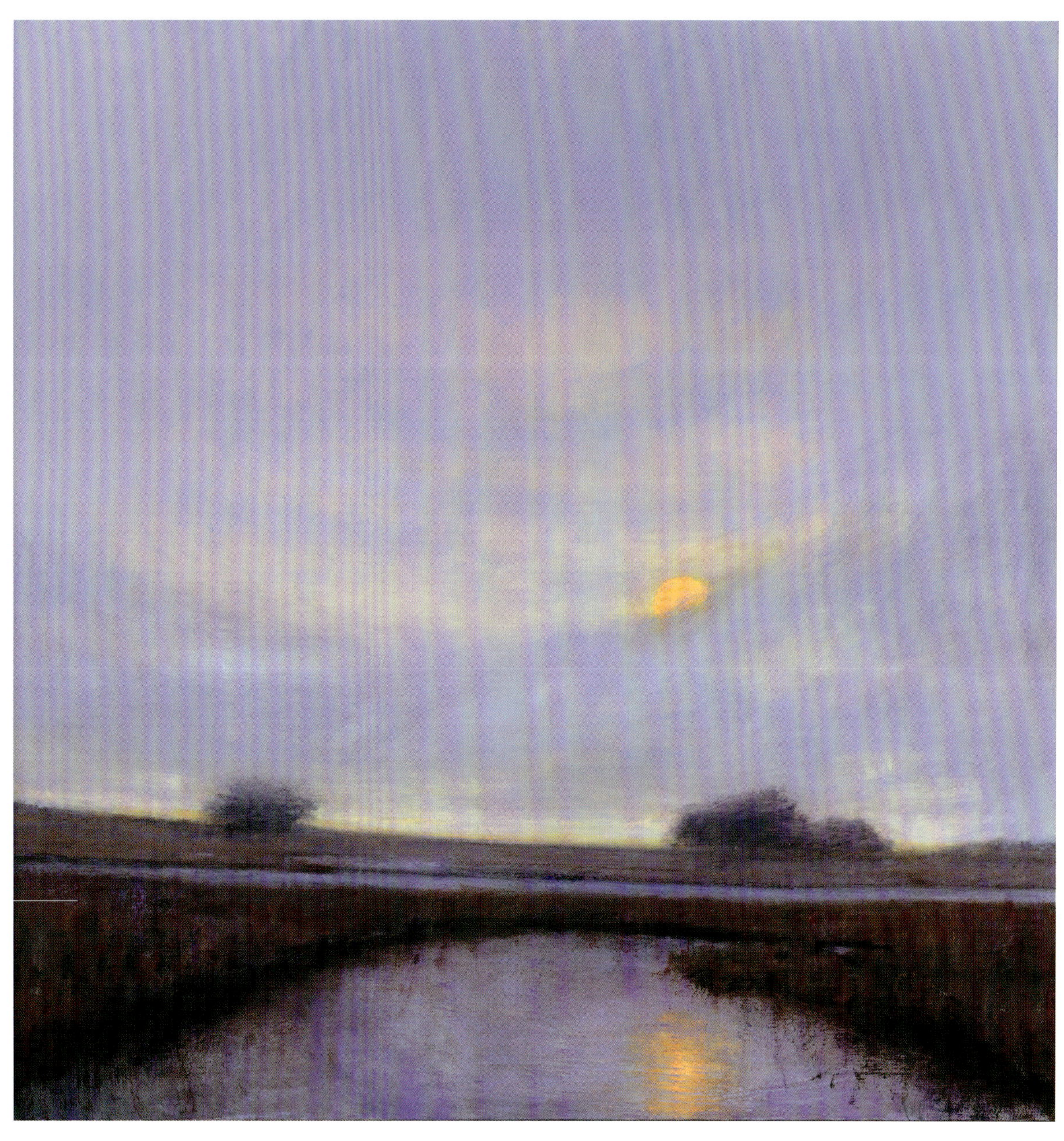

SALT MARSH, MATTAKESSET, 2000.

Oil on linen, 46 x 46 in. (116.8 x 116.8 cm).
Private collection.

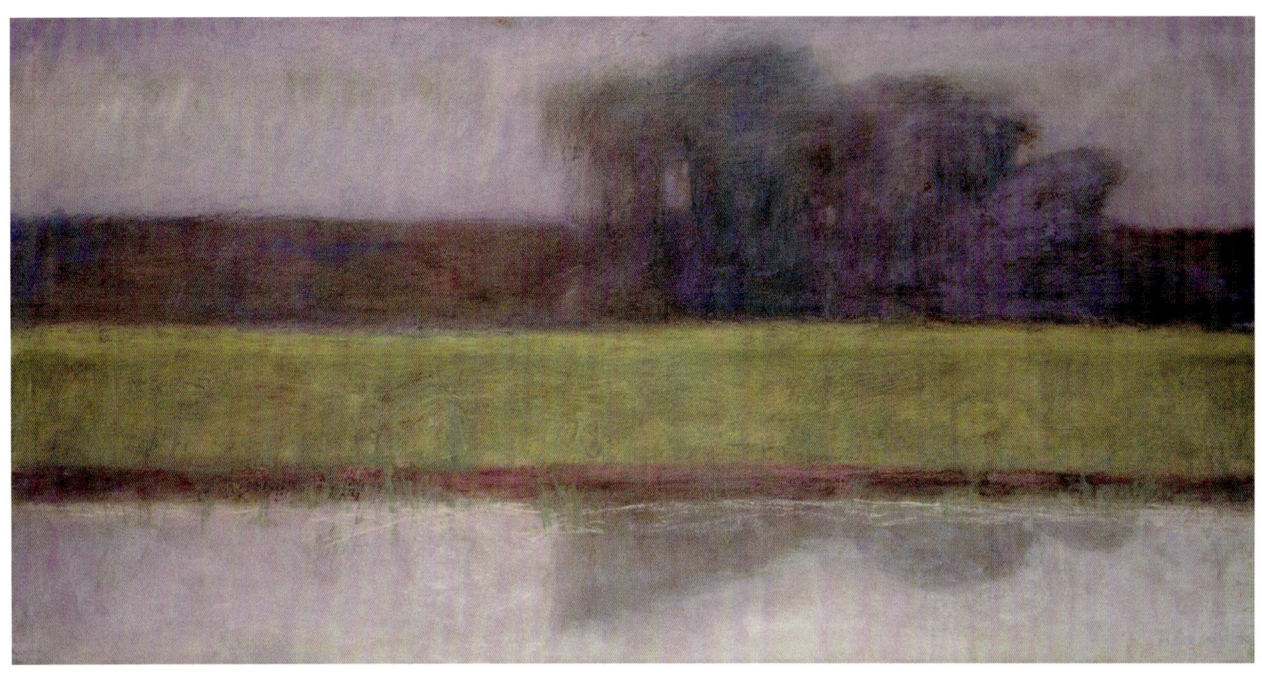

ALONG THE FARMINGTON, 1995.

Oil on linen, 11 x 24 in. (27.9 x 61 cm).
Private collection.

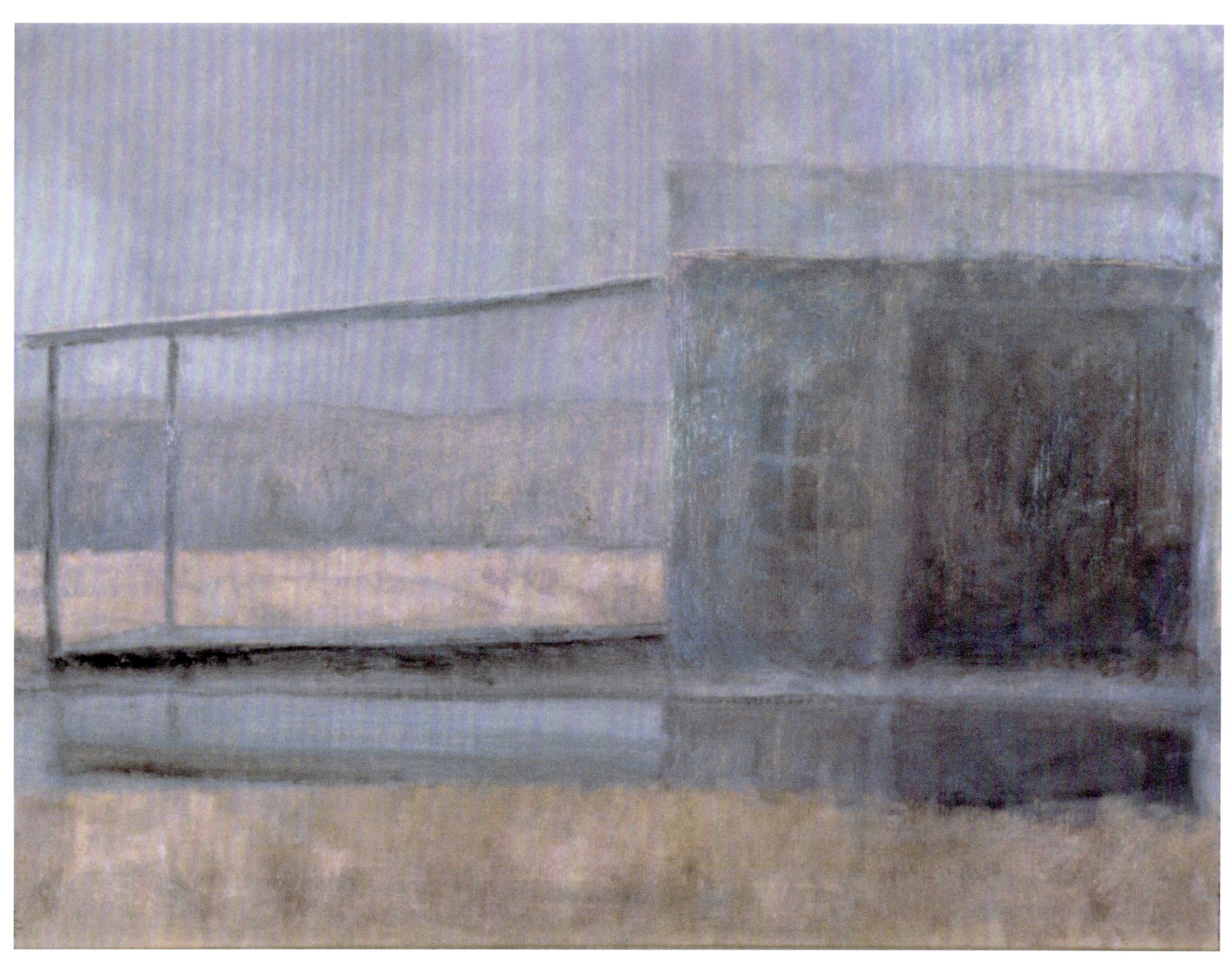

RIVER HOUSE, 1988.
Oil on linen, 27 x 38 in. (68.6 x 96.5 cm).
Artist's collection.

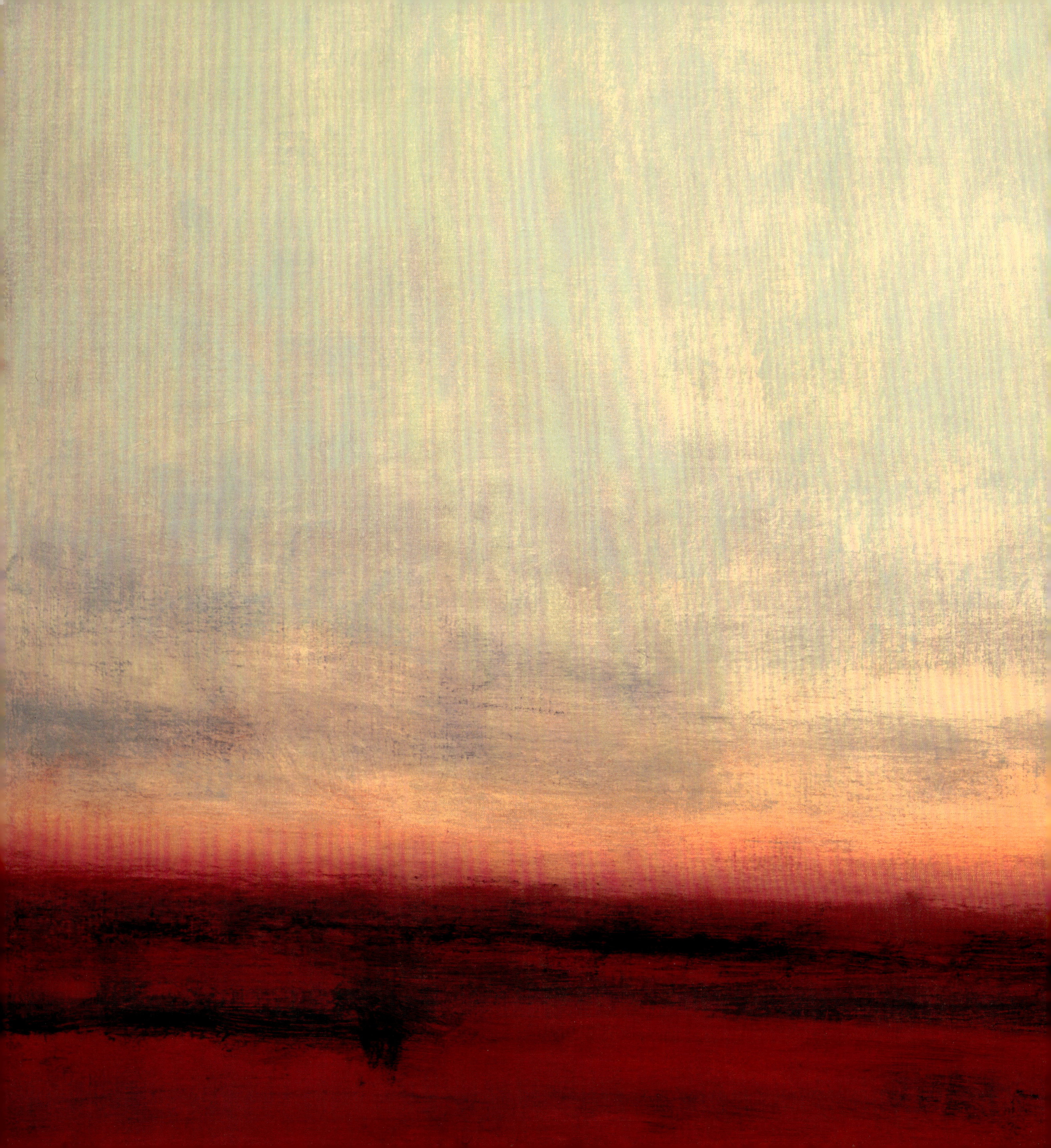

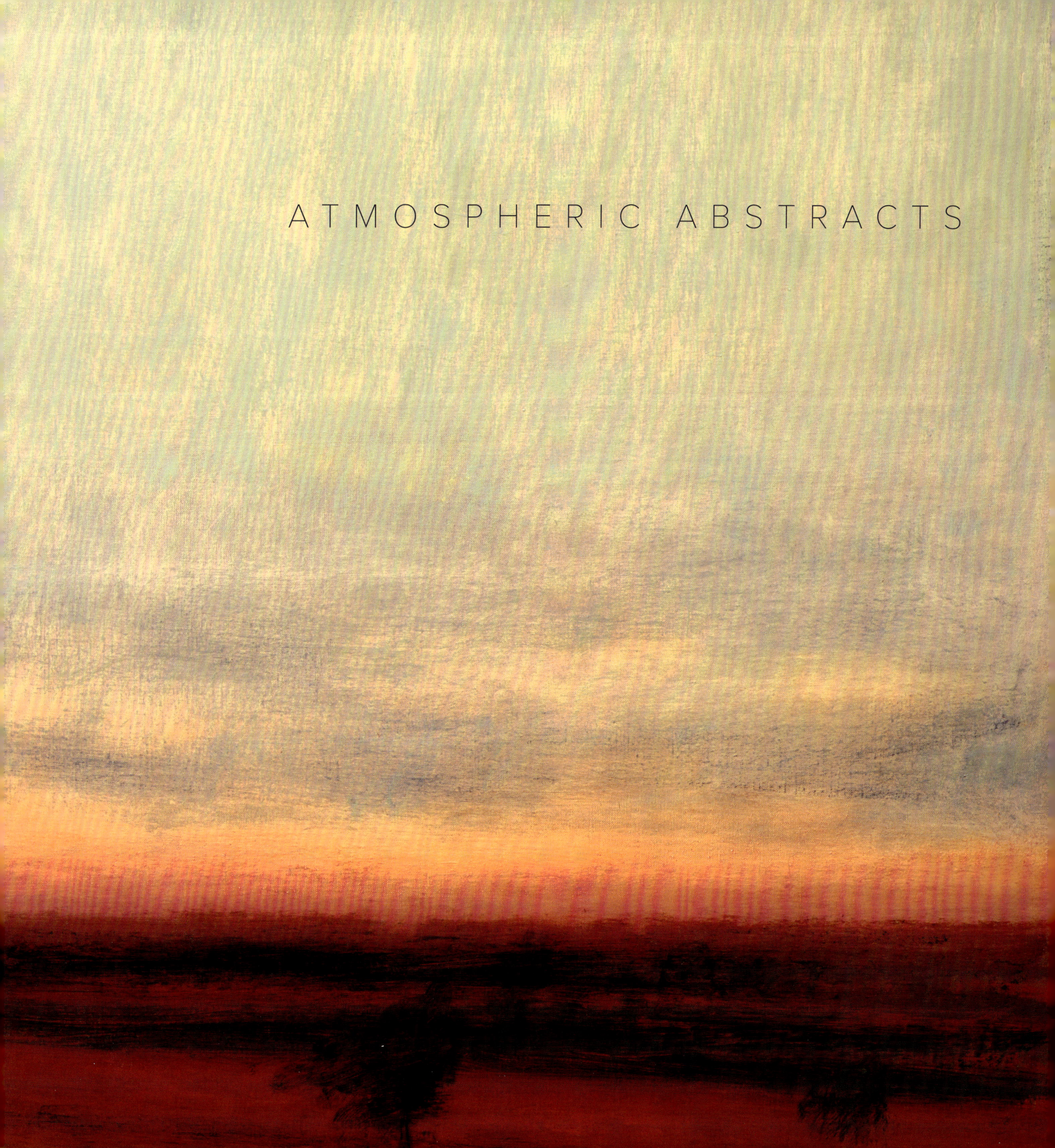
ATMOSPHERIC ABSTRACTS

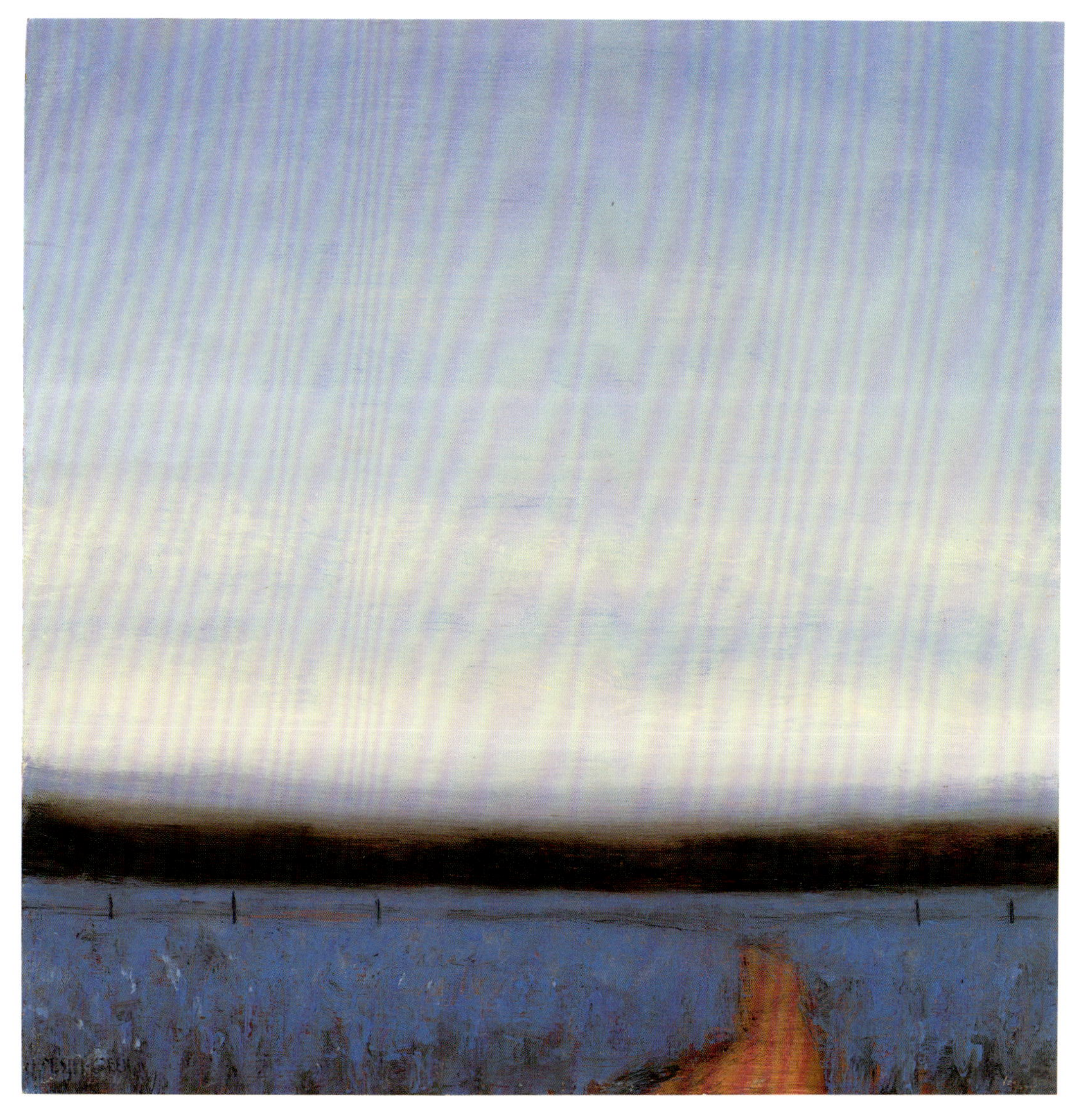

Oil on panel, 16 x 16 in. (40.6 x 40.6 cm).
Private collection.

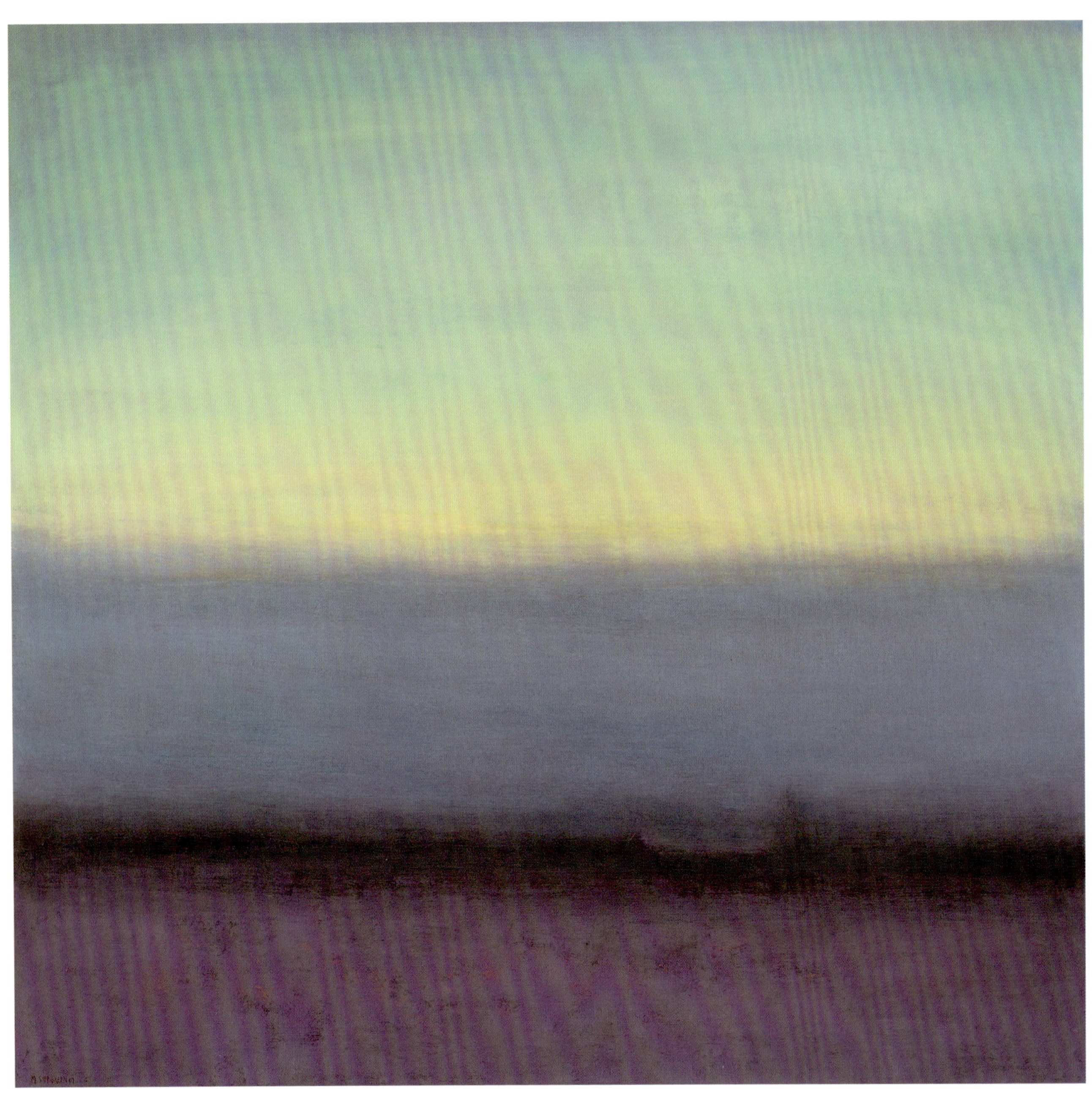

MALLOW FIELD IN TUSCANY, 2009.

Oil on linen, 48 x 46 in. (121.9 x 116.8 cm).
Artist's collection.

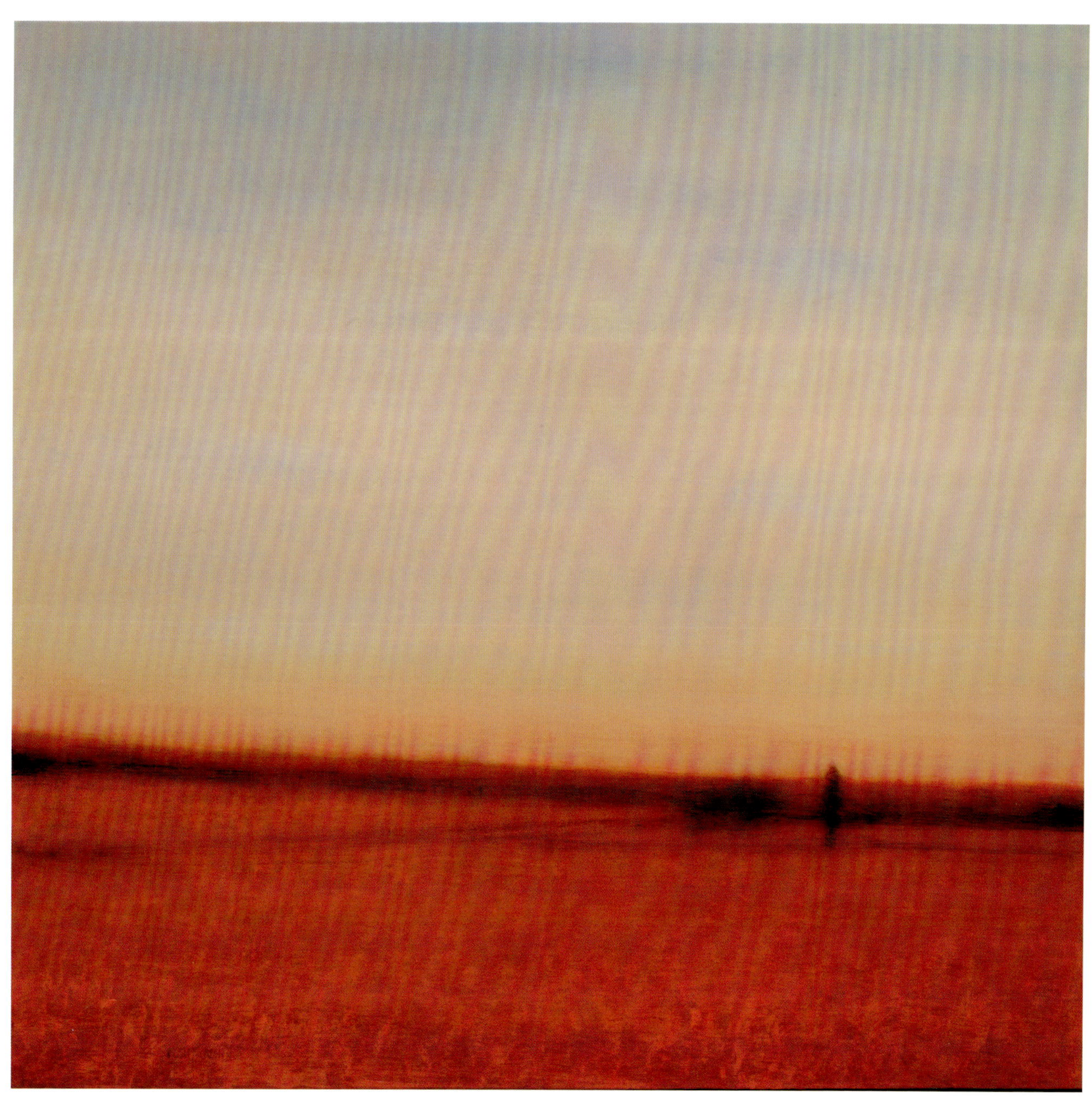

POPPIES, NEAR ASCIANO, 2007.

Oil on linen, 48 x 46 in. (121.9 x 116.8 cm).
Private collection.

AUTUMN LIGHT, CAPE POGE, 2002.
Oil on panel, 14 x 14¼ in. (35.6 x 36.8 cm).
Private collection.

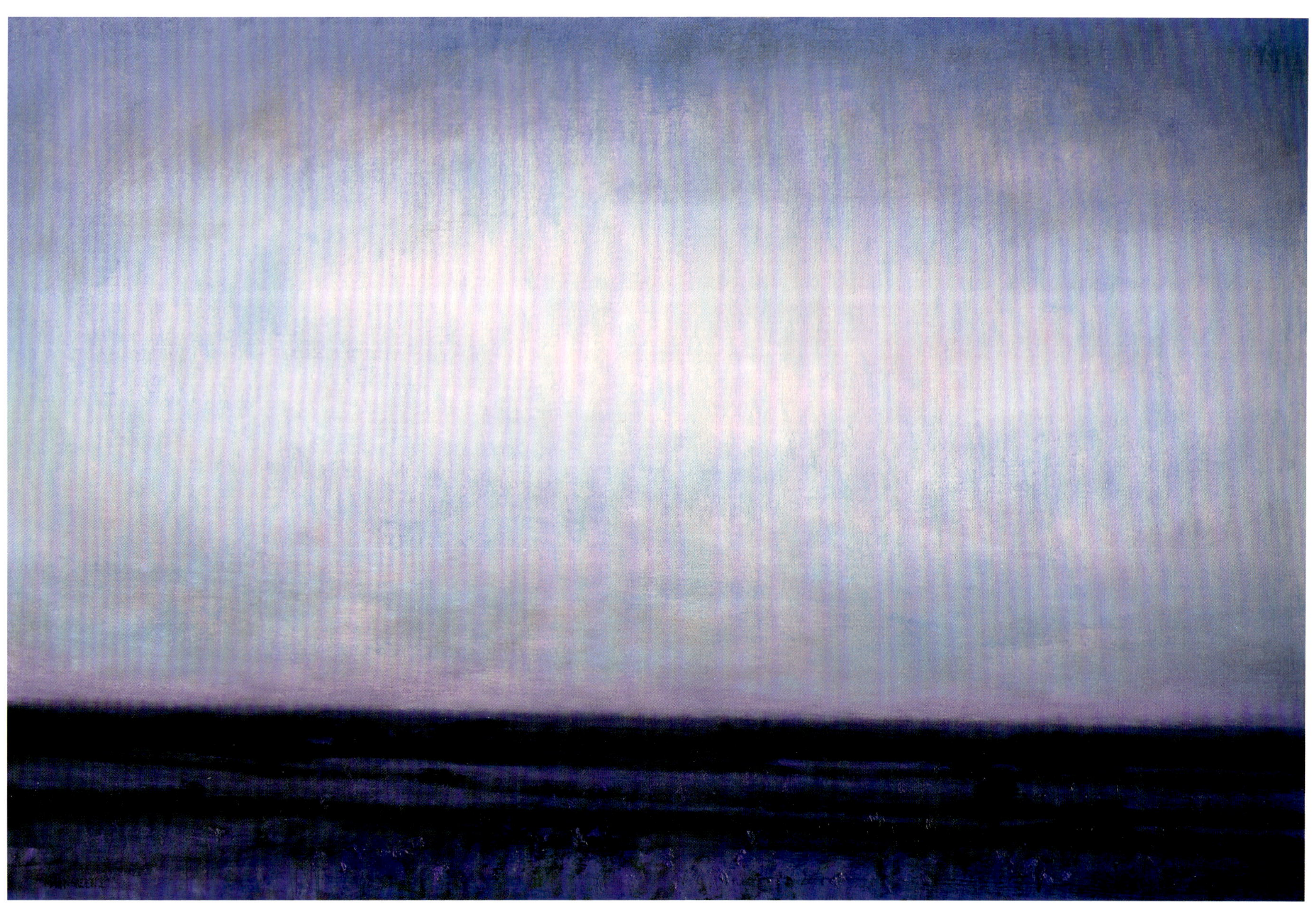

Oil on linen, 40 x 50 in. (101.6 x 127 cm).
Private collection.

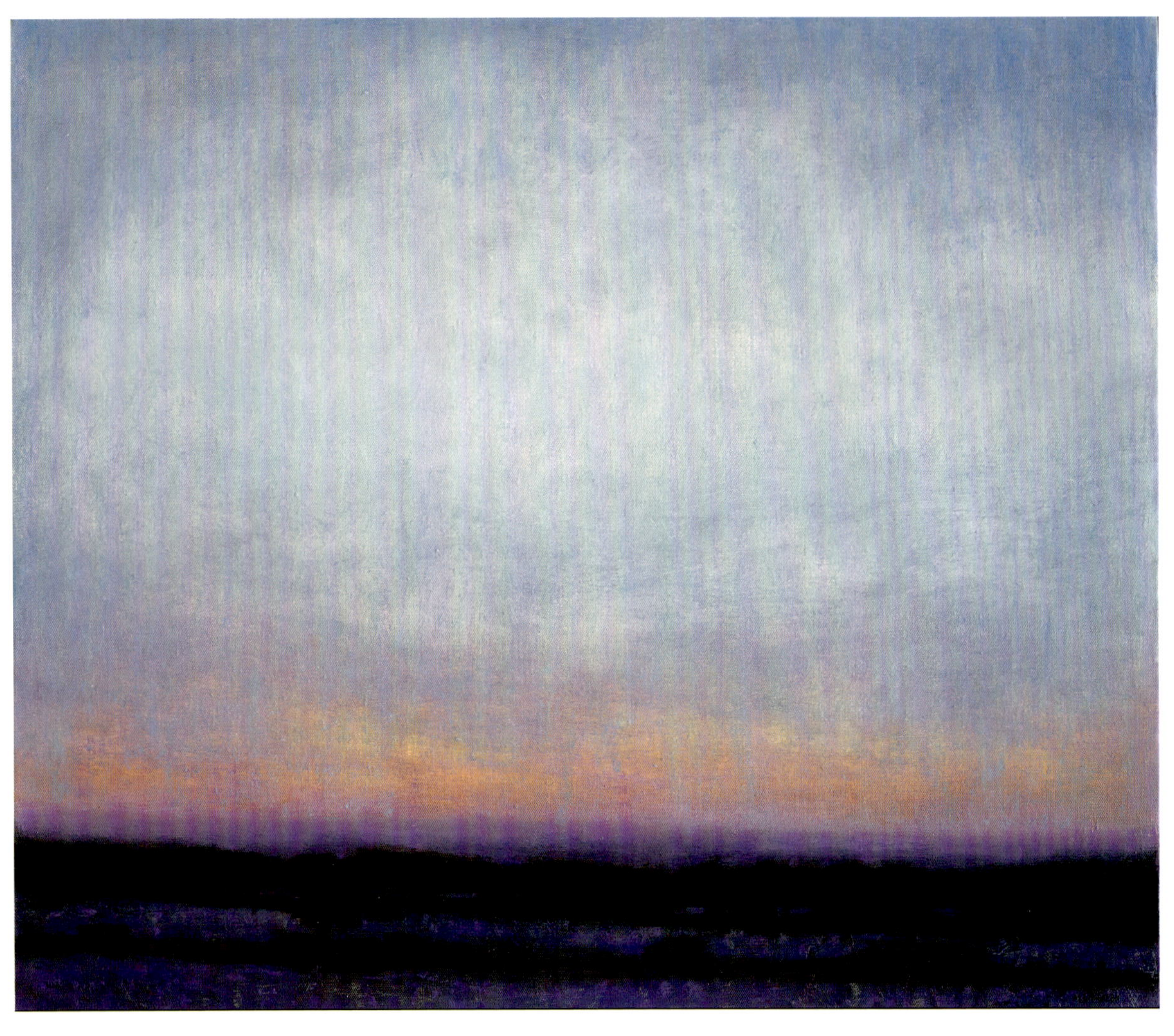

SUNSET IN IRIS FIELD, 2000.

Oil on linen, 26 x 30 in. (66 x 76.2 cm).
Private collection.

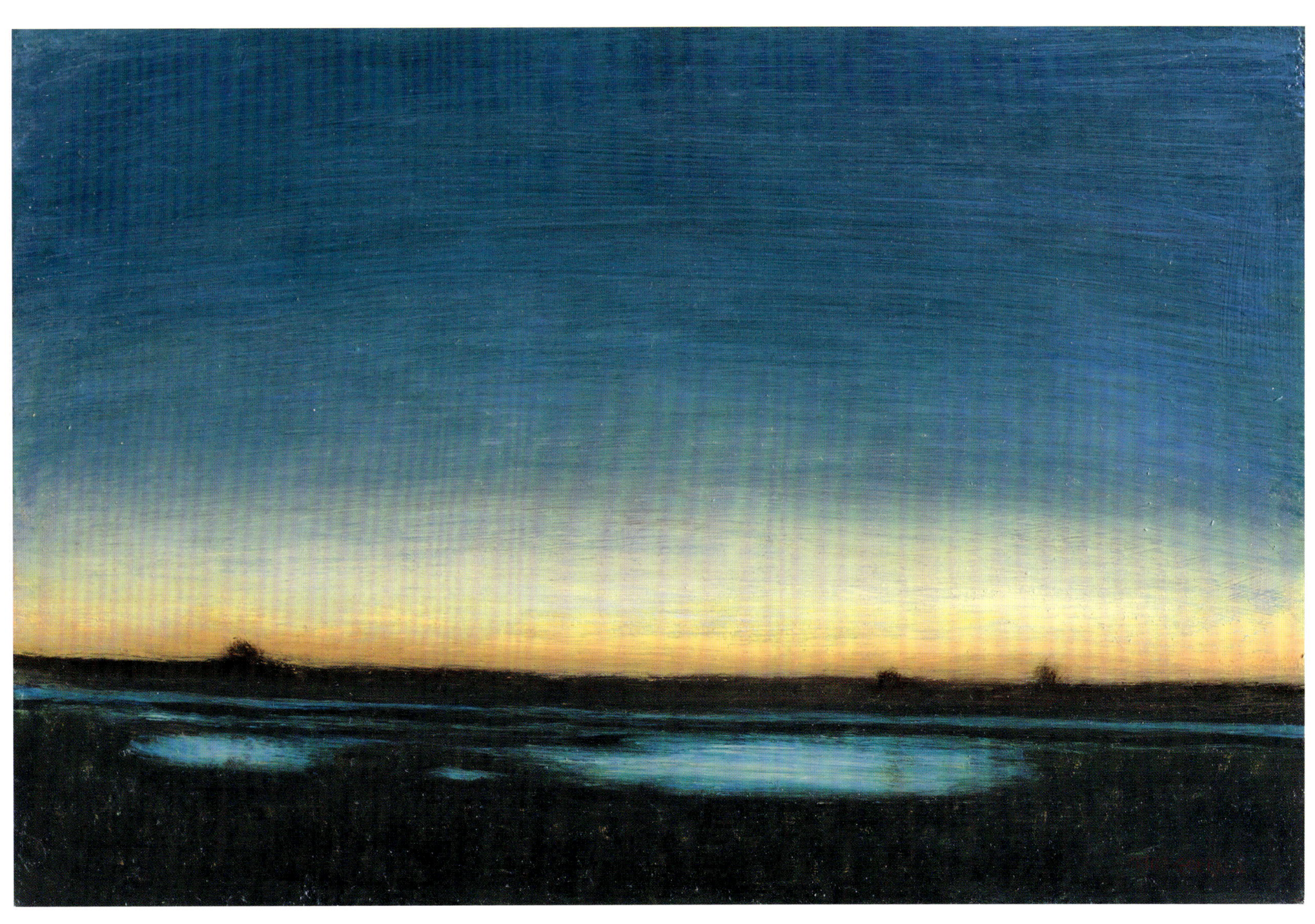

AFTER GLOW AT MATTAKESSET, 2000.
Oil on linen, 34 x 50 in. (86.4 x 127 cm).
Private collection.

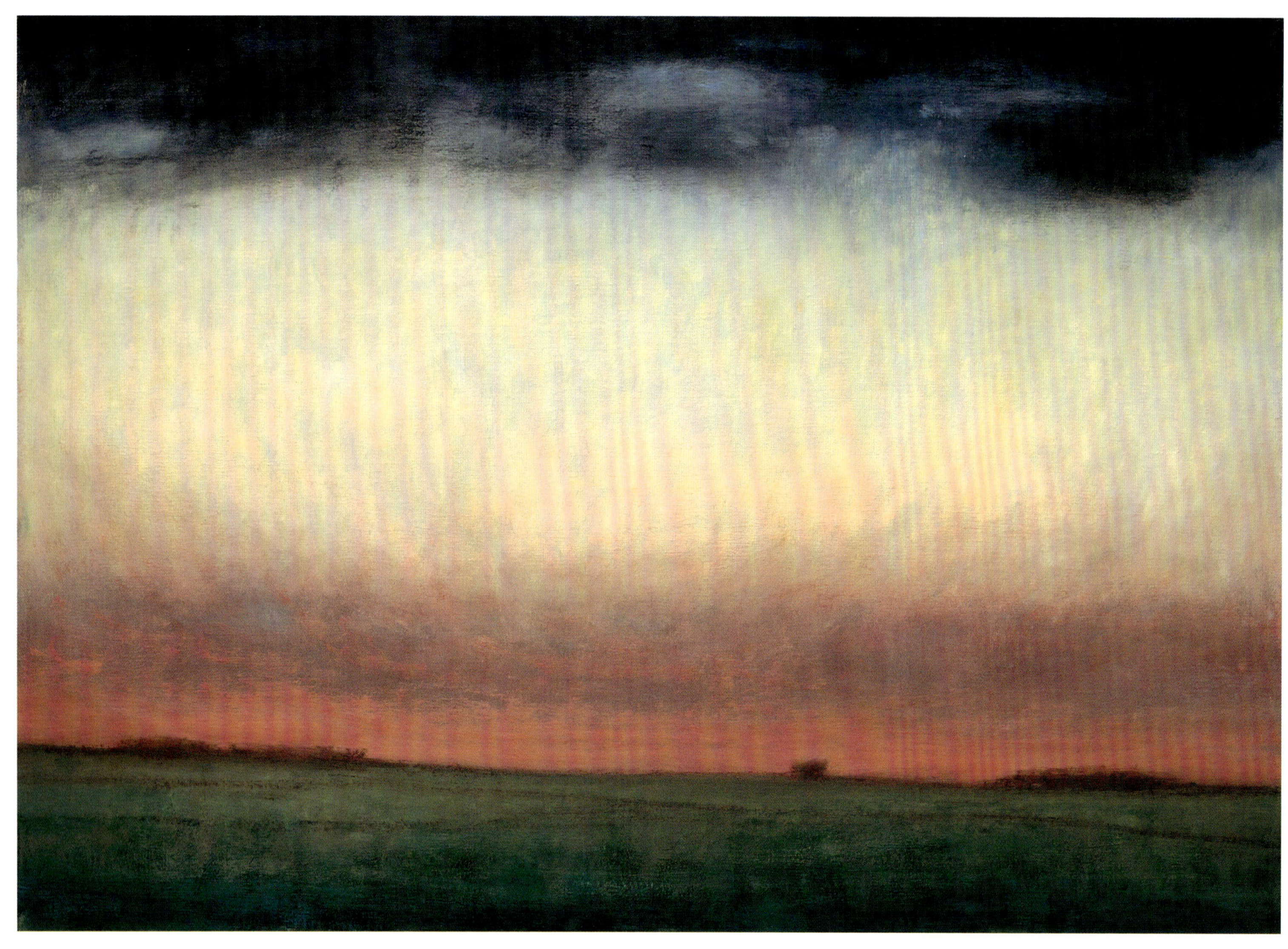

DARK CLOUDS PASSING, 1997.
Oil on linen, 34 x 48 in. (86.4 x 121.9 cm).
Private collection.

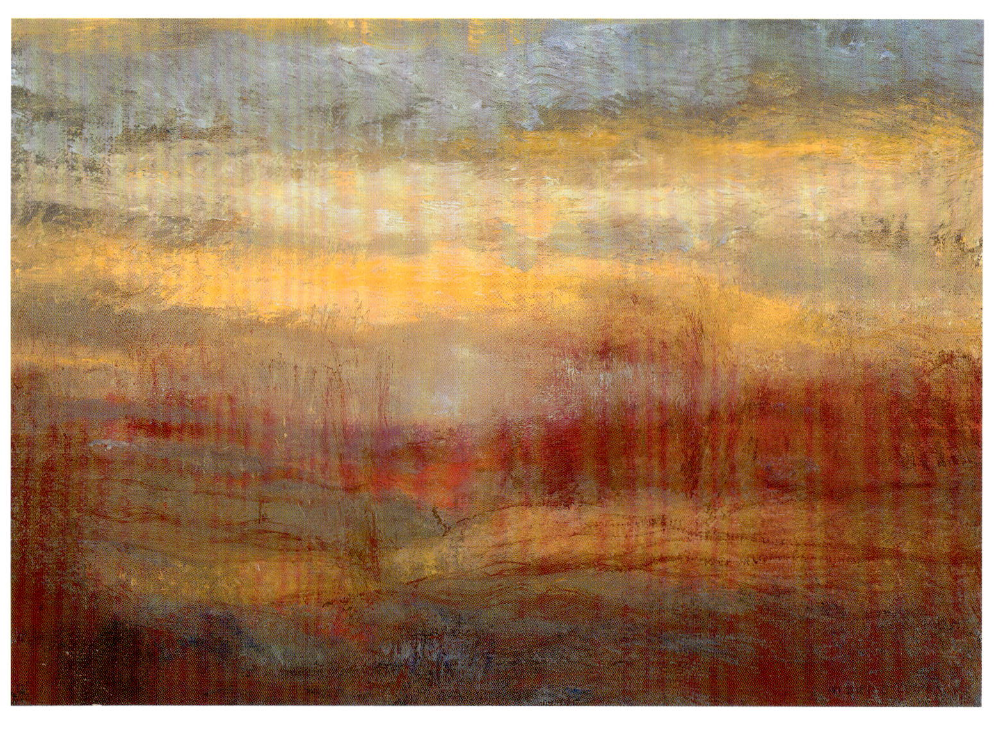

GOULD MEADOW, 1986.
Oil on linen, 11 x 16½ in. (27.9 x 41.9 cm).
Artist's collection.

WORKS ON PAPER

APPROACHING STORM, 1992.
Gouache, 6 x 8¾ in. (15.2 x 22.2 cm).
Artist's collection.

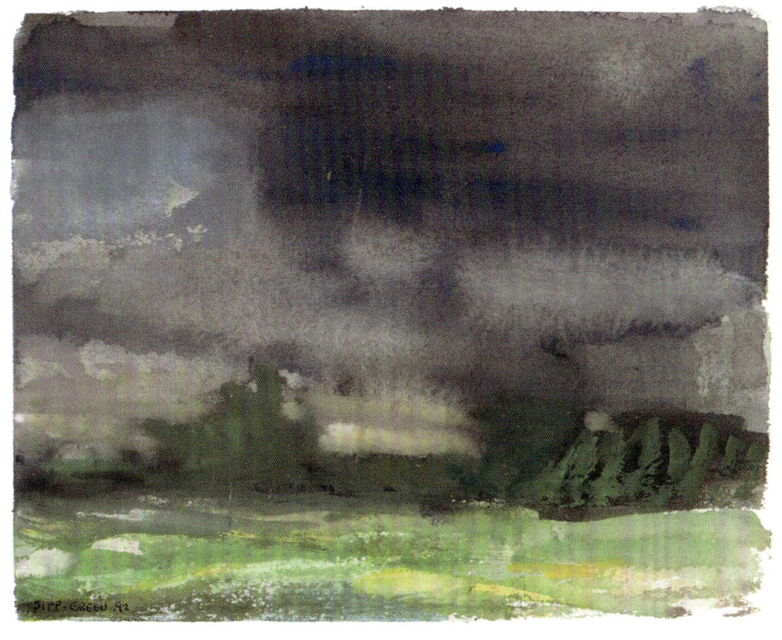

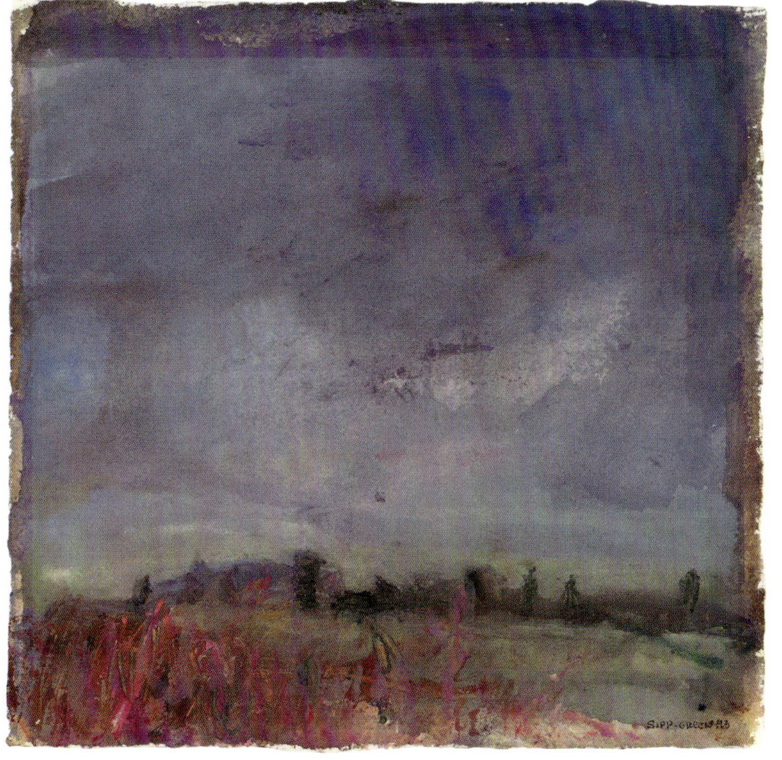

DARK CLOUDS, 1992.
Gouache, 6 x 7½ in. (15.2 x 19.1 cm).
Artist's collection.

CLEARING, 1992.
Gouache, 7½ x 8 in. (19.1 x 20.3 cm).
Artist's collection.

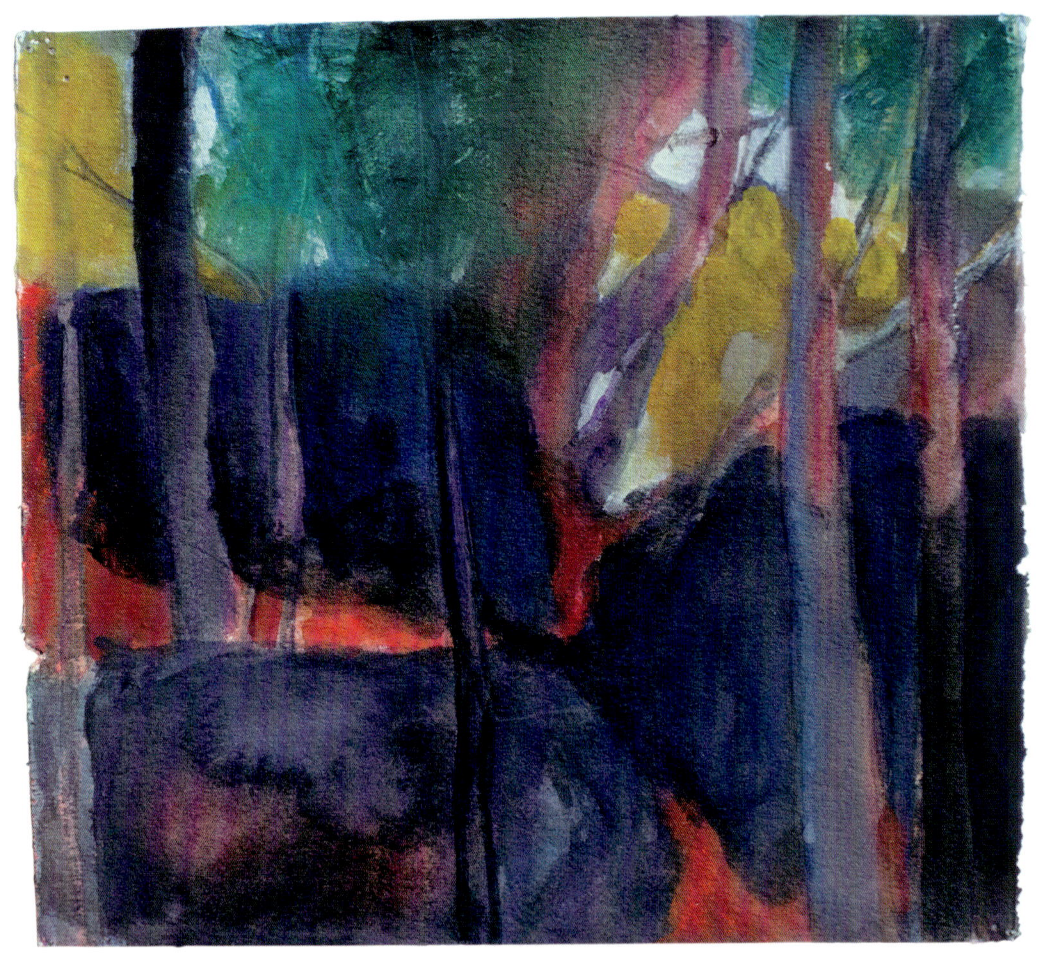

ICE GLEN, 1993.
Gouache, 8¾ x 8 in. (22.2 x 20.3 cm).
Private collection.

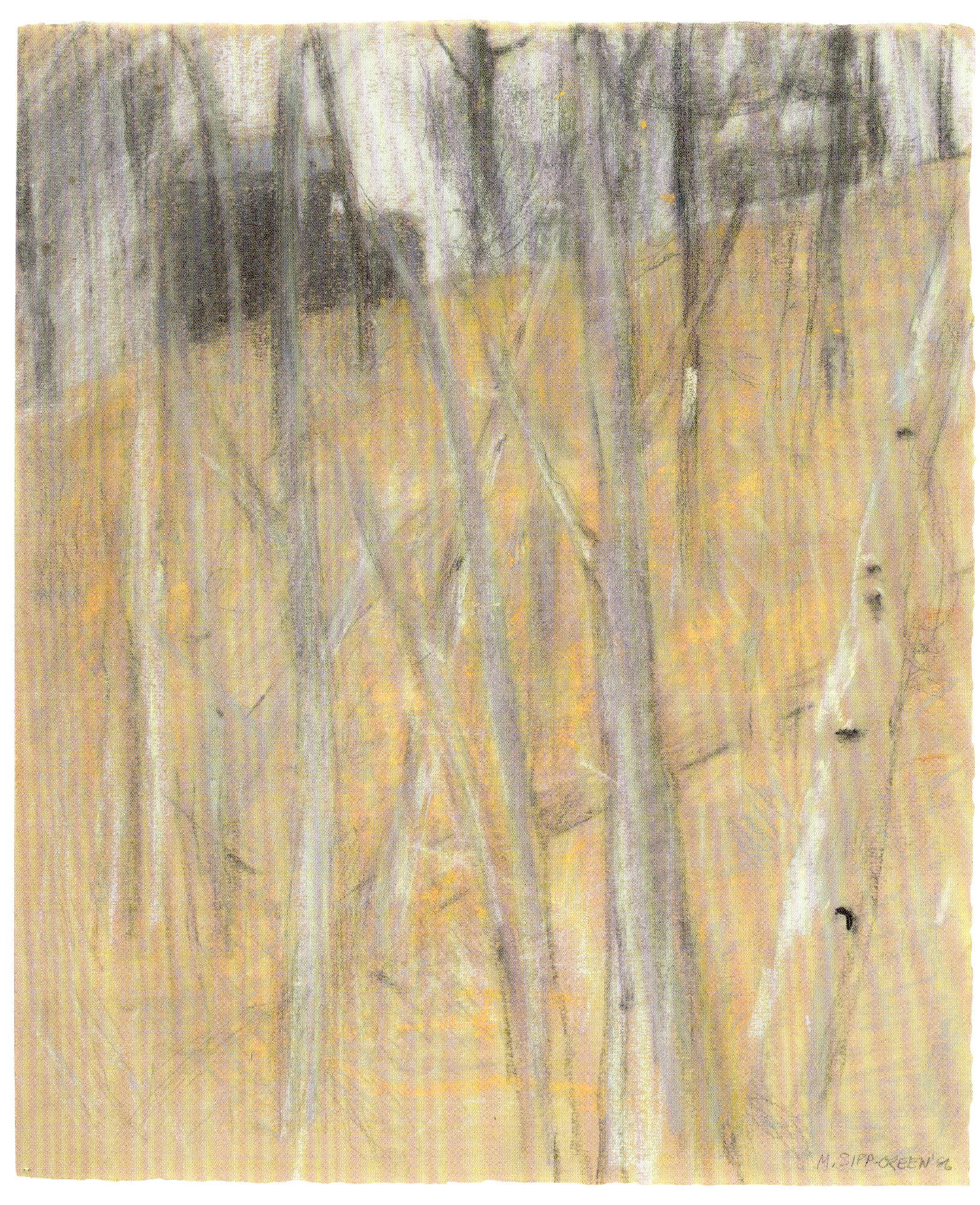

BIRCHES, 1986.

Pastel, 11 x 9½ in. (27.9 x 24.1 cm).
Private collection.

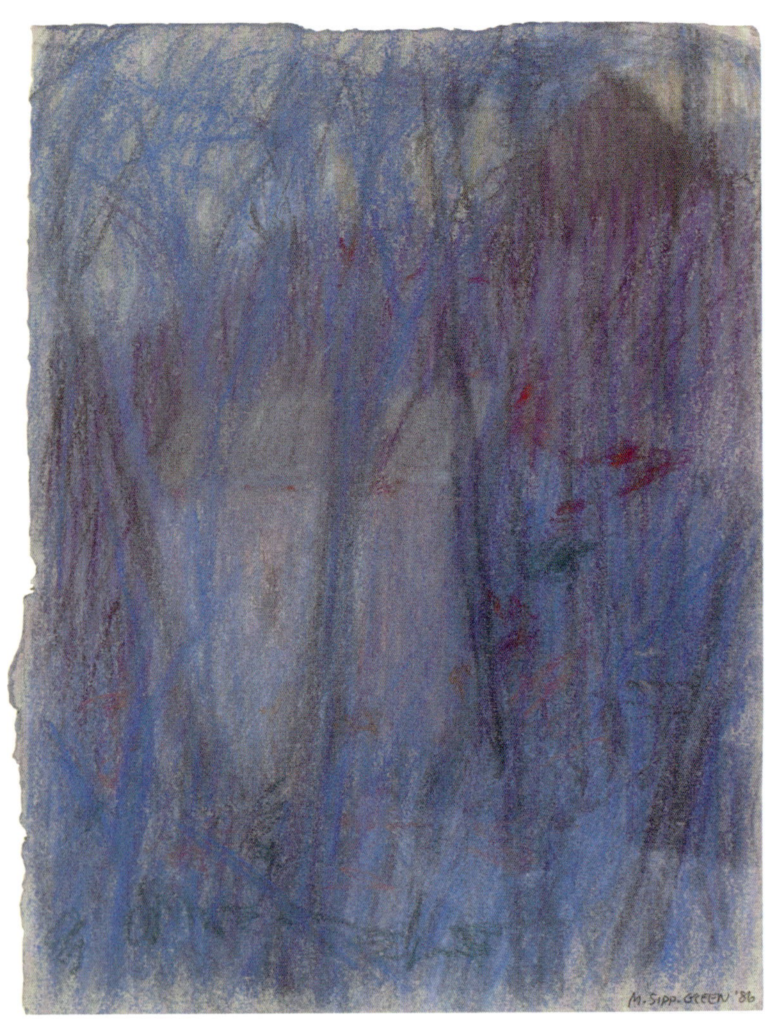

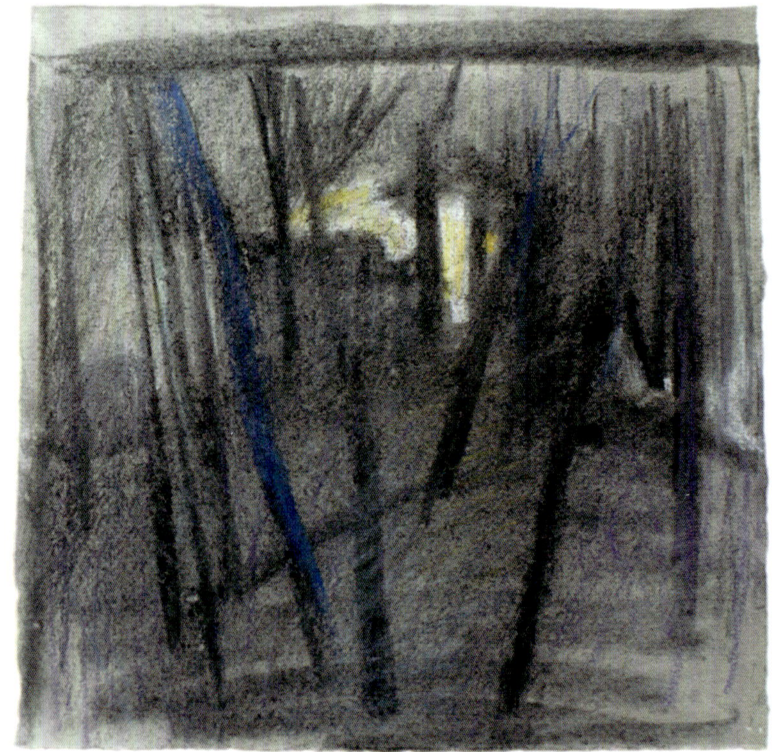

MORNING ON HILLSIDE, 1986.

Pastel, 8 x 6¼ in. (20.3 x 15.9 cm).
Private collection.

LAST LIGHT, 1986.

Pastel, 8 x 7¾ in. (20.3 x 19.7 cm).
Artist's collection.

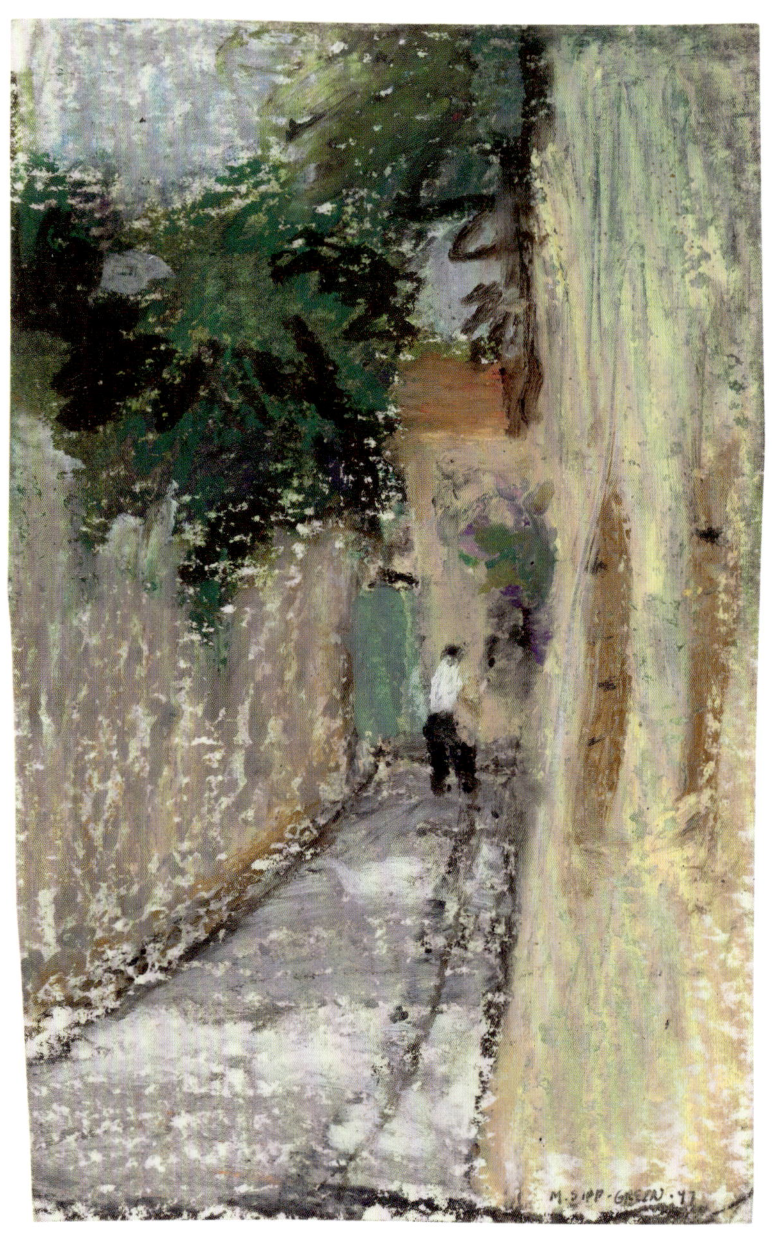

CASSIS, 1997.
Oil pastel, 6¼ x 4 in. (15.9 x 10.2 cm).
Private collection.

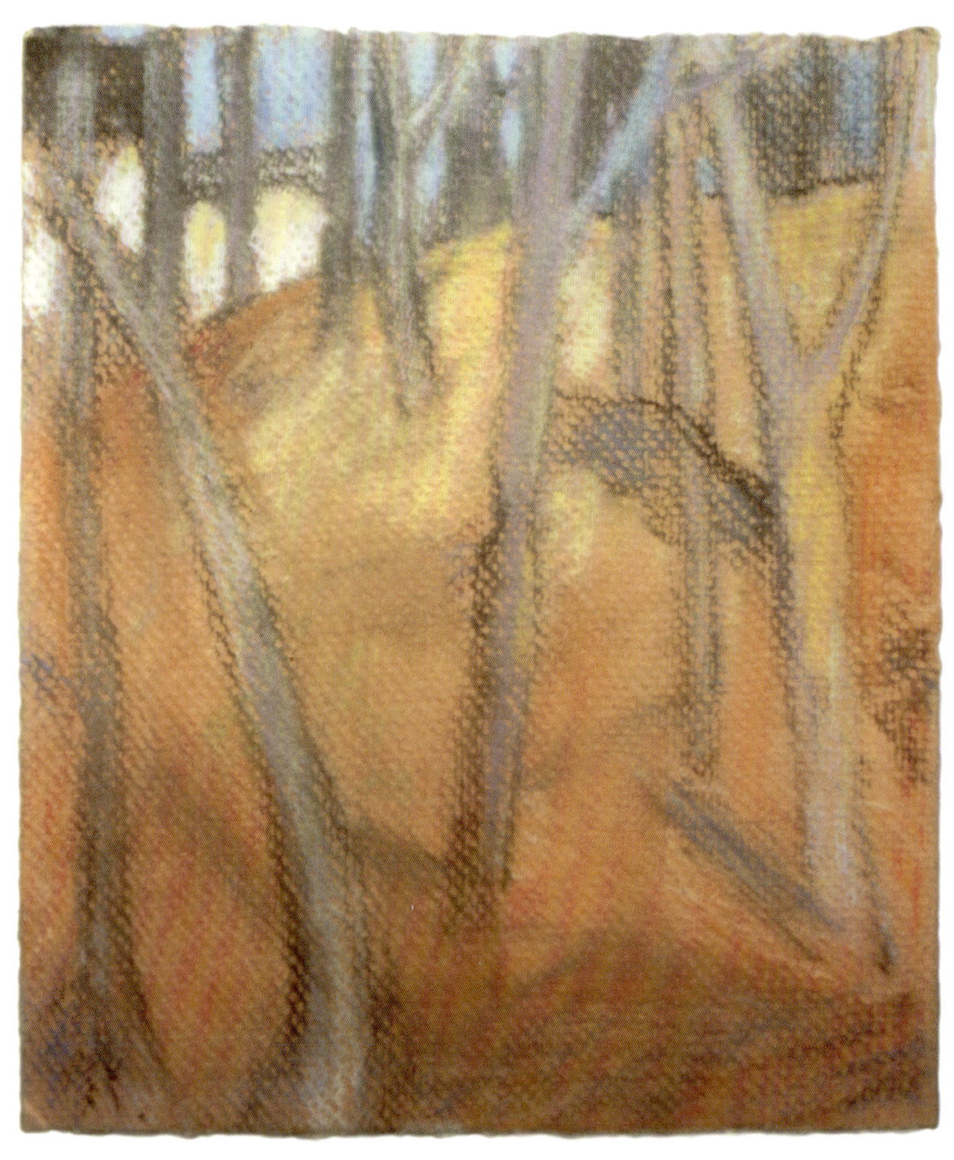

FALLEN LEAVES, 1986.
Pastel, 7½ x 5¼ in. (19.1 x 13.3 cm).
Artist's collection.

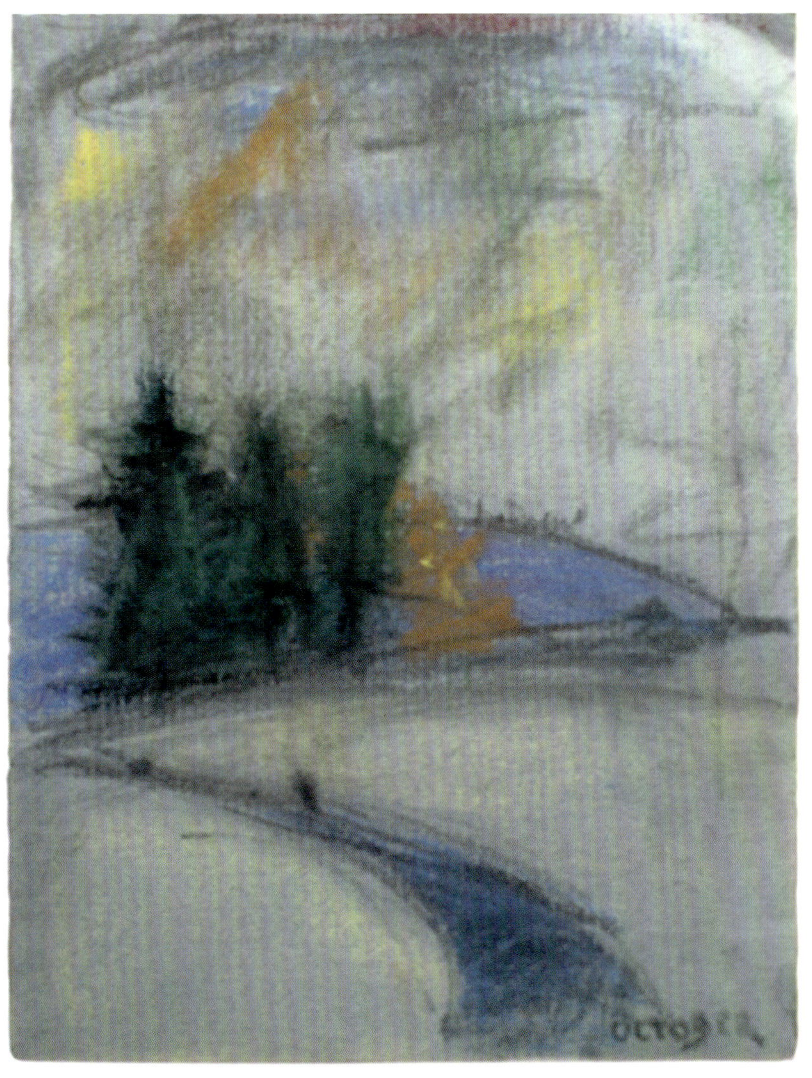

AUTUMN WALK (I), 1986.
Pastel, 5⅝ x 4¼ in. (14.3 x 10.8 cm).
Artist's collection.

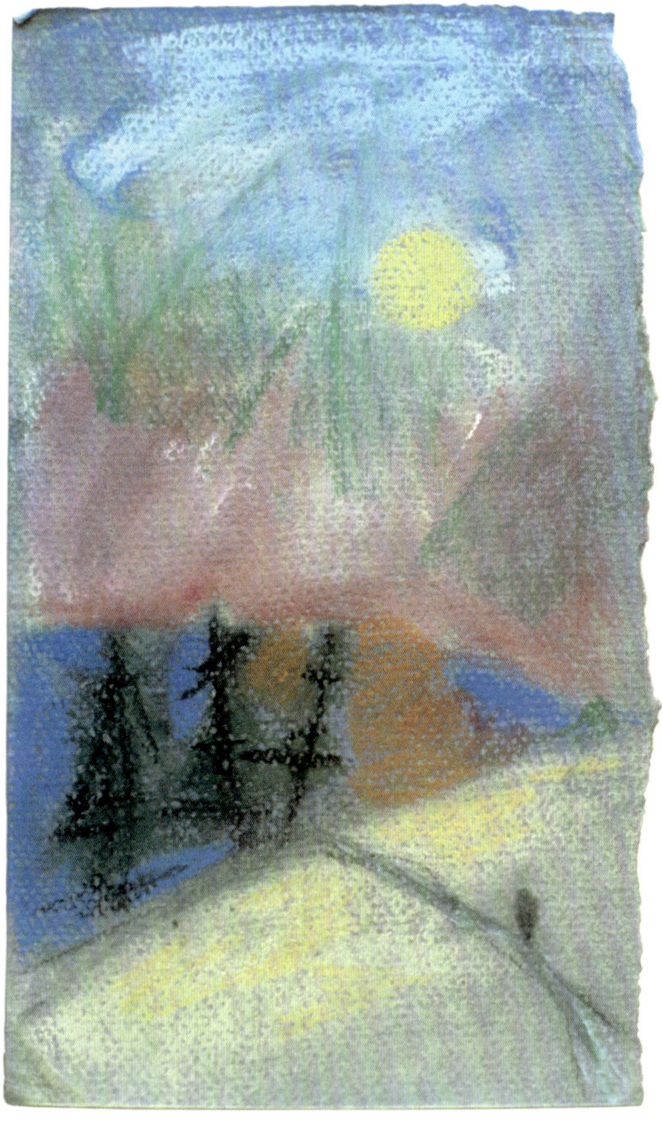

AUTUMN WALK (II), 1986.
Pastel, 8½ x 5 in. (21.6 x 12.7 cm).
Artist's collection.

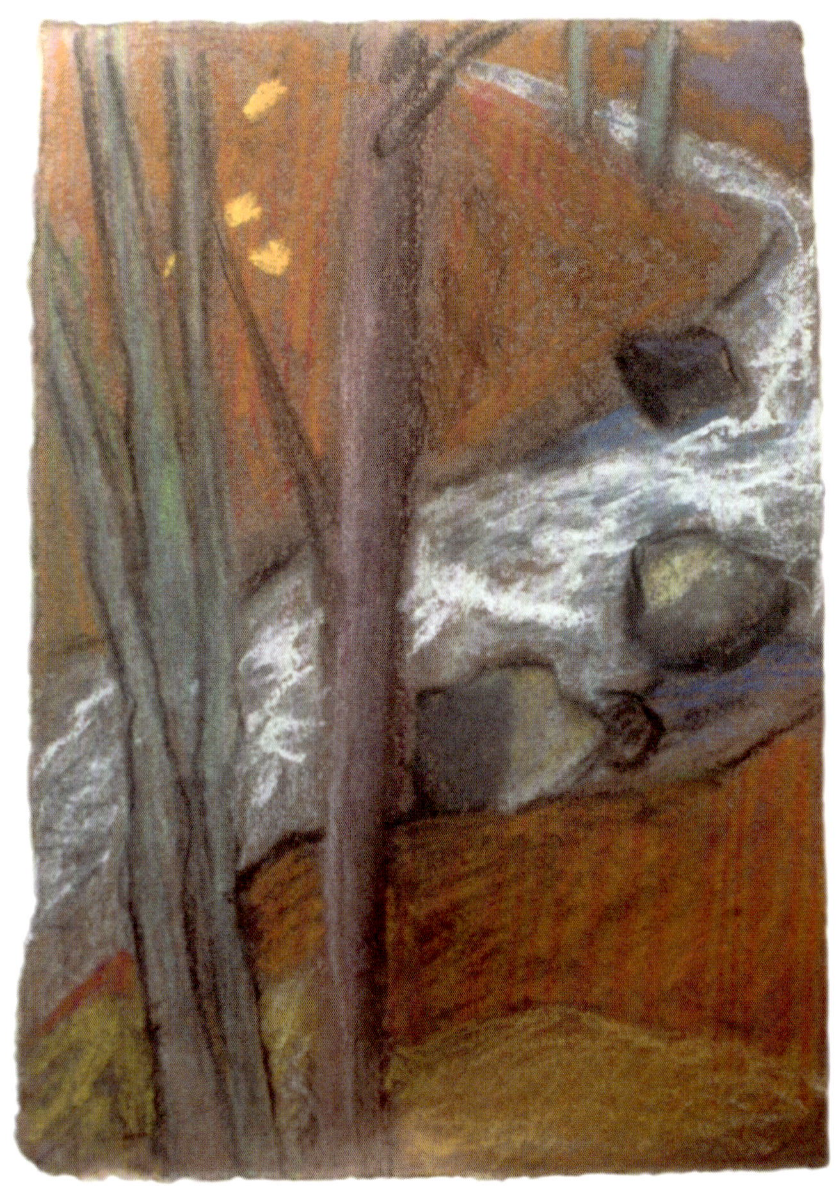

RTE. 183, AUTUMN, 1986.
Pastel, 10 x 8½ in. (25.4 x 21.6 cm).
Artist's collection.

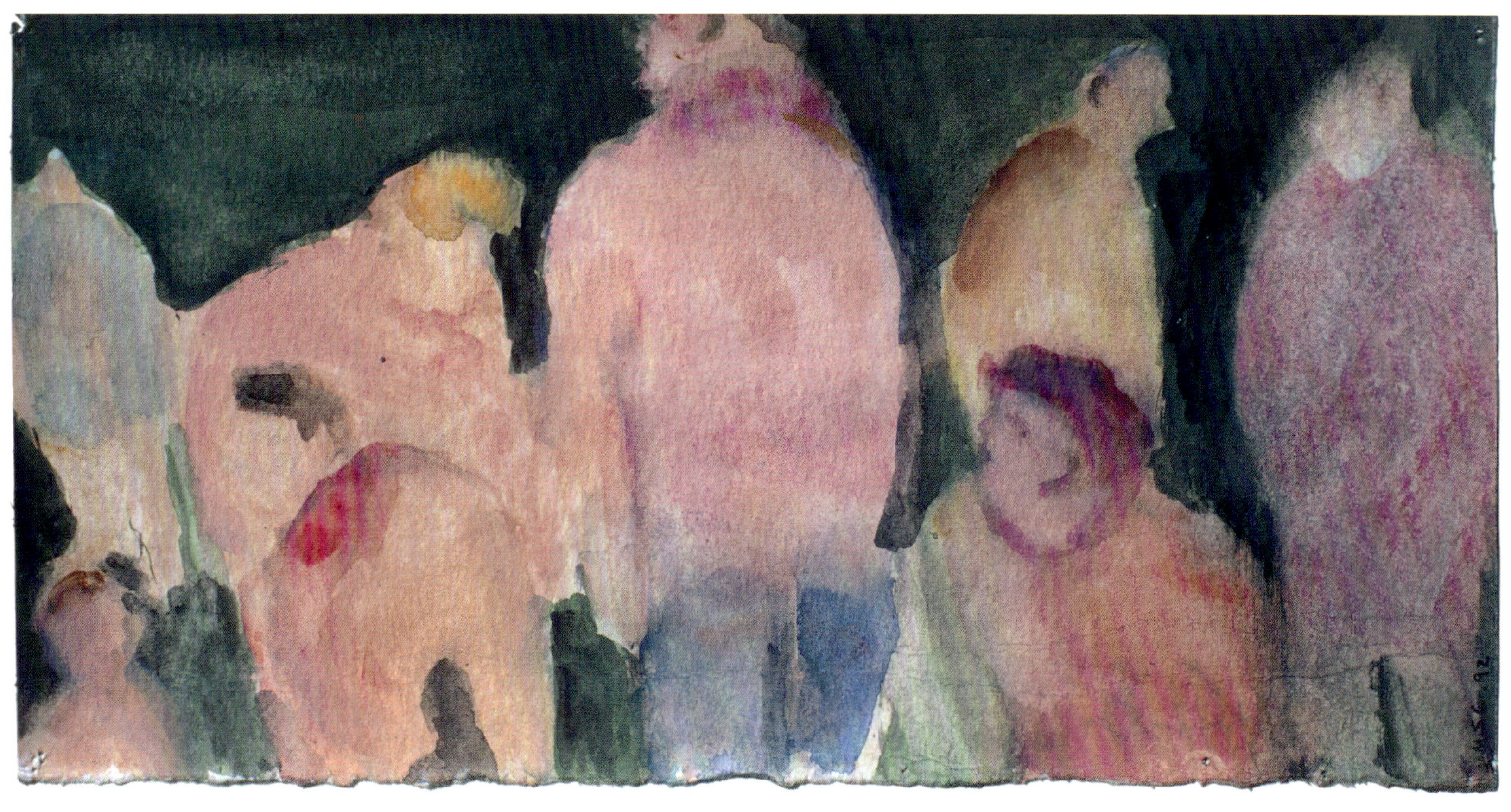

RUSH HOUR, 1992.
Gouache, 4¾ x 9½ in. (12.1 x 24.1 cm).
Artist's collection.

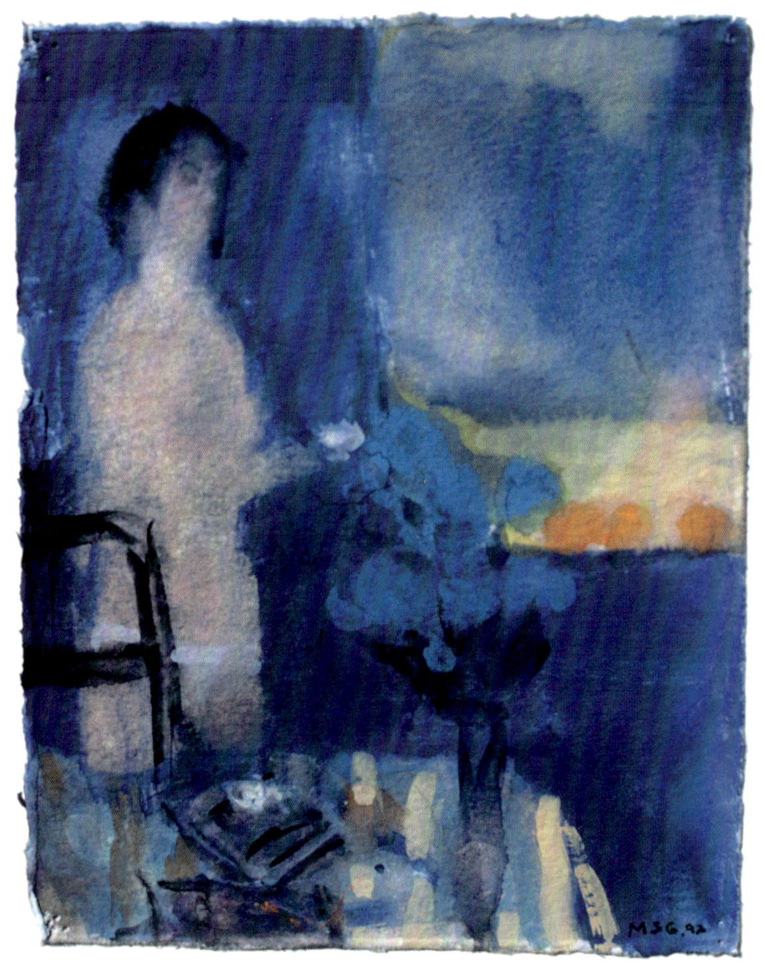

SUNDAY MORNING, 1993.
Gouache, 6 x 4¾ in. (15.2 x 12.1 cm).
Artist's collection.

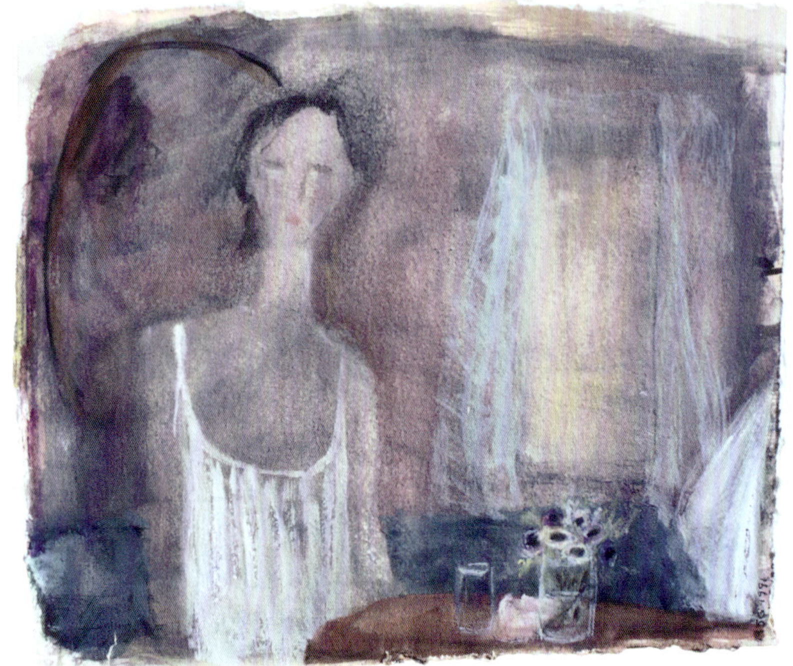

8 A.M., 1991.
Gouache, 7¼ x 8¾ in. (18.4 x 22.2 cm).
Artist's collection.

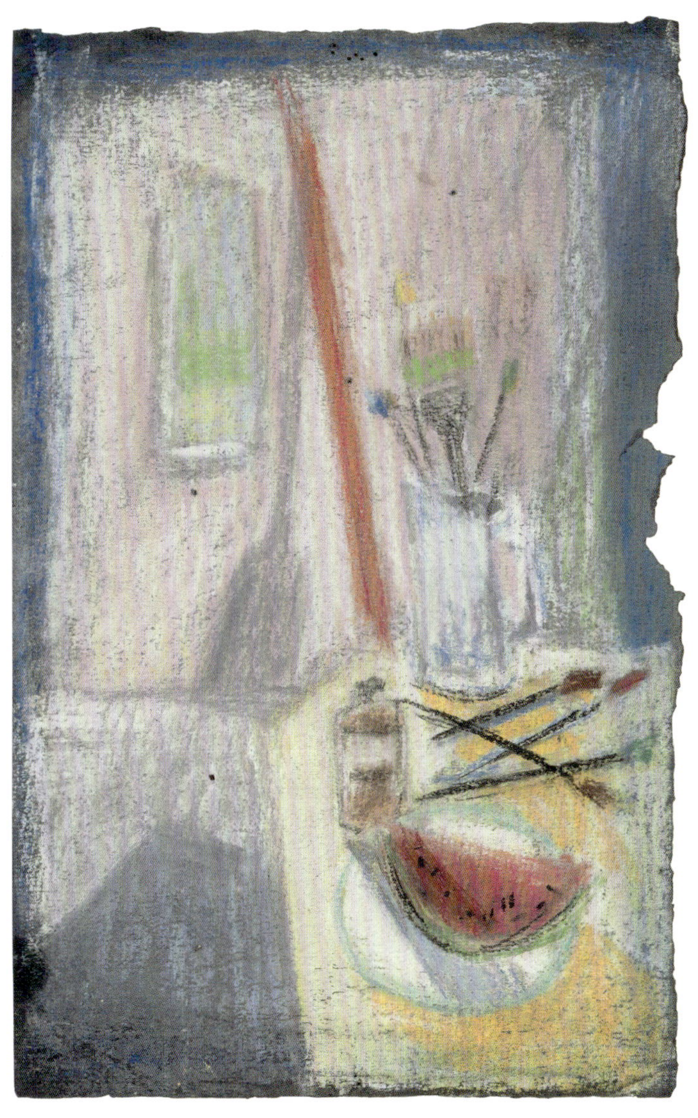

SUMMER STUDIO (I), 1988.
Pastel, 8¼ x 7 in. (21 x 17.8 cm).
Artist's collection.

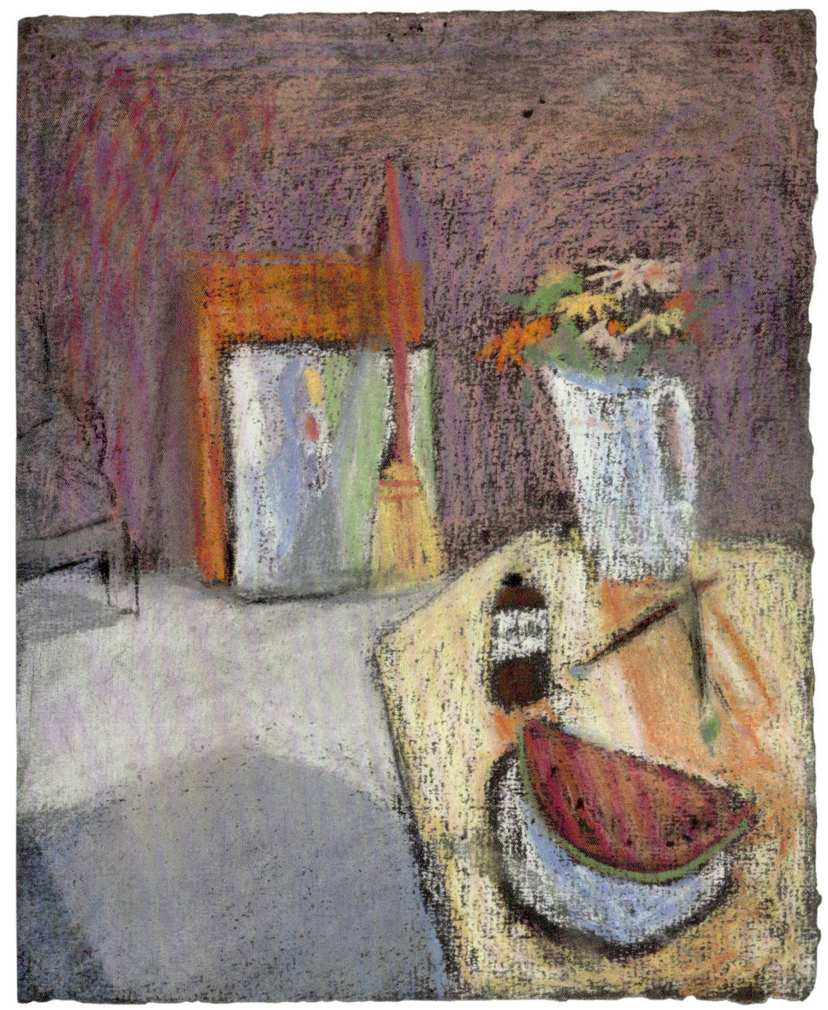

SUMMER STUDIO (II), 1988.
Pastel, 8 x 5 in. (20.3 x 12.7 cm).
Artist's collection.

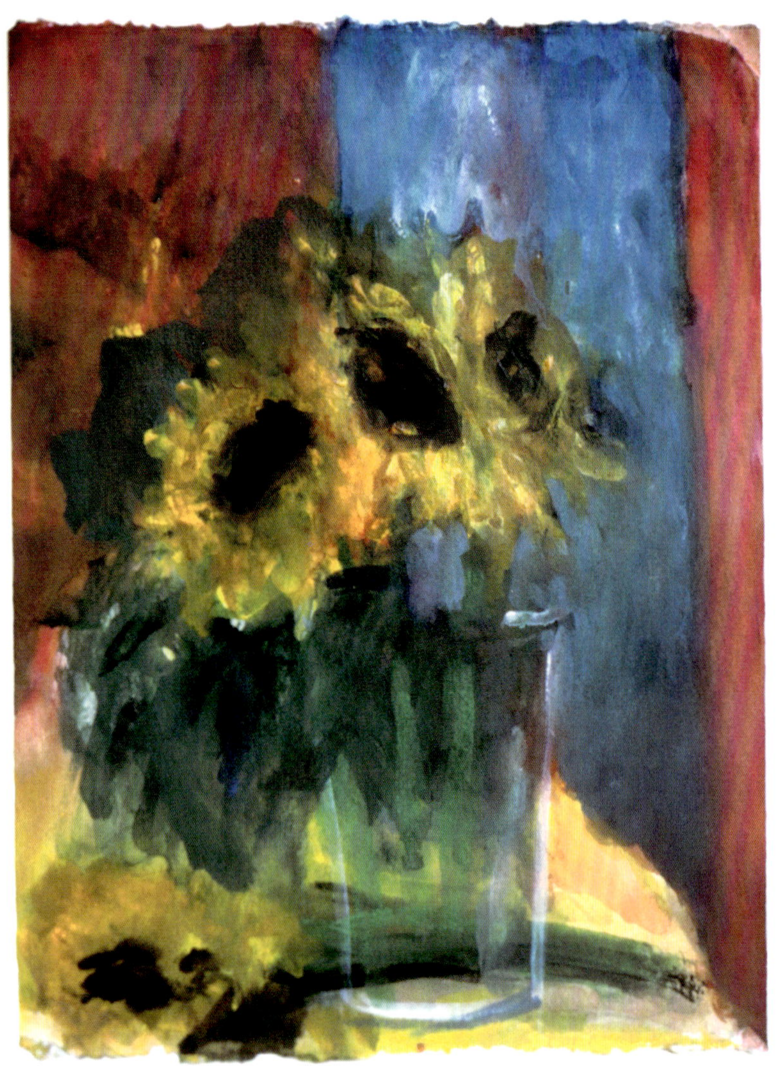

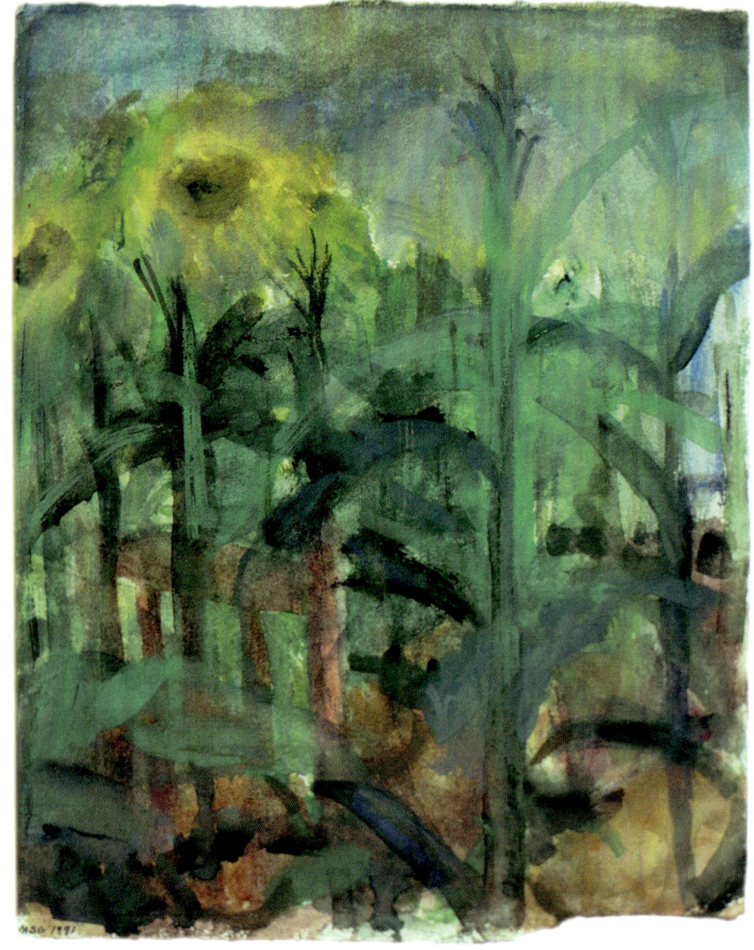

CUT FLOWERS, 1992.
Gouache, 10 x 8 in. (25.4 x 20.3 cm).
Artist's collection.

SUNFLOWER BED, 1991.
Gouache, 10¾ x 8½ in. (27.3 x 21.6 cm).
Artist's collection.

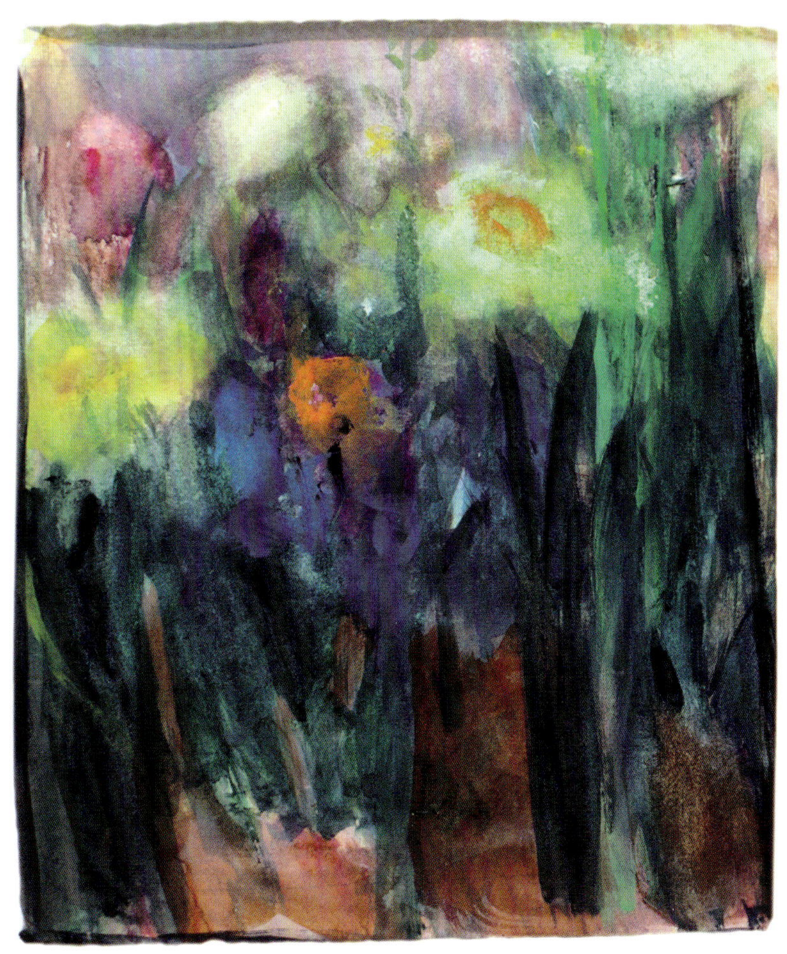

FLOWER BED, 1991.
Gouache, 10 x 9¼ in. (25.4 x 23.5 cm).
Artist's collection.

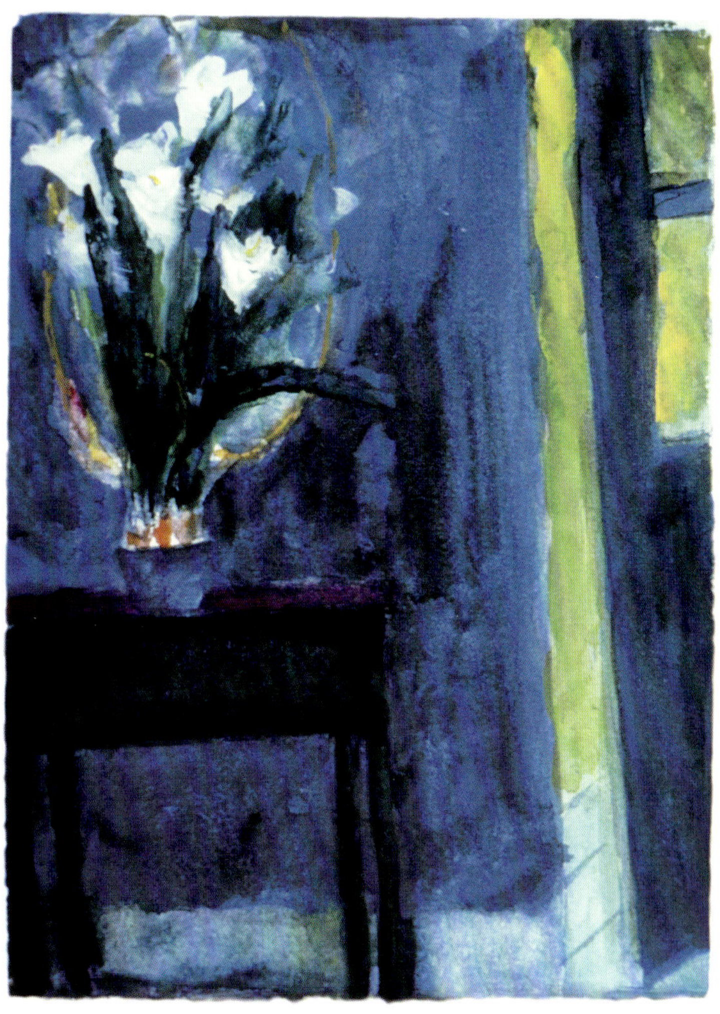

POTTED LILIES, 1991.
Gouache, 10 x 7½ in. (25.4 x 19.1 cm).
Artist's collection.

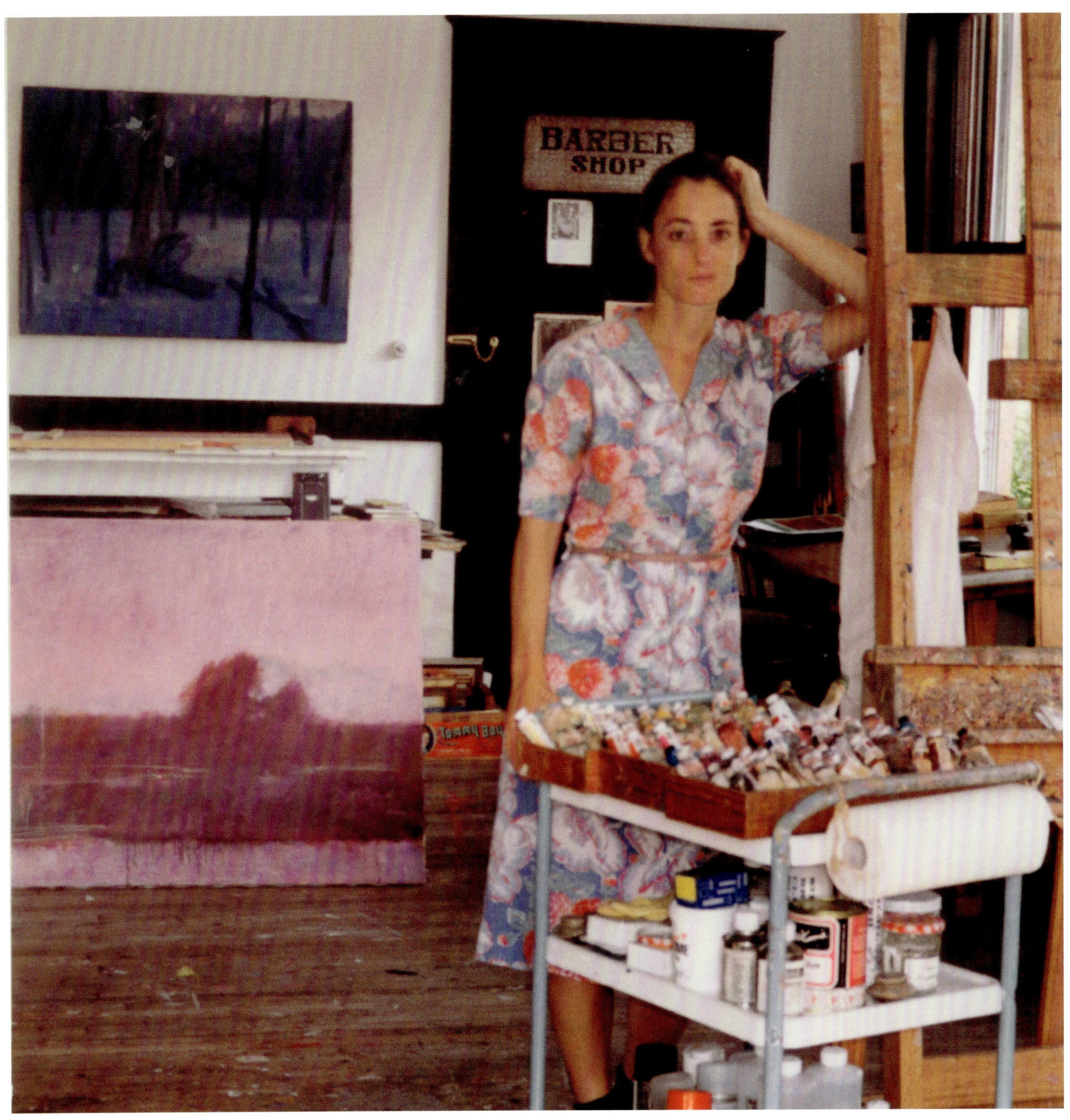

Barber shop studio, Housatonic, Massachusetts, Summer 1991.

1947
Born on June 2 in Brooklyn, New York, to parents Herbert H. Sipp (artist/graphic designer and owner of Rapecis and Sipp, art and advertising studio, New York City) and Anna C. Thristino (apparel designer and teacher).

1949–1965
Resides in Valley Stream, New York (Long Island).

1965–1967
Studies apparel design and illustration at the Fashion Institute of Technology, New York City.

1966
Moves to New York City.

1967–1969
Works as a freelance designer for her own label, L'Esprit, whose clothes are sold in Henri Bendel, Abracadabra, and other boutiques in New York City.

1968
Travels through England, France, Spain, and Italy.

Marries Martin Green.

1968–1970
Owns and is sole designer for Xanadu boutique, New York City (West Village).

Studies sculpture at The New School, New York, New York.

1970
Travels to Paris, France, and Barcelona and Ibiza, Spain.

Buys a house and moves to rural Cherry Plain, New York.

1971
Son Jared is born.

1972–1975
Owns and is sole designer for Bumpkins Clothing Co., whose apparel is distributed to boutiques and department stores across the United States.

1976
Buys a house and moves to Stockbridge, Massachusetts.

1979–1984
Studies photography at Berkshire Community College, Pittsfield, Massachusetts and printmaking and painting through individual instruction.

1979–1982
Rents and maintains in Stockbridge first studio, which has no heat or plumbing.

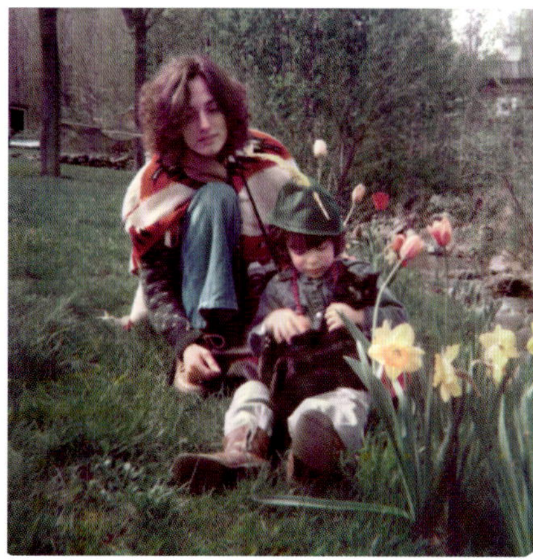

Mary and son Jared, Cherry Plain, New York, 1976.

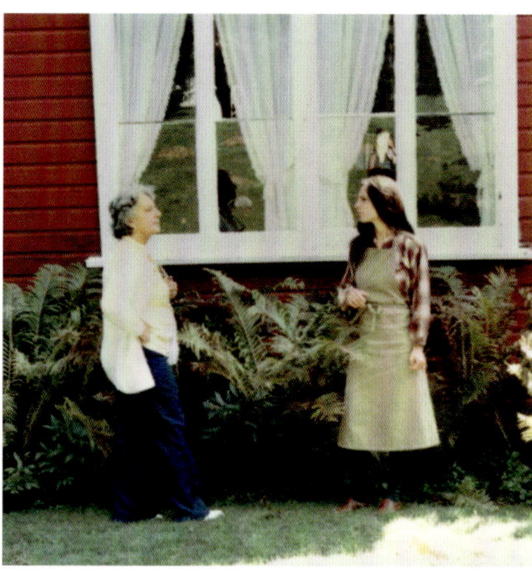

First studio in Stockbridge, Massachusetts, 1980. Mary with her mother Anna.

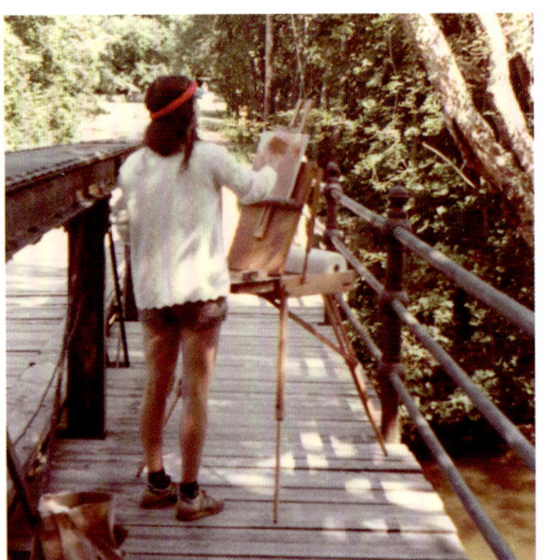

Painting along the Housatonic River, Stockbridge, Massachusetts, 1982.

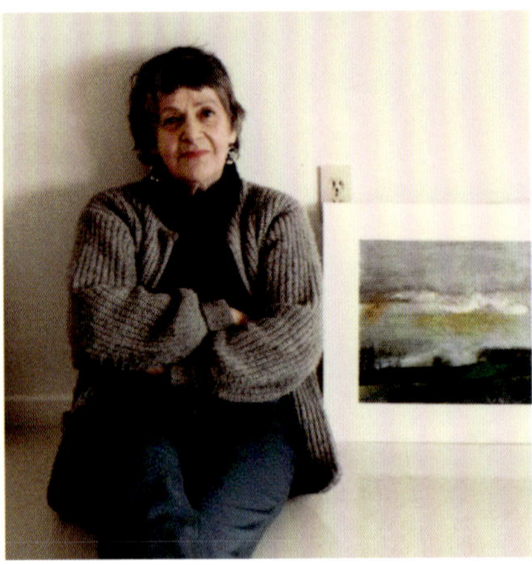

Bessie Boris, Stockbridge, Massachusetts, 1988.

1982
Makes first trip to Martha's Vineyard, Massachusetts, and sketches fields in Chilmark, Massachusetts.

1982–1988
Works in various, temporary studios and paints en plein air throughout Berkshire County, Massachusetts.

1986
Meets mentor Bessie Boris, whose work Sipp Green first discovered in the permanent collection of Smith College Museum of Art; Boris lived and worked in Stockbridge, Massachusetts.

1986–1991
Meets and studies with mentor Leo Garel in Stockbridge, Massachusetts.

1988
Maintains in Lenox, Massachusetts, a summer studio, which had been a peacock shed; there is no heat, plumbing, or electricity, and Sipp Green paints the pounded-dirt floor gray.

1988–2006
Maintains in the mill town of Housatonic, Massachusetts, her "barber shop" studio, a large loft space that was once a barber shop above a market.

1999
Travels to London, England, and Côte d'Azur, Paris, and Provence, France; sketches poppy fields in Provence.

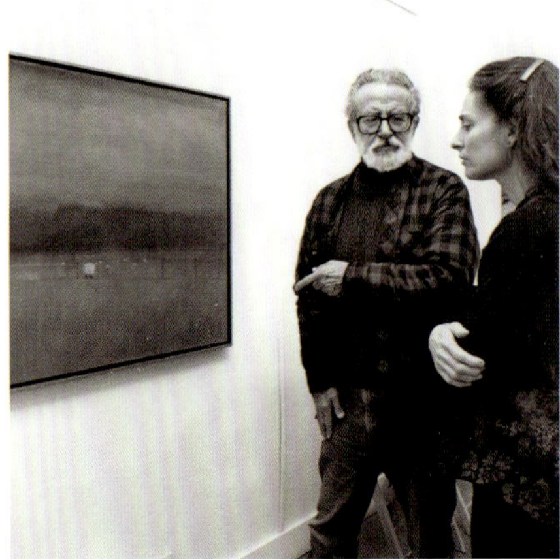

Leo Garel and Mary, mentor and protégé, Stockbridge, Massachusetts, 1992.

2004
First grandchild, Zoé Claire, is born.

2005
Sketches in Paris, France, and Florence, Naples, Rome, Tuscany, and Venice, Italy.

2007
Visits Normandy and Paris, France, and makes sketches in Pays d'Auge (Normandy).

Travels to Calabria, Naples, and Tuscany, Italy, and sketches in canola, sunflower, and poppy fields.

Buys a house in Stockbridge, Massachusetts.

2008
Studio is built in Stockbridge, Massachusetts.

2009

Travels to Calabria, Naples, Rome, and
Tuscany, Italy, and creates sketches in
sunflower and other flower fields.

2010

Second grandchild, Juliette Cécile, is born.

2012

Visits Budapest, Hungary; Prague, Czech
Republic; and Vienna, Austria.

Travels to Paris, France, and sketches views
along the Seine.

2013

Oil painting *Twilight Falls, in South County*
enters permanent collection of Springfield
Museum of Art, Massachusetts.

Pastel paintings *Quiet Morning* and
Twilight enter the permanent collection
of The Butler Institute of American Art,
Youngstown, Ohio.

2014

Travels to Côte d'Azur, Paris, and Provence,
France; makes sketches in the lavender
fields and villages of The Vaucluse and the
Valensole plateau.

Visits Calabria, Rome, Umbria, and
Tuscany, Italy, and makes sketches in the
countryside.

Major monograph, *Every Hour of the Light:
The Paintings of Mary Sipp Green*, published
by The Artist Book Foundation.

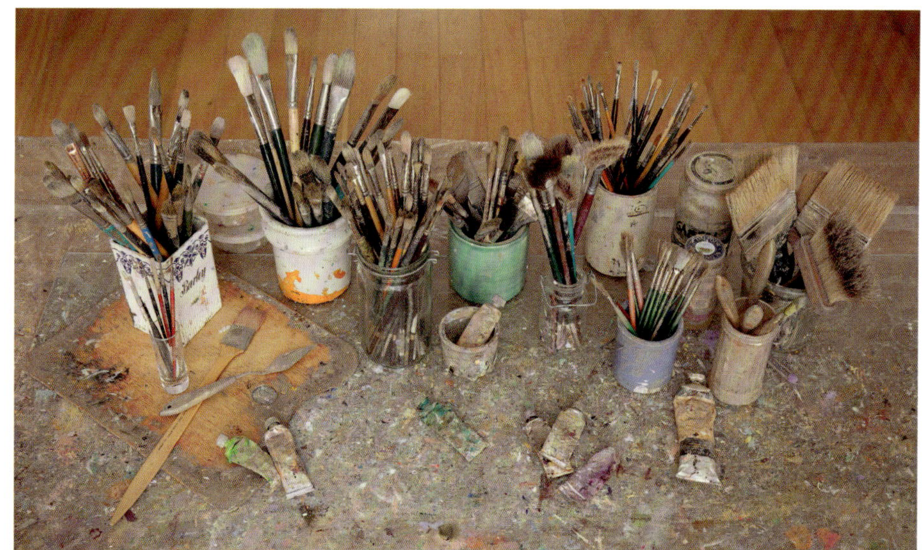

Studio tabletop, 2014.

Wally Findlay Galleries International, New York, New York, 2014
Mary Sipp Green: The Poetic Landscape; Selected Paintings

The Harrison Gallery, Williamstown, Massachusetts, 2012
Mary Sipp Green

Wally Findlay Galleries International, New York, New York, 2011
Under Western Skies

Wally Findlay Galleries International, Palm Beach, Florida, 2011
Ethereal Twilight

Wally Findlay Galleries International, New York, New York, 2010
Mary Sipp Green: Landscapes

Wally Findlay Galleries International, Palm Beach, Florida, 2010
Mary Sipp Green: Recent Works

The Harrison Gallery, Williamstown, Massachusetts, 2009
Mary Sipp Green: New Works; Italy

The Harrison Gallery, Williamstown, Massachusetts, 2008
Mary Sipp Green: Recent Landscapes

Wally Findlay Galleries International, Palm Beach, Florida, 2008
Mary Sipp Green: Poetic Landscape

Wally Findlay Galleries International, New York, New York, 2007
Coloritura: Paintings of the Italian Landscape

The Harrison Gallery, Williamstown, Massachusetts, 2006
Mary Sipp Green: Recent Paintings

Springfield Museum of Fine Art, Springfield, Massachusetts, 2005
Mary Sipp Green, Selected Works (1990–2004)

Multiple Impressions, New York, New York, 2003
Recent Landscapes

Arden Gallery, Boston, Massachusetts, 2002
Mary Sipp Green: Landscapes

Multiple Impressions, New York, New York, 2001
Mary Sipp Green: Recent Landscapes

Arden Gallery, Boston, Massachusetts, 2000
Mary Sipp Green: Landscapes

Arden Gallery, Boston, Massachusetts, 1998
Mary Sipp Green: Landscapes

Arden Gallery, Boston, Massachusetts, 1995
Mary Sipp Green: Landscapes

Ute Stebich Gallery, Lenox, Massachusetts, 1993
Mary Sipp Green: Gouaches, Oils, Pastels

Welles Gallery, Lenox, Massachusetts, 1986
Mary Sipp Green: Drawings and Paintings

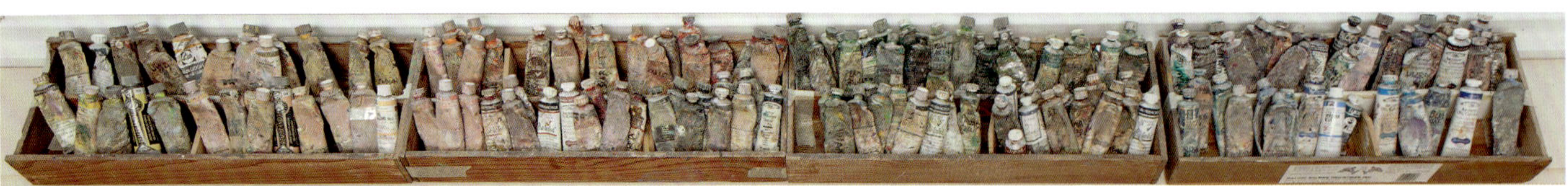

The Butler Institute of American Art,
Youngstown, Ohio, 2014
*Recent Acquisitions: Butler Pastel
Collection*

The Granary Gallery, West Tisbury,
Massachusetts, 2014
Group Summer Show

The Granary Gallery, West Tisbury,
Massachusetts, 2013, 2012, 2011, 2010,
2009, 2007, 2006, 2005, 2004, 2003, 2002,
2001, 2000, 1999, 1998, 1997
Summer Show

Lichtenstein Center for the Arts, Pittsfield,
Massachusetts, 2013
FRESH: Farm to Gallery

International Juried Competition, Grand
Rapids, Michigan, 2012
ArtPrize

Wally Findlay Galleries International,
Barcelona, Spain, 2007
Group Exhibition

Arnot Art Museum, Elmira, New York, 2005
Re-Presenting Representation

Berkshire Museum, Pittsfield,
Massachusetts, 2005
The Power of Place: The Berkshires

Cavalier Galleries, Inc., Greenwich,
Connecticut, and Nantucket,
Massachusetts, 2005
Summer Exhibition

Wally Findlay Galleries International,
New York, New York, 2005
Four Americans

Wally Findlay Galleries International,
Palm Beach, Florida, 2005
Luminous Landscapes

Norman Rockwell Museum, Stockbridge,
Massachusetts, 2004
Housatonic River Reflections

Vose Galleries LLC, Boston,
Massachusetts, 2004
*Realism Now: Traditions and Departures,
Mentors and Protégés, Part II*

Weber Fine Art, Chatham, New York, 2004
*A Lineage of Influence: Hans Hofmann,
Vaclav Vytlacil, Bessie Boris,
Mary Sipp Green*

Cavalier Galleries, Inc., Nantucket,
Massachusetts, 2001
Summer Exhibition

Hemphill Fine Arts, Washington, District
of Columbia, 1999
*Our Good Earth: The Landscape at the
End of the Century*

The Union League Club, New York,
New York, 1997
Winter Group Exhibition

The Brush Art Gallery, Lowell,
Massachusetts, 1996
Group Exhibition

Gardner Colby Galleries, Martha's
Vineyard, Massachusetts, 1996
Group Exhibition

RICA Gallery, Housatonic,
Massachusetts, 1996
Berkshire Artist Invitational

National Academy Museum, New York,
New York, 1994
169th Annual Juried Exhibition

Gay Head Gallery, Aquinnah,
Massachusetts, 1993
Island Landscapes

National Academy Museum, New York,
New York, 1992
167th Annual Juried Exhibition

Forum Gallery, New York, New York, 1990
Three American Landscape Painters

National Academy Museum, New York,
New York, 1990
165th Annual Juried Exhibition

Edgartown Art Gallery, Edgartown,
Massachusetts, 1988
Mary Sipp Green

Store Hill Gallery, South Egremont,
Massachusetts, 1987
Mary Sipp Green

Honey Sharp Gallery, Lenox,
Massachusetts, 1983
Mary Sipp Green

BIBLIOGRAPHY

Amato, Lisa. "Regional Art Reviews: The Springfield Museum of Art, Springfield, MA: Mary Sipp Green." *Art New England*, September/October 2005.

Beckett, Wendy. *The Mystical Now: Art and the Sacred.* London: Ryder Press, 1992.

Doherty, M. Stephen. "Respond to What Paintings Need." *American Artist*, vol. 73, no. 798, May 2009.

Evans, Sara. "Artists Making Their Mark: MARY SIPP GREEN." *Fine Art Connoisseur*, vol. 11, no. 4, August 2014.

Gillet, Michelle. "Luminous Landscapes: The Art of Mary Sipp Green." *Art of the Times*, November 10, 2012, http://artofthetimes.com/2012/11/10/season-2012–2013.

Grover, Eliott, and Susan Dewey, ed. "Mary Sipp Green." *Cape Cod Life*, "Cape Cod ART Profile" supplement, June 10, 2014.

Hickey, Maureen Johnson. *The Power of Place: The Berkshires.* Pittsfield, MA: Berkshire Museum, 2005.

Landscapes of Mary Sipp Green, exhibition catalogue. Foreword by S. Lane Faison, Jr. Boston: Arden Gallery, 2002.

Mayers, Gwen. "Mary Sipp Green: Inner and Outer Nature." *The Artful Mind* magazine, November 2004.

New American Paintings: Juried Exhibition in Print, no. 20. Wellesley, MA: The Open Studios Press, 1999.

O'Hern, John. *Re-presenting Representation VII*. Elmira, NY: Arnot Art Museum, 2005.

169th Annual Exhibition, exhibition catalogue. New York: National Academy Museum, 1994.

167th Annual Exhibition, exhibition catalogue. New York: National Academy Museum, 1992.

165th Annual Exhibition, exhibition catalogue. New York: National Academy Museum, 1990.

Perlman, Sar. "Collector Central." *Art & Antiques*, vol. 29, no. 1, January 2006.

Realism Now: Traditions & Departures, Mentors and Protégés, Part II, exhibition catalogue. Boston: Vose Galleries, 2004.

"Romance Restored." *Look* magazine, June 11, 1968.

Rose, Joshua. "Destination, Martha's Vineyard, MA: Mary Sipp Green." *American Art Collector*, January 2006.

Williams, Austin, ed. "Artist Roundup." *The Complete Painter's Handbook* magazine, April 2012.

Young, Geoffrey. "Recent Readings of the Housatonic" in *Art and the River: Views and Visions of the Housatonic*. Sheffield, MA: Sheffield Art League, 2004.

Zaffanella, Anna Biasin. "C'era Una Volta in Italia: La famosa pittrice statunitense porta l'Italia nel mondo." *Wealth Planet*, issue 3, edition 35, May/June 2014.

PHOTOGRAPH CREDITS

The Art Institute of Chicago, p. 37

Steve Blanchard, p. 92

Brilliant Graphics, pp. 36 (fig. 19), 42–43, 56, 58, 61, 62, 91, 106, 107

Fred Collins, Collins Editions, cover, pp. 4, 8, 18, 21, 22, 23, 24, 25, 27, 28, 30, 31, 32, 38, 54, 55, 59, 60, 66, 69, 76, 100, 109, 123, 124, 131, 134, 135, 137, 138, 139, 145, 151, 152

Stephen G. Donaldson, pp. 86, 87, 88, 89, 108

Arthur Evans, pp. 2–3, 10, 20, 29, 34, 36 (fig. 21), 45, 46, 47, 49, 50, 51, 52, 53, 63, 64, 65, 67, 68, 70, 71, 72, 73, 74, 75, 77, 78, 79, 80, 81, 82–83, 90, 93, 94–95, 97, 98, 99, 101, 102, 103, 104, 110, 111, 112, 113, 114, 115, 116, 117, 118, 119, 120–121, 125, 126, 127, 128, 129, 130, 136, 140, 141, 142, 143, 144, 146, 147

Lee Everett/ Fine Line Lenox, p.105

John Fulop, p. 16

Jo Ellen Harrison, The Harrison Gallery, pp. 35, 85

Gloria Henry, p. 6

Clemens Kalischer, p. 150 (top right)

Larry Klein, p. 150 (bottom left)

Gary Mirando, p. 57

Louise O'Rourke, p. 48

The Phillips Collection, Washington, DC, p. 33

Joe Rudenic, p. 12

Anna C. Sipp, pp. 148, 149 (top), 150 (top left)

Herbert H. Sipp, p. 149 (bottom)

Greg Staley, p. 14

First Edition

© 2014 The Artist Book Foundation

Published in the United States by The Artist Book Foundation
115 East 57th Street, 11th floor, New York, New York 10022

Distributed in the United States, its territories and possessions, and Canada by
ARTBOOK LLC D.A.P. | Distributed Art Publishers, Inc.
www.artbook.com
Distributed outside North America by ACC Distribution
www.accdistribution.com/uk

Publisher and Co-founder: Leslie Pell van Breen
Co-founder: H. Gibbs Taylor, Jr.
Production Manager: David Skolkin
Design: Irene Cole
Editor: Amanda Sparrow
Production Editor: Marisa Crumb
Printed and bound by Graphicom srl

Manufactured in Vicenza, Italy

ISBN 978-0-9888557-6-2

Library of Congress Cataloging-in-Publication Data:

Every hour of the light : the paintings of Mary Sipp Green / foreword by Louis Zona, Phd ; essay by Beth Venn. — First Edition.
pages cm
Includes bibliographical references and index.
ISBN 978-0-9888557-6-2 (alk. paper)
1. Green, Mary Sipp—Themes, motives. I. Zona, Louis, writer of supplementary textual content. II. Venn, Beth.
Mysterious dimensions of the everyday. III. Green, Mary Sipp. Paintings. Selections.
ND237.G61693A4 2014
759.13—dc23
2014022520

Cover: *Upper Meadow*, 2014 (detail). Oil on linen, 38 x 56 in. (96.5 x 142.2 cm). Private collection.
pp. 2–3: *Dusk on Goldenrod*, 1991 (detail of fig. 12).
p. 4: *Quitsa Mooring*, 2013. Oil on linen, 44 x 48 in. (111.8 x 121.9 cm). Private collection.
p. 6: Mary Sipp Green sketching in poppy fields, Tuscany, 2007.
p. 10: *Grandma's Teapot*, 1983. Oil on linen, 12 x 14 in. (30.5 x 35.6 cm). Artist's collection.
p. 12: *Summer Sunset*, 2009. Oil on panel, 19½ x 19¼ in. (49.5 x 48.9 cm). Private collection.